The Ethical Dimensions of Marxist Thought

The Ethical Dimensions of Marxist Thought

◇ ◇ ◇

Cornel West

Monthly Review Press
New York

Library of Congress Cataloging-in-Publication Data

West, Cornel.
    The ethical dimensions of Marxist thought / Cornel West.
        p.   cm.
    Includes index.
    ISBN 0-85345-817-0 : $36.00.—ISBN 0-85345-818-9 (pbk.) : $18.00
    1. Marx, Karl, 1818–1883—Ethics.   2. Socialist ethics—History.
3. Philosophy, Marxist—History.   I. Title.
B3305.M74W473   1991
171'.7—dc20
                                                            90-24357
                                                            CIP

Monthly Review Press
122 West 27th Street
New York, NY 10001

Manufactured in the United States of America

10 9 8 7 6 5 4 3 2 1

To my loving sisters
Cynthia and Cheryl

Contents

Acknowledgments

This essay was long in the making and it bears the stamp of this longevity. Parts of it were written in Harvard's Widener Library, Yale's Sterling Library, Princeton's Firestone Library, Columbia University Library, Union Theological Seminary Library, and the Library at California State University at Sacramento in the late 1970s. I extend my gratitude to Raymond Geuss and Sheldon Wolin for their perceptive comments, insightful criticisms, and patient guidance. I also am grateful for the invaluable encouragement from my former colleagues at Union Theological Seminary, especially the incredible inspiration and support from my closest friend, James Washington, Professor of Church History.

Harry Magdoff and Paul Sweezy—my personal friends and political comrades—kindly suggested that this essay should see the light of day. Susan Lowes did a superb job preparing it for publication. This essay was made possible—as are all my writings—by my loving family: my inimitable parents, Clifton L. West, Jr. and Irene Bias West; my steadfast brother, Clifton L. West III; my supportive sisters, Cynthia Cole and Cheryl West; and my marvelous son, Clifton Louis West. And, lastly, without the presence of my precious life companion, Elleni Gebre Amlak, this essay would have remained dormant.

◇ *Introduction* ◇

The Making of an American Democratic Socialist of African Descent

America is in the midst of a massive social breakdown. Never before in U.S. history has national decline and cultural decay so thoroughly shaken peoples' confidence in their capacity to respond to present-day problems. America remains the premier military power in the world, yet has a waning influence on the global scene. American big business can no longer compete with that of Japan, West Germany, and others as a result of bad management, myopic profiteering, insufficient productive investments, and a refusal to educate its workers adequately. The mediocrity of American leaders is horrendous. Money-driven elections and packaged politicians (turned fundraisers) have made the political system virtually an ugly joke—whose punchline is on the American people.

Cultural decay is pervasive. The erosion of civil society—shattered families, neighborhoods, schools, and voluntary associations—has contributed to a monumental eclipse of hope and to a collapse of meaning across the country. Civic terrorism—the sheer avalanche of mindless and calculated violence in our social fabric—haunts many urban, suburban, and rural streets. Deteriorating physical infrastructures—unkept highways, subways, bridges, and buildings—are everywhere. Escalating class inequality (including growing gaps between rich and poor), xenophobic violence (especially men against women, whites against people of color and against Jews, straights against lesbians and gays), and ecological devastation frighten most Americans.

Consumer culture—a way of life that spawns addictive personalities and passive citizens—promotes a profound spiritual impoverishment and moral shallowness. The culture industries of TV, radio, film, and video bombard Americans with degrading stereotypes—especially of women and people of color—and saturate leisure time with seductive images of sexual foreplay and orgiastic pleasures. Never before have Americans been so ill-equipped to confront the traumas of despair, dread, and death, even as so many, especially those among the political and economic elite, ignore the social chaos and self-destruction eating at the core of American society.

In short, there is a growing nihilism and cynicism afoot in the country. This nihilism—the lived experience of meaninglessness, hopelessness, and lovelessness—encourages social anomie (drugs, crime) and therapeutic forms of escape (sports, sex). This cynicism, often masquerading as patriotic lore, traditional "commonsense," and nostalgic posturing, is a form of paralysis; the body politic shrugs its shoulders while it waddles in private opulence and public squalor.

This present moment of massive social breakdown in America occurs at a time of epochal change in the Soviet Union and Eastern Europe: the revolutionary shift of authoritarian regimes with command economies to parliamentary political systems with capitalist economies. This collapse of bureaucratic elitist forms of communism—encouraged by the courageous and visionary Mikhail Gorbachev of the U.S.S.R. and enacted by heroic working peoples in these countries—has helped revivify the spirit of revolution in our day. Yet this epochal change warrants both support and suspicion. It is salutary because it reasserts the autonomy and integrity of civil society (e.g., individual liberties to speak, organize, publish, travel, and worship). It also is frightening in that it rekindles ugly xenophobia (such as anti-Semitism and chauvinistic nationalism) and unleashes harsh "free market" forces. To put it crudely, the breathtaking anti-communist revolutions of 1989 affirm and accent the libertarian—not egalitarian—aspects of the capitalist revolutions of 1776, 1789, and 1848. Like those revolutions of old—and like the present moment of the major capitalist power in the world, the United States—fundamental issues of employment, health care, housing, child care, and education for all are being ignored and overlooked.

The profound tragedy of the epochal change in the Soviet Union and Eastern Europe may be a turning away from these fundamental issues—a kind of global erasure of egalitarian and democratic concern for jobs, food, shelter, literacy, and health care for all. This would mean that along with the unleashing of capitalist market forces on an international scale goes an unleashing of despair for those caught within or concerned about the world's ill-fed, ill-clad, and ill-housed, especially those in "invisible" Africa, Asia, and Latin America. This tidal wave of popular cynicism and nihilism about the capacities of people to imagine, create, and sustain alternatives to the world-encompassing capitalist order is the spectre now haunting the globe.

This enormous obstacle of cynicism and nihilism is the starting point for freedom fighters who defend and promote egalitarian and democratic possibilities in our time. How do we put the fundamental issues of employment, health and child care, housing, ecology, and education on the agenda of the powers that be in a world disproportionately shaped by transnational corporations and nation-state elites in a global multipolar capitalist order? How do we keep a focus on these issues while we fight racism, patriarchy, homophobia, and ecological abuse? What effective forms of progressive politics can emerge in this new moment of history?

The present tasks for the remaking of the left are threefold. First, given the extraordinary power of capitalism and the pervasive cynicism and skepticism toward fundamental social change it breeds, we should try to understand and support all egalitarian and democratic concerns, efforts, and movements that focus on more and better jobs, food, shelter, education, child and health care, and ecological balance. This means, in part, a wholesale critical inventory of ourselves and our communities of struggle. More pointedly, the existential and ethical dimensions of our lives require serious scrutiny. Why do we still fight and hope for social change? What really sustains our faith in struggle and our hope for change in these barbaric times? How do we analyze and account for the egalitarian values and democratic sensibilities we act upon?

I am suggesting here neither moral confession nor personal therapy. Rather, I am calling for a historical assessment and political reading of our morality and morale, in order to shed light on how we can make them more contagious to others captive to the prevailing cynicism and nihilism. This assessment and reading should disclose some of the cultural sources of critique and resistance still extant in a society saturated by market ways of life.

Second, we must confront candidly the intellectual crisis of the left. How do we best analyze and explain our society and world? Which moral visions and values apply? What do we mean by such precious ideals as equality, democracy, freedom, and justice? What are the complex dynamics of such ugly phenomena as racism, patriarchy, ageism, homophobia, class exploitation, bureaucratic domination, and ecological abuse? How do we best mobilize and organize both victims and people of good will? What are the appropriate responses to the collapse of communist regimes, the new developments in southern Africa and Brazil, the economic power of Japan and Europe, and the diverse yet devastated state of most of Africa, Asia, the Middle East, and Latin America?

These crucial questions and urgent challenges require a careful evaluation of past and present efforts of those social theorists, historical sociologists, and cultural critics who have grappled seriously with them. I am convinced that, despite its blindnesses and inadequacies—especially in regard to racism, patriarchy, homophobia, and ecological abuse—Marxist thought is an indispensable tradition for freedom fighters who focus on the fundamental issues of jobs, food, shelter, literacy, health and child care for all. One of the major ironies of our time is that Marxist thought becomes even more relevant after the collapse of communism in the Soviet Union and Eastern Europe than it was before. The explosion of capitalist market forces on a global scale—concomitant with open class conflict, aggressive consumerism, rapacious individualism, xenophobic tribalism, and chauvinistic nationalism—makes Marxist thought an inescapable part of the intellectual weaponry for present-day freedom fighters.

Third, we have to specify the kind of credible strategies and tactics for progressive politics in the United States. The existential and ethical dimensions of struggle—linked to subtle analyses and sophisticated explanations of power, wealth, status, and prestige—must yield concrete ways that people's pressure can be brought to bear to change American society. This entails a fresh examination of the crisis of leadership, mobilization, and organization of the left. I shall now elaborate on each of the three tasks for the remaking of the left in the present global capitalist epoch in light of my own critical self-inventory over time and space.

◇ ◇ ◇

A wholesale critical inventory of ourselves and our communities of struggle is neither self-indulgent autobiography nor self-righteous reminiscence. Rather, it is a historical situating and locating of our choices, sufferings, anxieties, and efforts in light of the circumscribed options and alternatives available to us. We all are born into and build on circumstances, traditions, and situations not of our own choosing; yet we do make certain choices that constitute who we are and how we live in light of these fluid circumstances, traditions, and situations.

The most significant stage-setting for my own life pilgrimage has been neither academic life nor political organizations, but rather my closely knit family and overlapping communities of church and friends. These pillars of civil society—my loving parents, siblings, and communities—transmitted to me ideals and images of dignity, integrity, majesty, and humility. These ideals and images—couched within Christian narratives, symbols, rituals, and, most importantly, concrete moral examples—provided existential and ethical equipment to confront the crises, terrors, and horrors of life. The three major components of this equipment were a Christian ethic of love-informed service to others, ego-deflating humility about oneself owing to the precious yet fallible humanity of others, and politically engaged struggle for social betterment. This Christian outlook, as exemplified in our time by Martin Luther King, Jr., serves as the basis for my life vocation. As a youth, I resonated with the sincere black militancy of Malcolm X, the defiant rage of the Black Panther Party, and the livid black theology of James Cone. Yet I did not fully agree with them. I always felt that they lacked the self-critical moment of humility I discerned in the grand example of Martin Luther King, Jr. Such humility has always been a benchmark of genuine love for, and gratitude to, ordinary people whose lives one is seeking to enhance. I witnessed this same kind of integrity and dignity in the humble attitude to black folk of my early heroes: the Godfather of Soul, James Brown; the legendary baseball player, Willie Mays; my pastor, Rev. Willie P. Cooke (of Shiloh Baptist Church in Sacramento, California); my grandfather, Rev. C. L. West, of Metropolitan Baptist Church in Tulsa, Oklahoma; and my older brother, Clifton L. West III, to me an exemplary human being. In this way, Martin Luther King, Jr.

has always been not so much a model to imitate but *the* touchstone for personal inspiration, moral wisdom, and existential insight. I heard him speak in person only once—when I was ten years old (1963)—and I remember not his words but his humble spirit and sense of urgency.

My first noteworthy political action—besides marching with my family in a civil rights demonstration in Sacramento—was the coordination of a city-wide strike of students demanding courses in black studies. At the time there were four black student body presidents in Sacramento high schools (including myself). My good friend Glenn Jordan and I decided to launch this effort during the 1969–1970 school year, and we had good results.

My critical self-inventory highlights the fact that I was born eight years after the end of the Age of Europe (1492–1945). Much of who and what we are has to do with where and with what our immediate ancestors confronted the advent of modernity during the Age of Europe. And for most of us there is no escape from the effects of European modernity in that by the early twentieth century the handful of states located between the Atlantic Ocean and the Ural mountains (in addition to the former British colony, the United States) controlled more than two-thirds of the land and peoples on the globe. My perspective on the achievements and deficiencies of this Age of Europe is shaped and colored by being a descendant of seven generations of Africans in the Western hemisphere, enslaved and exploited, devalued and despised by Euro-Americans; and three generations of African-Americans, subordinated and terrorized by legal racist practices in the South. Both of my parents were born in Jim (and Jane) Crow Louisiana in the late 1920s and early 1930s. With the post-World War II decentering of Europe, the dwarfing of European populations, the demystifying of European cultural hegemony, the deconstruction of European philosophical systems and, most importantly, the decolonization of the third world, I came of age during the eclipse of one epoch and the emergence of another.

My early formative years were spent during what Henry Luce called the "American century"—a period of unprecedented economic boom in the United States, the creation of a large middle class, i.e., a prosperous working class with a bourgeois identity and a mass culture primarily based on African-American cultural products (music, style, etc.). I arrived on the scene just when black, and some white, blood, sweat, and tears broke the back of an apartheid-like rule of law in the South and overturned discriminatory laws (though not *de facto* practices) in employment, housing, and education. In 1970, when I entered Harvard College, I became part of the first generation of young black people to attend prestigious lily-white institutions of higher learning in significant numbers—institutions still coping with the new wave of Jewish faculty and students who had confronted an earlier tribal civility, snobbish gentility, and institutional loyalty of primarily well-to-do white Anglo-Saxon Protestants. Owing to my family, church, and the black social movements of the 1960s, I arrived at Harvard unashamed of my African, Christian, and militant decolonized outlooks. More pointedly, I acknowledged and accented the empowerment of my black styles, mannerisms, and viewpoints, my Christian values of service, love, humility, and struggle, and my anti-colonial sense of self-determination for oppressed people and nations around the world. But I soon discovered that this positive black identity, these persuasive Christian values, and this deep commitment to struggles for freedom were not enough. Given my privileged position (as a student—only about 18 percent of black young people were enrolled in college at the time) and grand opportunities, I needed a more profound understanding of history, a deeper grasp of the complex, conflict-ridden dynamics of societies and cultures, and a more flexible perspective on human life.

My passionate interest in philosophy was—and remains—primarily motivated by the radical historical *conditionedness* of human existence and the ways in which possibilities and potentialities are created, seized, and missed by individuals and communities within this ever changing conditionedness, including our inescapable death, illness, and disappointment. This attention to the historical character of all thought and action has led me to be suspicious of intellectual quests for truth unwilling to be truthful about themselves, including my own. So though I find delight in the life of the mind—inseparable from, yet not identical with, struggles for freedom—I do not put primary value on intelligence or book knowledge. Rather, I believe we have a moral obligation—for the quality of human life and protection of the environment—to be wise, especially about the pitfalls and shortcomings of mere intelligence and book knowledge.

My three decisive years at Harvard College empowered me in a variety of ways. Although I first majored in philosophy and then changed to Near Eastern Languages and Literature (especially Biblical Hebrew and Aramaic) in order to graduate a year early, my major focus was on history and social thought. I learned much of the former from Samuel Beer, H. Stuart Hughes, and Martin Kilson; of the latter from Talcott Parsons, Hilary Putnam, Preston Williams, Terry Irwin, and John Rawls. My political involvement consisted of daily work (beginning at 6:00 a.m.) in the breakfast program in Jamaica Plain with left black friends like Steven Pitts; weekly trips to Norfolk State Prison with fellow supporters like Valerie Hepburn; and campus activism led by the Black Student Organization. The major action of this student group was the legendary 1972 takeover of Massachusetts Hall (including the president's office) to oppose Harvard's investments in Gulf Oil and to support the anti-imperialist forces in Angola. Randall Robinson, founder of TransAfrica but at that time Harvard law student, played a crucial and courageous leadership role, as did the chief undergraduate spokesman, Harvard Stephens. I could not go into the building with my comrades because of trumped-up charges brought by the Cambridge Police Department, and two Hebrew tests I had to take in order to catch up with my class. Instead I joined the support work outside, which culminated in a march of 5,000 people on the first weekend of the takeover.

In the early 1970s, varieties of black nationalism were predominant at Harvard. Imamu Amiri Baraka's Congress of African People (CAP), Ron Karenga's early writings, the politics of the Republic of New Africa (RNA), and, to some extent, the Nation of Islam were attractive to black student activists. As a product of the Black Church I have always acknowledged some of the tenets of black nationalism, namely, black intelligence, beauty, character, and capacity, and their subjection to vicious attack by white supremacist practices. The fundamental issue of black identity—the affirmation of African humanity and ability—is a precondition for any black progressive politics. Yet my Christian universalist moral vision and my progressive international political perspective—derived from my readings of Frantz Fanon, Kwame Nkrumah, and Karl Marx (promoted by the Black Panther Party over what Huey Newton called "porkchop nationalism")—made me deeply suspicious of the politics of black nationalists. I worked with them on anti-racist issues—and we discussed, laughed, and partied together weekly—but I always staked out my Christian version of democratic socialist values and politics. My conversations with Trotskyists—especially the provocative lectures given by Peter Camejo—reinforced an anti-Stalinist stance I had already adopted, exposed me to a Leninist view I remained unpersuaded of, and promoted an appreciation of black nationalist insights within a larger multiracial organization. I learned much from readings of Trotskyist intellectuals like Leon Trotsky himself, C.L.R. James, Perry Anderson, and others, but I was not convinced. At this time, my major intellectual influences on political matters were the early Reinhold Niebuhr (of *Moral Man and Immoral Society*), R. H. Tawney (especially *The Acquisitive Society* and *Equality*), Julius K. Nyerere *(Essays on Socialism)*, the early Leszek Kolakowski *(Towards a Marxist Humanism)*, and the dissenting Marxist humanists Marković and Stojanović. I was most excited by the powerful essays by Harold Cruse in *Rebellion or Revolution*—a book I much preferred over his classic, *The Crisis of the Negro Intellectual*. Yet I remained critical of Cruse's cultural nationalist followers at Harvard, most of whom were my close friends. At that time, Martin Luther King, Jr. was a grand example of integrity and sacrifice but, in sharp contrast to Malcolm X, not a distinct voice with a credible politics in our Harvard conversations. Malcolm X's voice was as fresh as ever. We were all convinced that Malcolm X would hold *our* position and have *our* politics if he were alive. We rarely if ever asked this question of King in those days, even Christians like myself, principally owing to our blindness to his affirmation of democratic socialist politics and our impatience (read: ignorance) of his anti-imperialist (not just anti-Vietnam war) stance. King was for us the Great Man who died for us—but not yet the voice to whom we had to listen, question, learn from, and build on. This would change in the next decade.

When I arrived at Princeton's philosophy department—by far the best in the country at the time—I anticipated three basic intellectual challenges: the undermining of my Christian faith by the powerful tools of analytical philosophy; the way in which the works of Ludwig Wittgenstein—my philosophic hero at the time—were interpreted by Princeton's philosophy department, and how the department's social philosophers might regard the Hegelian Marxist tradition, i.e., Georg Lukács and the Frankfurt School, whom I had recently been seduced by. I quickly discovered the first issue was an irrelevant one for my teachers and peers. Nobody cared about religious faith—though Walter

Kaufmann and Richard Rorty regarded the issue with historic curiosity. So I kept my Pascal, Kierkegaard, Montaigne, Thurman, and Unamuno close to my heart and read Frege, Carnap, Quine, and Kuhn. My eye-opening and horizon-broadening encounter with Richard Rorty made me an even stronger Wittgensteinian, although with gestures toward Dewey. Rorty's historicist turn was like music to my ears—nearly as sweet as The Dramatics, The Spinners, or The Main Ingredient, whom I then listened to daily for sanity. My allegiance to the Hegelian Marxist tradition was deepened by Sheldon Wolin—the major influence, along with Rorty and C. B. MacPherson—on my thought at the time. It was during the two short years at Princeton that I became convinced that the values of individuality—the sanctity and dignity of all individuals shaped in and by communities—and of democracy—as a way of life and mode of being-in-the-world, not just a form of governance—were most precious to me. This is why, when I returned to Harvard as a DuBois Fellow to write my dissertation, I turned first to T. H. Green, the British neo-Hegelian of the late nineteenth century, and then to the ethical dimensions of Marxist thought. Marx's own debts to the Romantics' preoccupation with many-sided personality and full-fledged individuality (as in Friedrich Schiller's *Letters on Aesthetic Education*) and to the early socialists' focus on universal suffrage, womens' rights, abolitionism, and workplace democracy intrigued me. I became convinced that Marx's own intellectual development should be understood in terms of this fascinating tension between the moral conviction of the flowering of individuality under wholesale democratic socioeconomic and political conditions and the theoretical concern of explaining scientifically the dynamics and tendencies of profit-driven capitalist societies that foster a narrow individualism and a truncated political democracy.

This book, *The Ethical Dimensions of Marxist Thought*—written over a decade ago when I was in my mid-twenties—was my attempt to understand Marxist thought as one grand stream, among others, of the larger modern articulation of historical consciousness, an articulation fanned by Romantic quests for harmony and wholeness and fueled by concrete revolutionary and reformist movements for freedom, equality, and democracy. Such quests and movements may result in aborted authoritarian arrangements or be crushed by powerful capitalist powers. Yet the precious values of individuality and democracy that can guide and regulate such quests and movements sit at the center of Marx's own thought. Hence I take the reader—step by step, text by text—through Marx's own intellectual development in order to show how he incorporated modern historical consciousness (as he constructed and understood it) in relation to his ethical values of individuality and democracy, and how these values clashed with what he viewed as the pernicious and vicious effects of the fundamental class-ridden capitalist processes of capital accumulation and the commodification of labor. My brief examinations of subsequent Marxists, like Friedrich Engels, Karl Kautsky, and Georg Lukács, try to show that their diverse conceptions of modern historical consciousness in relation to ethical issues differ greatly from that of Marx.

The scope of this essay is limited, yet its focus on Marxist ethical reflection—regarding methodology and substance—is timely. There is not only a paucity of highly detailed interpretations of Marx's intellectual development, but also a need for more investigation of the kind of turn toward history and social theory Marx made and how it contrasts with that of subsequent noteworthy disciples and followers. And though I wrote *The American Evasion of Philosophy: A Genealogy of Pragmatism* six years after my dissertation, there is no doubt that my interpretation of Marxist thought is influenced by the works of John Dewey, the early Sidney Hook, and Richard Rorty. My basic claim is that Marx's turn toward history resembles the anti-foundationalist arguments of the American pragmatists, yet Marx wants to retain a warranted-assertability status for social explanatory claims in order to understand and change the world.

Marx wisely shuns any epistemic skepticism (as promoted by the deconstructive critics of our day) and explanatory agnosticism or nihilism (as intimated by those descriptivist anthropologists and historians bitten by the bug of epistemic skepticism). Instead, Marx refuses to conflate epistemic and methodological issues, philosophic and social theoretical ones, matters of justification for the certain or absolute grounds for knowledge—claims and matters of explanation that provide persuasive yet provisional (or revisable) accounts of social and historical phenomena. Like so many critics today, Marx's immediate followers often made a "category mistake" of collapsing epistemological concerns of justification in philosophy into methodological concerns of explanation in social theory. This unwarranted collapse is the basic reason why anti-foundationalists in epistemology became full-fledged skeptics and why descriptivists in the social sciences shun subtle explanations of change and conflict in society and culture. Needless to say, the complex relation of epistemic skepticism and explanatory nihilism to the sense of political impotence and historical cynicism among such critics—even as they monotonously invoke slogans that knowledge is culturally constructed, historically constituted, and politically-laden— cries out for explanation. One major reason is that they are reacting against narrow conceptions of social theory, especially positivistic, economistic, and reductionist versions of Marxism. This book shows that, despite the deep tensions in Marx's thought, there are other and better versions of Marxism put forward by Marx himself in his best moments. My point here is not that Marx's social theory fully accounts for all social and historical phenomena; rather, it is that social theory wedded in a nuanced manner to concrete historical analyses must be defended in our present moment of epistemic skepticism, explanatory agnosticism, political impotence (among progressives), and historical cynicism.

So it is necessary to discredit the fashionable trashing of Marxist thought in the liberal academy. Besides predictable caricatures of Marxist thought by conservatives, this trashing principally proceeds from ironic skeptics and aesthetic historicists. The former shun any theory that promotes political action with purpose; for them, any social project of transformation reeks of authoritarian aims. The latter highlight wholesale contingency and indeterminacy, with little concern with how and why change and conflict take place. So we have disciples of Jacques Derrida and Michel Foucault who talk about the subtle relations of rhetoric, knowledge, and power, yet remain silent about concrete ways in which people are empowered to resist and what can be gained by such resistance. In addition, we have the so-called "new historicists," preoccupied with "thick descriptions" of the relativity of cultural products, including those formerly neglected by traditional bourgeois male critics—while thoroughly distrustful of social *explanatory* accounts of cultural practices.

Needless to say, crude Marxist perspectives warrant scrutiny and rejection. Yet in these days of Marxist-bashing, it is often assumed that vulgar Marxist thought exhausts the Marxist tradition—as if mono-causal accounts of history, essentialist conceptions of society, or reductionist readings of culture are all Marxist thought has to offer. One wonders whether any such critics have read Marx's *Eighteenth Brumaire, Class Struggles in France,* or the *Grundrisse.*

Faddish ironic skepticism and aesthetic historicism are contemporary assaults on the twin pillars of Marxist social theory: historically specific accounts of structures such as modes of production, state apparatuses and bureaucracies, and socially detailed analyses of how such structures shape and are shaped by cultural agents. These pillars require that one's understanding of history, society, and culture highlight latent and manifest multifarious human struggles for identity, power, status, and resources. More pointedly, it demands that one bite the explanatory bullet and give analytical priority to specific forms of struggle over others. For sophisticated Marxists, this does not mean that class explains every major event in the past or present, or that economic struggles supersede all others. It simply suggests that in capitalist societies, the dynamic processes of capital accumulation and the commodification of labor condition social and cultural practices in an *inescapable* manner. How such practices are played out in various countries and regions for different races, classes, and genders in light of the fundamental capitalist processes will be determined in an experimental and empirical manner. Like other refined forms of historical sociology, Marxist theory proceeds within the boundaries of warranted assertable claims and rationally acceptable conclusions. Its assertions can be wrong in part because they are believed to be right.

The high intellectual moments of Marxist theory—Marx's own historical and economic analyses, Georg Lukács' theory of reification, and Antonio Gramsci's conceptions of hegemony—are those that bring together explanatory power, analytical flexibility, and a passion for social freedom. Yet certain crucial phenomena of the modern world—nationalism, racism, gender oppression, homophobia, ecological devastation—have not been adequately understood by Marxist theorists. My rejoinder simply is that these complex phenomena cannot be grasped, or changed, without the insights of Marxist theory, although we do need other theories to account for them fully.

Efforts to link the fundamental capitalist processes of capital accumulation and the commodification of labor to progressive traditions of ordinary people are not a call to revive old debates about base and superstructure. Similar to the best work of Raymond Williams, W.E.B. DuBois, Eugene Genovese, and Simone de Beauvoir, I am suggesting that we focus on the oppositional cultures of oppressed peoples that extend far beyond their workplaces. In other words, we need a serious *Simmelian* moment (as in Georg Simmel's *The Philosophy of Money*) in Marxist theory that probes into the lived experiences of people in light of fundamental capitalist processes. The aim here is not to reduce cultural efforts to ideological battles, but rather to discern and determine the distinctive elements of the structures of feeling, structures of meaning, ways of life and struggle under dynamic circumstances not of peoples' own choosing. In this way, Marxist theory can give social substance and political content to postmodern themes of otherness, difference, and marginality. And limited epistemological debates about foundationalism and skepticism, realism and pragmatism can give way to more fruitful exchanges about clashing methodological, theoretical, and political conceptions of how to understand and change contemporary cultures and societies.

When I arrived as Assistant Professor of Philosophy of Religion at Union Theological Seminary in New York City in 1977, one of my concerns was precisely this issue: defending sophisticated Marxist theory as an indispensable—though by itself inadequate—intellectual weapon in the struggle for individuality and democracy. I decided to teach at Union Seminary for three reasons: it was (and still is) the center of liberation theology in the country, it was one of the best places for black theological education in the country, and it allowed me to teach and read widely in philosophy, social theory, history, literary criticism, and cultural thought. Union was the perfect place to become a broadly engaged cultural critic with a strong grounding in the history of philosophy and criticism. In fact, I received another education at Union from my supportive colleagues—especially my closest friend James Washington, Professor of Church History. My faith was tested and deepened, my mind was stretched and refined, my soul was refreshed and readied for battle. After serious intellectual exchanges with James Cone, Beverly Harrison, Dorothea Sölle, Tom Driver, James Forbes, Jr., David Lotz, Milton Gatch, and Donald Shriver—and trips to Brazil, Jamaica, Costa Rica, Mexico, Europe, and later South Africa—the incarnation of progressive thought in concrete struggles for freedom was no mere dream. Despite a relative quietism on the U.S. left, I witnessed and participated in an intellectual and political ferment in these places reminiscent of our 1960s. At home, the Theology in the Americas movement—the major national progressive multiracial and religious activity in the country in the 1970s—culminated in a historic gathering in Detroit. The results were published in 1982 by Orbis Press in a volume entitled *Theology in the Americas: Detroit II,* co-edited by Caridàd Guidote (a professor and Filipina nun), Margaret Coakley (a white American nun), and myself. The same year I published *Prophesy Deliverance! An Afro-American Revolutionary Christianity* (Westminster Press), based in part on lectures I gave at Rev. Herbert Daughtry's House of the Lord Pentecostal Church in Brooklyn, New York. Rev. Daughtry was the founder and then head of the National Black United Front—one of the few progressive organized responses to the conservative Reaganite policies of the early 1980s.

Two crucial encounters shaped the kind of democratic socialism I would promote: the intense intellectual exchanges with Stanley Aronowitz and my membership in Michael Harrington's new organization, Democratic Socialists of America (DSA). In addition to James Washington and to my younger colleagues—Mark Ridley-Thomas, Anders Stephanson, Farah Griffin, Jerry Watts, Anthony Cook, and Michael Dyson—I have never had a more enhancing intellectual interlocutor than Stanley Aronowitz. We read voraciously and talked incessantly about the impasse of the left and the crisis of Marxism—he was then writing his important work, *The Crisis in Historical Materialism.* His leadership of *Social Text*—the major journal in which Marxism encountered cultural politics in the 1980s and 1990s—pushed me toward a serious engagement with the works and lives of Fredric Jameson, Antonio Gramsci, Raymond Williams, Cedric Robinson, Anders Stephanson, Edward Said, Bertell Ollman, Barbara Fields, Stuart Hall, Ellen Willis, Audre Lorde, Eric Foner, bell hooks, Rick Wolfe, Sohnya Sayres, and Michel Foucault. This engagement still sets the framework for how I relate Marxist thought to the cultural politics of difference, i.e., race, gender, sexual orientation, age. This framework is an integral part of my work with the editorial collective of *Boundary 2: An International Journal of Literature and Culture*—Paul Bové, Jonathan Arac, William Spanos, Michael Hays, Daniel O'Hara, Donald Pease, Joseph Buttigieg, Margaret Ferguson, and Nancy Fraser.

Michael Harrington's DSA in 1982 was the first multiracial, socialist organization close enough to my kind of politics that I could join. I was then, and remain, a sharp critic and staunch defender of DSA. After seven years on the national political committee—and many protracted ideological struggles—I now serve as an honorary chairperson. My own Gramscian democratic socialism is not in the mainstream of DSA, but it is an acceptable and legitimate perspective within the organization, and one that is sharpened and refined by defenders of other versions of democratic socialism.

I put forward my own critiques of the late Michael Harrington's conception of democratic socialism in my book, *Prophetic Fragments* (Africa World Press, 1988) and in my review of his last book, *Socialism: Past and Future*, in *The Nation* (6–13 January 1990). Michael Harrington meant much to me as a person and I learned tangible and intangible lessons from him as we interacted in meetings and on trips together. We shared three fundamental points: the necessity of rethinking and reinterpreting the insights of the Marxist tradition in the light of new circumstances; the need for a national multiracial democratic socialist organization that puts a premium on intellectual exchange and political relevance; and the necessity of articulating a distinctive U.S. road to greater freedom, justice, and equality. Harrington was, despite some political faults and intellectual flaws, a masterful organic intellectual who held these three points together in creative tension better than anyone else of his generation.

My close friendships with Harry Magdoff and Paul Sweezy—the long distance runners of the American Marxist left—began just as I was moving from Union to Yale Divinity School in 1984. In our work together on a special issue on religion and the left for *Monthly Review* (July–August 1984), we realized that our versions of Marxist theory overlapped in significant ways. Their critical allegiance to historical materialist analyses that are magnanimously global in character yet meticulously specific in content fit well with my Gramscian accounts that link the rule of capital—the powers of transnational corporations, banks, and political elites—to the racial and gender-skewed ill-fed, ill-housed, and ill-clad. As the caretakers of one of the oldest Marxist journals in the United States, they have defended and updated Marxist theory while opening its pages to non-Marxist socialists like myself who share their concern about the significance of Marxist theory as an indispensable intellectual weapon for freedom fighters in the present.

I am a non-Marxist socialist in that as a Christian, I recognize certain irreconcilable differences between Marxists of whatever sort and Christians of whatever sort. Since my conception of Christian faith is deeply, though not absolutely, historical, this disagreement is not primarily a metaphysical issue; rather, it is a basic existential difference in the weight I put on certain biblical narratives, symbols, and rituals that generate sanity and meaning for me. My Christian perspective—mediated by the rich traditions of the Black Church that produced and sustains me—embraces depths of despair, layers of dread, encounters with the sheer absurdity of the human condition, and ungrounded leaps of faith alien to the Marxist tradition. Like so much of black music, Christian insights speak on existential and visceral levels neglected by the Marxist tradition. This is not so because the Marxist tradition is Eurocentric—for there are traditions and figures in Europe that do speak to existential issues, e.g., Samuel Beckett, T. S. Eliot, Martin Buber, Susanne Langer. Rather, the Marxist tradition is silent about the existential meaning of death, suffering, love, and friendship owing to its preoccupation with improving the social circumstances under which people pursue love, revel in friendship, and confront death. I share this concern.

Yet like both Russian novelists and blues singers, I also stress the concrete lived experience of despair and tragedy and the cultural equipment requisite for coping with the absurdities, anxieties, and frustrations, as well as the joys, laughter, and gaiety of life. In this deep sense, Marxism is not and cannot serve as a religion. And if it is cast as a religion, it is a shallow secular ideology of social change that fails to speak to us about the ultimate facts of human existence. To put it charitably, Marxist thought does not purport to be existential wisdom—of how to live one's life day by day. Rather, it claims to be a social theory of histories, societies, and cultures. Social theory is not the same as existential wisdom. Those theories that try to take the place of wisdom disempower people on existential matters, just as those wisdoms that try to shun theory usually subordinate people to the political powers that be.

My writings constitute a perennial struggle between my African and American identities, my democratic socialist convictions, and my Christian sense of the profound tragedy and possible triumph in life and history. I am a prophetic Christian freedom fighter principally because of distinctive Christian conceptions of what it is to be human, how we should act toward one another, and what we should hope for. These conceptions—put forward in a variety of diverse streams and strains of the Christian tradition stretching back over centuries—has to do with the indispensable yet never adequate capacities of human beings to create error-proof or problem-free situations, theories, or traditions— hence the strong anti-dogmatic or fallible character of prophetic Christian thought and practice which encourage relentless critical consciousness; the moral claim to view each and every individual as having equal status, as warranting dignity, respect, and love, especially those who are denied such dignity, respect, and love by individuals, families, groups, social structures, economic systems, or political regimes— hence the prophetic Christian identification and solidarity with the downtrodden and disinherited, the degraded and dispossessed; and lastly, the good news of Jesus Christ which lures and links human struggles to the coming of the kingdom—hence the warding off of disempowering responses to despair, dread, disappointment, and death.

Prophetic Christianity has a distinctive, though not exclusive, capacity to highlight critical, historical, and universal consciousness that yields a vigilant disposition toward prevailing forms of individual and institutional evil, an unceasing suspicion of ossified and petrified forms of dogmatism, and a strong propensity to resist various types of cynicism and nihilism.

Prophetic Christian conceptions of what it is to be human, how we should act, and what we should hope for are neither rationally demonstrable nor empirically verifiable in a necessary and universal manner. Rather, they are embedded and enacted in a form of life—a dynamic set of communities that constitute a diverse tradition—that mediates how I interpret my experiences, sufferings, joys, and undertakings. There are indeed good reasons to accept prophetic Christian claims, yet they are good not because they result from logical necessity or conform to transcendental criteria. Rather, these reasons are good (persuasive to some, nonsense to others) because they are rationally acceptable and existentially enabling for many self-critical finite and fallible creatures who are condemned to choose traditions under circumstances not of our own choosing. To choose a tradition (a version of it) is more than to be convinced by a set of arguments; it is also to decide to live alongside the slippery edge of life's abyss with the support of the dynamic stories, symbols, interpretations, and insights bequeathed by communities that came before.

I have always shunned the role of theologian because I have little interest in systematizing the dogmas and doctrines, insights and intuitions of the Christian tradition. Nor do I think that they can be rendered coherent and consistent. The theological task is a noteworthy endeavor—especially for the life of the church—yet my vocation uses Christian resources, among others, to speak to the multilayered crises of contemporary society and culture. So I am more a cultural critic with philosophic training who works out of the Christian tradition than a theologian who focuses on the systematic coherency or epistemic validity of Christian claims.

This vocation puts social theory, historiography, cultural criticism, and political engagement at the center of my prophetic Christian outlook. I do not believe that there are such things as Christian social theory, Christian historiography, Christian cultural criticism, or Christian politics—just as there are no such things as Christian mathematics, Christian physics, or Christian economics. Rather, there is prophetic Christian thought and practice informed by the best of these disciplines that highlights and enhances the plight of the loveless, luckless, landless, and other victims of social structural arrangements. In this way, my prophetic vocation overlaps in significant ways with such Marxists as Harry Magdoff and Paul Sweezy. In the present methodological debate against ironic skeptics, aesthetic historicists, political cynics, and explanatory agnostics, we stand together in defense of Marxist theory and socialist politics—even as we may disagree on how we conceive of Marxist theory or the kind of socialism we promote.

My move to Yale Divinity School in 1984 afforded me the opportunity to reflect on the crisis in American philosophy—as in *Post-Analytic Philosophy* (1985), edited by my good friend John Rajchman and myself, and in my book *The American Evasion of Philosophy* (1989). This coincided with an intense campus drive for clerical unionism at Yale (one of the few labor victories of the 1980s) and against Yale's investments in South African companies. Again, my arrest and jail resulted. This action served as a fine example for my wonderful son, Clifton, quickly approaching adolescence—an example he has followed as a progressive student body president of his predominantly black middle school in Atlanta. Partly owing to this action, my request for leave was denied and I was forced to teach a full program at Yale (two courses) and the University of Paris VIII (three courses) in the spring of 1987. I commuted every five to seven days from New Haven to Paris from February to April. To be on the same faculty with Gilles Deleuze (who retired that spring) and Jean-François Lyotard was an honor. Yet I was amazed at the French students' ignorance of U.S. philosophy and the hunger for Afro-American history and culture. In my graduate seminar on John Dewey, Hilary Putnam, Stanley Cavell, and Richard Rorty, brilliant students had never heard of Dewey—in fact, one wanted to study with him (unaware he had died in 1952)! My Afro-American intellectual history course was scheduled for twenty, but over a hundred students (many from African and Arab countries) enrolled. Student activism regarding educational reform was increasing at the time and I participated in many lively discussions and actions. When I returned from Paris I decided to leave Yale—for personal reasons linked with my lovely African wife-to-be Elleni Gebre Amlak—and went back to Union. But after a short year I decided to go to Princeton University, to teach in the religion department and direct the Afro-American studies program. My major motivation was to constitute a critical mass of black scholars—with the great Toni Morrison at the center—although I also was eager to learn from other superb scholars there.

At present, besides completing *Breakin' Bread,* a book written with bell hooks on the black crisis (including black male/female relations), a collection of essays *(Prophetic Criticism),* and a work on David Hume (seven years in the making), my focus is twofold: the battle in the arts, popular culture, and the academy over Eurocentrism and multiculturalism, and the crisis in black and progressive leadership. In 1990, I co-edited (with Russell Ferguson, Martha Gever, and Trinh T. Minh-ha) *Out There: Marginalization and Contemporary Cultures* (MIT) for the New Museum of Contemporary Art. This landmark text may set the framework for the debate between conservatives like Allan Bloom, Africanist thinkers such as Leonard Jeffries, feminist theorists countering patriarchal canons like Elaine Showalter, and democratic socialists of African descent like myself. This battle will continue to rage well into the twenty-first century. My major aim is to rescue the ambiguous legacy of the European age from conservatives, to accent the racist, patriarchal, and homophobic currents that still run through American intellectual and cultural life while criticizing any separatist politics or parochial outlook, and linking the new cultural politics of difference to a democratic socialist perspective. My critical appreciation of the hip-hop culture of American youth, especially black youth, reflects this dialectical reading of our present moment. I applaud the spirit of resistance against racism yet condemn its misogynist and homophobic elements.

The crisis of leadership in black and progressive communities is symptomatic of the paucity of credible strategies and tactics for social change in the United States. It also reflects the relative inability of the left to mobilize and organize over time and space. Needless to say, there is no easy way out of this impasse.

The effort is more difficult due to the pervasive disarray of the progressive movement in the United States. Never before in our history has the U.S. left been so bereft of courageous leaders of vision, intelligence, and integrity. We simply do not have formidable figures that the public identifies with progressive causes. Aside from those preoccupied with electoral politics and admirable local activists with little national attention, there are no major leaders who articulate in bold and defiant terms—with genuine passion and analytical clarity—the moral imperative to address the maldistribution of resources, wealth, and power, escalating xenophobia, ecological devastation, national decline, and spiritual impoverishment we are facing. This crisis of leadership adds to the balkanization of U.S. progressive politics—its fragmentation, isolation, and insularity. Given the power of big business and cultural conservatism, the U.S. left has potency primarily when strong leadership—rooted in extra-parliamentary organizational activity—energizes and galvanizes demoralized progressives and liberals across racial, class, regional, age, and gender lines. This usually does not last long—so the propitious moment must be seized.

We find it hard to seize this moment not only because of the establishment's strategies of repression and incorporation but also owing to the consumer culture—with its addictive seductions and pacifying pastimes—that often saps and disperses our energies for collective struggle. Market morality engulfs us in such a way that it is difficult to arrange our lives so that communal activity supersedes personal pursuits. Market mentality makes it hard for us to believe our sacrificial progressive efforts will make a real difference in our busy and short lives. And since there can be no substantive progressive politics without oppositional subcultures, institutions, and networks, the predominant "market way of life" presents a—maybe *the*—major challenge for progressive politics.

At the moment, the most *explosive* issues in U.S. society revolve around black bodies and womens' wombs—race and abortion. And, in a fundamental sense, the starting points—through not landing grounds—for progressive politics in the 1990s may be *enhancement* of the poor, especially those of color, and protection of womens' rights. Yet reform measures such as progressive taxation and appointment of liberal judges fall far short of what is required. We also need a progressive cultural renaissance that reshapes our values, restructures how we live, and puts struggle and sacrifice closer to the center of what we think and do. Only then will our fight to turn back a market-driven, conservative United States—already far down the road to social chaos and self-destruction—be not only desirable but also credible. The defense of the relevance of Marxist thought, including its ethical dimensions, after the Cold War is an indispensable weapon in this fight.

At the forefront of this fight stands Jesse Jackson. His historic presidential campaigns were the major progressive responses to Reagan's conservative policies. His 1988 bid was the first time since the last days of Martin Luther King, Jr.'s Poor People's campaign—with the grand exception of Mayor Harold Washington's election in Chicago—that the nearly *de facto* segregation in U.S. progressive politics was confronted and partly surmounted.

Yet Jackson's courageous leadership is problematic. His televisual style—a style too preoccupied with TV cameras—relies on personal charisma at the expense of grassroots organizing. His brilliance and energy sustain his public visibility at the expense of programmatic follow-through. This style downplays peoples' participatory possibilities—at the level of followership and leadership. More pointedly, it shuns democratic accountability. Pure democracy must never be a fetish for progressives. Work must get done; decisions must be made. But criticism and democratic practices are the lifeblood of any progressive organization worthy of the name. Jackson's televisual style not only mitigates against this; it tends to preclude it. So despite his salutary social democratic politics, Jackson's televisual style may be reaching the point at which it undermines his crucial message.

This televisual style must give way to a collective model of progressive leadership that puts a premium on grassroots organizing, criticism, and democratic accountability. The future of U.S. progressive politics lies with those engaged local activists who have made a difference yet who also have little interest in being in the national limelight. They engage in protracted organizing in principled coalitions that bring power and pressure to bear on specific issues—especially issues of jobs, housing, health and child care, education, and ecological protection. Without such activists there can be no progressive politics. Yet state, regional, and national networks are also necessary for an effective progressive politics. This is why locally based collective (and especially multiracial and multigender) models of leadership are needed. These models must shun the idea of one national progressive leader; they must highlight critical dialogue and democratic accountability within and across organizations. These models of collective leadership will more than likely not be part of the lethargic electoral system riddled with decreasing revenues (i.e., debt), loss of public confidence, self-perpetuating mediocrity, and pervasive corruption. Rather, the future of U.S. progressive politics lies in the capacity of a collective leadership to energize, mobilize, and organize working and poor people. Democratic socialists can play a crucial role in projecting an all-embracing moral vision of freedom, justice, and equality, and making social analyses that connect and link activists together. In this way we can be a socialist leaven in a larger progressive loaf. Yet this loaf will never get baked if we remain separate, isolated, insular, and fragmented. America's massive social breakdown requires that we come together—for the sake of our lives, our children, and our sacred honor.

The Ethical Dimensions
of Marxist Thought

◇ 1 ◇

Radical Historicism

The radical historicist approach to ethics claims that the search for *philosophic* criteria, grounds, or foundations for moral principles is doomed. By "philosophic" I mean criteria, grounds, or foundations that carry the weight of rational necessity and/or universal obligation— that we are compelled to accept by some kind of philosophic rationality, or that we are all obliged to endorse by some overarching law or rule. The radical historicist approach calls into question the very possibility of an ethics (Kantian ethics, for example) that claims to rest upon philosophic notions of rational necessity and/or universal obligations.

There are two reasons for this radical historicist claim. First, the radical historicist sees the dynamic historical processes as subjecting all criteria, grounds, and foundations to revision and modification. Whereas notions such as "rational necessity" and "universal obligation" are employed by philosophers precisely in order to secure immunity from revision and modification. By rejecting these notions, the radical historicist is precluding the possibility of either timeless criteria, necessary grounds, or universal foundations for ethics. Second, for the radical historicist, the only plausible candidates for the criteria, grounds, or foundations in question would be the *contingent, community-specific* agreements people make in relation to particular norms, aims, goals, and objectives. These agreements, owing to their dynamic character, do not carry the weight of rational necessity or universal obligation.

By calling into question the possibility of securing either timeless criteria, necessary grounds, or universal foundations for moral principles, the radical historicist approach is calling into question a particular

1

conception of objectivity in ethics and hence the possibility of ethics as a *philosophic* discipline. Without such criteria, grounds, or foundations to serve as a last court of appeal for adjudicating between rival moral principles, *objectivity* in ethics or *valid* justification of moral principles becomes but a dream, a philosopher's dream which results from an obsession with philosophic certainty and security in the flux of historical change and development. In this sense, ethics as a *philosophic* discipline has no subject matter.

The radical historicist approach to ethics holds that people make ethical judgments in light of moral principles, employ criteria to undergird such principles and give reasons to justify their criteria, principles, and judgments. But it claims that these judgments, principles, and criteria are philosophically groundless or that they do not rest upon philosophic foundations.

Therefore, for the radical historicist, the search for philosophic foundations or grounds for moral principles is but an edifying way of reminding (and possibly further committing) oneself and others to what particular (old or new) moral community or group of believers one belongs to. Instead of focusing on the *status* (objective or subjective, necessary or contingent, universal or particular) of moral principles, the radical historicist approach stresses the *role* and *function* these principles (or any principles) play in various cultures and societies. Instead of accenting the *validity* or *objectivity* of the justification of moral principles, the radical historicist approach highlights the plausible *descriptions* and *explanations* of the emergence, dominance, and decline of particular moral principles under specific social conditions in the historical process. Instead of *philosophic* notions such as status, validity, objectivity, the radical historicist approach prefers *theoretic* notions such as role, function, description, and explanation.

The radical historicist approach discards the quest for philosophic certainty and the search for philosophic foundations because, it claims, this quest and search rests upon a misguided picture of philosophy—a picture of philosophy as the discipline that enables us to grasp necessary and universal forms, essences, substances, categories, or grounds upon which fleeting cultural and historical phenomena can rest. For the radical historicist, philosophy itself is but a part of the fleeting cultural and historical phenomena, and it is hence incapable of grounding anything else. The vision of philosophy as a quest for philosophic certainty and search for philosophic foundations is an ahistorical vision, a hapless attempt to escape from the flux of history by being philosophic, that is, by being bound to certainty, tied to necessity, or linked to universality.

Two noteworthy implications for moral philosophy result from the radical historicist approach to ethics. First, the distinction between moral philosopher and social critic breaks down. The moral philosopher is no longer viewed as either engaging in an investigation into the nature of the "logic of moral discourse" or generating timeless criteria, necessary grounds, or universal foundations for moral principles which should regulate human behavior. Rather the moral philosopher attempts to put forward "moral" guidelines or insights as to how to solve particular pressing problems, overcome urgent dilemmas, and alleviate specific hardships. Of course, the moral philosopher must still "justify" guidelines or insights, but the notion of justification is understood in a new way.

This new way of understanding the notion of justification is the second noteworthy implication for moral philosophy which results from the radical historicist viewpoint. No longer does the idea of justification serve as the last court of appeal which stands above the contingent and variable world of fleeting morals. Instead, as we noted earlier, the notion of justification is understood to be a way of reminding ourselves and others which particular community or set of we-intentions (e.g., "we would that . . .") we identify with.

Since the radical historicist approach to ethics rejects the idea of philosophic grounds or foundations for moral principles, the idea of a last philosophic court of appeal that stands above contingent and variable morals is precluded. The point is not to lift oneself out of the flux of history—an impossible task—but rather to immerse oneself more deeply into history by consciously identifying with—and digesting *critically* the values of—a particular community or tradition.

For the radical historicist, the task of ethics is not *philosophic,* it is not to put forward irrefutable justifications of particular moral viewpoints. Rather the task of ethics is *theoretic:* the task is to discover ways in which to develop a larger consensus and community, such as through example and exposure, through pressure and persuasion, without the idea of a last philosophic court of appeal in the background. If one disagrees with a particular consensus or community, the task is not to seek philosophic foundations for one's view, but rather to put forward a realizable alternative, a new possibility for consensus and community, and then to make it attractive to others.

Radical Historicism and Moral Relativism

The radical historicist approach in ethics is often understood to be identical with moral relativism. In this section, I shall try to show that this identity-claim is misleading—not primarily because the radical historicist makes claims different from those of the moral relativist about objectivity and validity in ethics, but rather because the radical historicist assumes a different conception of philosophy than does the moral relativist. To put it crudely, the moral relativist is on the right track but is still captive to the vision of philosophy as the quest for certainty and the search for foundations, whereas the radical historicist is a moral relativist liberated from this vision and hence no longer to be labelled by terms which presuppose it.

Before I examine moral relativism, I shall briefly define what ethical view moral relativism is reacting against, namely, *hard objectivism,* or solid foundationalist ethics. This viewpoint takes many forms. I shall note only two forms. First, *absolutism,* which claims it is possible to generate and justify rationally necessary or universally obligatory, moral standards against which to judge rival ethical judgments (or beliefs). Second, *scientific naturalism,* which holds that it is possible to reduce moral truths or facts to nonmoral, i.e., scientific, truths or facts, and thereby be as "objective" as scientists. Although the absolutist view posits the radical autonomy of ethics and the scientific naturalist view posits a radical reduction of ethics, both subscribe to the basic claim of hard objectivism: that there must be necessary grounds, universal foundations, for moral principles.

I will present three versions of moral relativism and examine the claims put forward in each version.[1] The first of these versions—descriptive relativism—is an empirical thesis that pertains to the diversity of fundamental ethical beliefs; the second—strong relativism—is a thesis about the existence of rational *procedures* or *standards* to adjudicate between conflicting ethical beliefs or judgments; the third—weak relativism—is a thesis about the existence of rational *criteria* to guide one's choice between rational procedures or standards that adjudicate between conflicting ethical beliefs or judgments. *Descriptive relativism* claims that the fundamental ethical beliefs of people in diverse cultures and societies differ and even conflict. *Strong relativism* holds that there are no rational procedures or objective (universal) standards that permit one to justify ethical beliefs or judgments against others. *Weak relativism* says that there are some rational procedures or objective standards for justifying certain ethical beliefs or judgments against others, but that there are no rational criteria for choosing between sets of rational procedures or standards. Let us briefly examine these three versions.

Descriptive relativism puts forward an empirical claim. It does not hold that people in different cultures and societies make different ethical judgments. This is obviously true. Rather it claims that people in different cultures and societies have different fundamental ethical beliefs. The distinction between ethical judgments and fundamental ethical beliefs is a crucial one. Ethical judgments are based on fundamental ethical beliefs and factual beliefs (about the self, the world, and God). Since factual beliefs are theory-laden, we can legitimately infer that ethical judgments appeal to fundamental ethical beliefs *in light of theories about the self, the world, and God.*

For example, imagine two societies—one secular, the other religious—which accept and follow the fundamental ethical belief that people should attend to the welfare of the physically handicapped. Suppose the first society is guided by a secular theory about the self and the world which denies life after death. Furthermore, it holds that physically handicapped people are biologically disabled human beings owing to discernible mishaps in nature. Only persistent and prolonged scientific investigations into the natural causes of such mishaps provide a clue for their cure. Until such cures are found, this society collectively decides that physically handicapped people should reside in the homes of loved ones or in hospitable public residences. This decision serves as evidence that this secular society accepts and follows the fundamental ethical belief that the welfare of physically handicapped people ought to be attended to.

Suppose the second society is regulated by a religious theory about the self, the world, and God which affirms life after death. Furthermore, it holds that physically handicapped people will have divine status in the hereafter if they are put to death before the age of one. So the society decides to kill all physically handicapped newborn infants. Despite this affront to our modern sensibilities, these killings serve as evidence that this society accepts and follows the same fundamental ethical belief as the secular society described above.

This crude example is *not* a case of descriptive relativism. It illustrates how different ethical judgments can be reached based on the same fundamental ethical belief and conflicting theories about the self, the world, and God. Both societies value the welfare of physically handicapped people, but they arrive at diverging ethical decisions owing to their different understandings of the notion of "welfare" within their different theories about the self, the world, and God.

Now imagine our societies one hundred years later. Suppose the religious society has now acquired the same theory about the self and the world as the secular society. The formerly religious society now denies life after death and no longer holds that physically handicapped infants under one year old will have divine status in any hereafter. Yet this society continues to kill physically handicapped newborn infants.

This second example, reconstructed from the first one, clearly is a case of descriptive relativism. The two societies share the same theory about the self and world, yet still arrive at different ethical judgments regarding the welfare of physically handicapped people. We are forced to conclude that the formerly religious society (now secular) no longer accepts and follows the fundamental ethical belief that the welfare of physically handicapped people ought to be attended to.

Strong relativism is a more complicated doctrine. Its basic claim is that there is no Archimedian point from which to adjudicate between conflicting ethical beliefs or judgments. It denies the possibility of *sub specie aeternitatis* from which to judge rival ethical beliefs of judgments.

This doctrine is complicated because its implications are diverse. First, it could yield an *extreme moral nihilism* which claims that there are no moral truths or facts. Admittedly, it is a bit misleading to call extreme nihilism a form of moral relativism since it denies even relativistic moral claims about right and wrong, just and unjust, good and bad. For the extreme moral nihlist (like Max Stirner, as we shall see in chapter 3), moral claims—relativistic or objectivistic—are mere illusions.

Second, strong relativism could lead to what is often called *normative relativism,* which holds that a particular ethical belief or judgment may be right for one person or society and not right for another person or society, given that there are no morally significant differences in the two societies. This doctrine differs from extreme moral nihilism in that it does not deny moral truths or facts. Instead, it claims that there are moral truths or facts and that these moral truths or facts are always relative to a given person, group, or society.

Normative relativism denies the universalizability of moral truths or facts, whereas extreme moral nihilism denies the existence of moral truths or facts. Of course, some objectivistic Kantians would claim that the denial of the universalizability of moral truths or facts is tantamount to denying the existence of moral truths or facts. But this claim only illustrates an affinity between some objectivistic Kantians and extreme moral nihilists: an obsession with universal foundations for moral facts or truths. The important point here is that both extreme moral nihilism and normative relativism reject the possibility of a rational, objective, universal standard from which to adjudicate between rival ethical judgments (or beliefs). In short, both fall under the rubric of strong relativism.

Finally, strong relativism could possibly yield a view which is usually referred to as *meta-ethical relativism,* namely, the view that rival ethical judgments (or beliefs) can *both* be right or equally valid. This view differs from extreme moral nihilism in that it accepts a notion of validity in regard to moral judgments, whereas the extreme moral nihilist does not. Meta-ethical relativism claims that it is possible for there to be conflicting ethical judgments (or beliefs) about a particular case, both judgments being fully correct.

This view indeed sounds counterintuitive, but it is possible if we were to imagine a relativist C overhearing two nonrelativists, A and B, putting forward conflicting ethical judgments about a specific issue. For example, if A says that the death penalty is right and B holds that the death penalty is wrong, they surely are both right from their own nonrelativist perspectives. But for the relativist C overhearing the conversation, the nonrelativistic ethical judgment of A is justified and valid for A but not for B and the nonrelativistic ethical judgment of B is justified and valid for B but not for A. In C's relativistic meta-ethical perspective, both conflicting ethical judgments of A and B would be correct.

It is important to note that being committed to strong relativism does not commit one to all of its sub-relativisms, but that it does commit one to at least one of them. That is, if one adheres to the doctrine of strong relativism, one is either a moral nihilist or a normative relativist and/or a meta-ethical relativist. Being a moral nihilist means that one cannot be a normative or meta-ethical relativist, whereas one can be both a normative relativist and a meta-ethical relativist.

Weak relativism holds that it is possible to arrive at rational procedures or objective, universal standards that justify certain ethical beliefs or judgments against others. It also claims that there can be a plurality of such procedures and standards between which there can be no adjudication. Therefore weak relativism puts forward a weaker claim than strong relativism. It would not yield moral nihilism, normative realism, or meta-ethical relativism.

Weak relativism would not yield moral nihilism because it affirms the existence of moral truths and facts. It would not lead to normative relativism because it endorses the universalizability of moral facts and truths. And it would not produce meta-ethical relativism because it assumes there to be a general convergence between the plurality of rational procedures and objective, universal standards regarding ethical judgments and also because it refuses to view nonrelativistic ethical judgments through a relativistic lens.

Weak relativism, like strong relativism, holds that there is no Archimedian point from which to adjudicate conflicting ethical beliefs or judgments. But unlike strong relativism, it does not go on to claim that there are no last philosophic courts of appeal. Instead, weak relativism holds that there are *philosophic* criteria—such as logical consistency, theoretical coherency, simplicity—which permit the affirmation of *some* rational procedures and objective, universal standards and the rejection of less rational procedures and less objective, universal standards. Weak relativism tries to cling to some threadbare notion of universal validity or ethical objectivity without appealing to a timeless standard or Archimedian point. In this sense, weak relativism may be called moderate historicism or soft objectivism. It is the halfway house between radical historicism and hard objectivism. It attempts to take history seriously, like radical historicism, yet like hard objectivism, to preserve philosophic notions of objectivity and validity in ethics.

Weak relativism can be viewed as endorsing a sifting process through which prospective moral procedures or standards must pass. Some are deemed more rational, objective, and universal than others, i.e., they pass the test and thereby deserve to be viewed as serious ethical viewpoints. The sifting process consists roughly of rigorously applying philosophic criteria (usually generated by professional moral philosophers) to prospective moral procedures and standards.

For example, the major contemporary prospective moral procedures or standards consist of various versions of Kantianism, act and rule utilitarianism, intuitionism, perfectionism, egoism, and forms of consequentialism. These all represent attempts to establish moral validity or ethical objectivity in the sense that they provide relevant reasons— reasons that carry weight, that can persuade and convince rational, impartial human beings—for arriving at ethical judgments. From the standpoint of the contemporary community of professional moral philosophers, the most logically consistent, theoretically coherent, and formulaically simple procedures provide good, relevant reasons and more logically inconsistent, theoretically incoherent, formulaically obscure procedures yield bad, unconvincing reasons.

At the present time in America, certain sophisticated forms of consequentialism (usually nonutilitarian versions) and of Kantianism are the most widely accepted moral procedures for generating philosophic justifications for ethical judgments. A recent example of the consequentialist view claims roughly that one must begin with a conception of human beings which highlights their capacity to anticipate pain, have memories of the past, and sustain ends, commitments, and projects over time. This conception of the person can be understood to be based on empirical evidence. These features become the morally relevant facts which serve as the starting point from which rational procedures of objective, universal standards for justifying ethical judgments can be constructed.

A current example of the Kantian viewpoint holds that one must begin with a conception of human beings which accents their capacity to act contrary to their natural desires, social interests, and capricious prejudices, i.e., their rationality and freedom. This conception of the person can be understood to be based on metaphysical features, or features about ourselves which are rationally indispensable if we are to make our own behavior comprehensible to ourselves. These features become morally relevant facts which serve as the starting point from which a rational procedure or objective, universal standard for justifying ethical judgments can be generated.

So weak relativism denies an Archimedian point from which to adjudicate rival ethical judgments (or beliefs), but it does permit philosophic objectivity in ethics. It promotes this thin notion of objectivity in that it does not claim that the starting points for agreed-upon rational procedures or objective, universal standards are absolute or immune from revision. Instead, it holds that these starting points can be shown to possess some kind of rational necessity and/or universal obligation upon which to rest one's moral viewpoints.

Weak relativism is still a version of moral relativism to the extent that it allows an open-ended pluralism among the procedures and standards deemed rational, objective, and universal. It says that there is no higher philosophic criteria that can be appealed to in deciding which particular rational procedures or objective, universal standard ought to be chosen from among the small set of such procedures and standards, only philosophic criteria to judge which procedures and standards belong to this small set. So weak relativism permits relativism only at the "higher" level.

It is important not to confuse the radical historicist approach to ethics with the most exhorbitant form of strong relativism, namely, extreme nihilism. As we noted earlier, the extreme moral nihilist holds that there are no moral truths or facts. The radical historicist view says that there are moral truths or facts, but that they are always subject to revision. The radical historicist view then goes on (sounding like a normative relativist) to claim that such moral truths or facts are always relative to specific aims, goals, or objectives of particular groups, communities, cultures, or societies. Yet the radical historicist perspective differs from normative relativism because the former, in stark contrast to the latter, affirms the universalizability of such moral truths or facts that are established relative to specific aims, goals, or objectives of particular groups, communities, cultures, or societies.

The fundamental difference between the radical historicist and the extreme moral nihilist is that the latter remains under the grip of the quest for philosophic certainty, the search for philosophic foundations. Since the extreme moral nihilist believes such a quest and search is hopeless, he or she throws in the towel and deems illusory what was once believed to be real, namely, universal moral truths or facts. In other words, the extreme moral nihilist is a deeply disenchanted and disappointed hard objectivist. For the extreme moral nihilist, like the hard objectivist, moral truths or facts are either rationally necessary, universally obligatory, and philosophically objective or they are capricious, arbitrary, and subjective. For both, it is an either/or affair—there are either philosophic foundations or there is the abyss.

This commitment to the vision of philosophy as the quest for certainty and search for foundations also is assumed by the normative and meta-ethical relativists. From the radical historicist point of view, these positions represent a failure of nerve, a lack of courage, in that the relativist preoccupation with an unattainable objectivity precludes the universalization of the ethical judgments which come from particular groups, communities, cultures, or societies. The normative relativist seems to believe that an Archimedian point is needed for ethical judgments to be universalizable, and that since there is no Archimedian point, we should not universalize relativist ethical judgments.

But for the radical historicist, universalizing particular ethical judgments has nothing to do with an Archimedian point. The nonexistence of an Archimedian point plays no role whatsoever in determining the scope and status of ethical judgments; it is not even a factor in the framework against which one understands one's own ethical position. For it is only plausible to assume, as do relativists, that an Archimedian point is required for universalizing ethical judgments when it is believed that universalization requires permission from philosophic criteria, grounds, or foundations.

It is at this point that we clearly begin to see the contrast between the forms of moral relativism and the radical historicist approach to ethics. The moral relativists are openly engaged in a fierce struggle against hard objectivism. Their response is either to radically reject hard objectivism and accept the consequences that the hard objectivist view claims will follow (as in the case of extreme moral nihilism), to liberally reject hard objectivism and preclude the possibility of universalizing ethical judgments (as in the case of normative relativism and meta-ethical relativism), or to conservatively reject hard objectivism and then water down notions of objectivity and validity to acceptable philosophic proportions (as in the case of weak relativism, moderate historicism, or soft objectivism). The important insight here is that all these forms of moral relativism allow hard objectivism to set the terms and dictate the

conditions as to what are the options and alternatives to hard objectivism. Moral relativism, in its various forms, refuses to ask the more
fundamental questions, namely, what would an ethical position look
like which did not merely *react* against hard objectivism? What would
constitute an approach to ethics which did not permit hard objectivism
to set the terms and dictate the conditions as to what are the options
and alternatives to hard objectivism?

Moral relativism does not ask these fundamental questions precisely
because it presupposes a vision of philosophy which precludes the
possibility of asking these questions. As long as moral relativists see
themselves in opposition to hard objectivism, they remain captive to
the vision of philosophy as the quest for philosophic certainty, the
search for philosophic foundations. As long as moral relativists remain
captive to this vision they remain locked into its fundamental distinctions of objectivism/relativism, necessary/arbitrary, essential/accidental,
universality/particularity, etc. The very ascription "relativist" bespeaks
an allegiance to these distinctions and to the metaphilosophical vision
which circumscribes them.

The radical historicist approach to ethics fundamentally differs from
moral relativism in that it rejects the vision of philosophy as the quest
for philosophic certainty, the search for philosophic foundations. This
rejection means that hard objectivism does not set the framework for
opposition, that the primary task is not to engage in a fierce struggle
against hard objectivism, that one's alternative position should not
affirm the fundamental distinctions of the metaphilosophical vision one
is rejecting.

The radical historicist is a moral relativist liberated from the vision of
philosophy which holds the moral relativist captive. This liberation
primarily consists of overcoming the fundamental distinctions of objec-
tivism/relativism, necessary/arbitrary, essential/accidental, universality/
particularity, etc., by understanding that these positions are but alter-
nate sides of the same coin, that both positions are tied to a common
picture of what philosophy is and ought to be, that both positions
become credible alternatives only by freezing the historical process or
by selecting a particular time slice in a specific culture and society.

Once more to put it crudely, the radical historicist is a moral relativist
who has made this metaphilosophical move. The radical historicist
discards the pejorative self-description "relativist" and rejects the objec-

tivist lens. The radical historicist does not see attainable or unattainable timeless criteria, necessary grounds, or universal foundations which cut through the flux of history, but rather different dynamic human agreements and disagreements and changing community-specific criteria constituting continuous and discontinuous traditions which are linked in highly complex ways to multiple human needs, interests, biases, aims, goals, and objectives. If there is to be an appropriate response to hard objectivism (and its various forms), the radical historicist approach would not be to reject its philosophic status, as does moral relativism, but rather to attempt to understand its historic emergence and its social function and cultural role during its dominance, and to describe and explain its decline.

◇ 2 ◇

Marx's Road to Radical Historicism

Marx's own radical historicist approach to ethics can be best explicated by first observing its evolution. For one thing, it is in the early writings that his preoccupation with the issues of objectivity and validity in ethics is intense. Then too, we will better understand Marx's specific radical historicist approach to ethics if we see it as a moment in the dynamic process of self-criticism, as a position critical of his earlier views. And this process of self criticism can be made clear only if we have some idea what his ethical viewpoints were before his adoption of the radical historicist approach.

Therefore this chapter will be interpretive in character and historical in content. It will focus on the development of Marx's understanding of ethics up to his adoption of the radical historicist approach to ethics, highlighting his famous schoolboy letter to his father, a section of his dissertation, a few of his journalistic articles and political essays, and portions of *The Economic and Philosophic Manuscripts*.

The underlying thesis of my explication and interpretation of Marx's early writings is that he becomes a radical historicist in ethics primarily because of his disillusionment and disenchantment with the conception of philosophy as the quest for certainty and search for foundations. His disillusionment and disenchantment is prompted by his acknowledgment of the importance of historical consciousness as found in Hegel's philosophy and by the significance of dynamic social practices and human activities as revealed by his political activism. The historical consciousness and the political activism finally lead Marx to reject the foundationalist conception of philosophy and its hard objectivist views

14

in ethics. This metaphilosophical move is the culmination of a tortuous journey. And in order to better understand where he finally arrives, we first shall briefly explore how he gets there.

The Famous Letter

The first text I shall consider in this section is the famous letter Marx wrote to his father while he was a student of law at the University of Berlin. This letter is an appropriate starting point for our consideration of Marx's road to the radical historicist approach to ethics, for it demonstrates Marx's preoccupation with overcoming the opposition between what is and what ought to be, between facts and values, and ultimately between science and ethics.

This opposition obsesses Marx in his study of law and is revealed clearly in his letter to his father. He first introduces this opposition within the context of his writing of romantic poetry.[1]

> In accordance with my state of mind at the time, lyrical poetry was found to be my first subject, at least the most pleasant and immediate one. But owing to my attitude and whole previous development it was purely idealistic. My heaven, my art, became a world beyond, as remote as my love. Everything real became hazy and what is hazy has no definite outlines. All the poems of the first three volumes I sent to Jenny are marked by attacks on our times, diffuse and inchoate expressions of feelings, nothing natural, everything built out of moonshine, *complete opposition between what is and what ought to be,* rhetorical reflections instead of poetic thoughts, but perhaps also a certain warmth of feeling and striving for poetic fire.[2]

The association of the is/ought opposition with romantic, idealistic poetry is significant. The key contrast here is between the reality and unreality of his love. This love is real in that he feels it deeply as an undeniable flow of desires, emotions, and passions; it is unreal in that it remains unfulfilled, unrealized, unconsummated. What is is his love and her absence; what ought to be is his love and her presence.

Marx attempts to overcome this opposition through his art, by creating an imaginary substitute that has no bounds or limits. In this way, he identifies the solution to the is/ought opposition with unregulated imagination, intense subjectivity, capricious arbitrariness, and fanciful illusions. He then proceeds,

> Poetry, however, could be and had to be only an accompaniment; I had to study law and above all felt the urge to wrestle with philosophy. The two were so closely linked that, on the one hand, I read through Heineccius, Thibaut, and the sources quite uncritically, in a mere schoolboy fashion; thus, for instance, I translated the first two books of the Pandect into German, and, on the other hand, tried to elaborate a philosophy of law covering the whole field of law. I prefaced this with some metaphysical propositions by way of introduction and continued this unhappy opus as far as public law, a work of almost 300 pages.[3]

It is essential to point out that this linking of law to philosophy is not Marx's idiosyncratic or novel approach. Rather, it was a common one for law students of his day. In fact, the very first sentence of the Pandects, the major text for law students then, was "Jurisprudence is the true philosophy" *(juris prudentia est vera philosophia)*. The law was conceived as both a science and a moral activity; it utilized causal language, applied to and held for all, and was concerned first and foremost with the common good of society.

Unfortunately, the three hundred page text on the philosophy of law is not extant, so we must take Marx's word as to what caused his dissatisfaction with it and what it looked like. In regard to the former question he writes,

> Here, above all, the same opposition between what is and what ought to be, which is characteristic of idealism, stood out as a serious defect and was the source of the hopelessly incorrect division of the subject-matter.[4]

In this important passage, he makes two claims. First, the is/ought opposition perplexed him. It served as a major obstacle to completing the work. The adjective "same" apparently refers to the opposition mentioned in relation to his romantic poetry, the opposition associated with illusions and arbitrariness. Second, the is/ought opposition was the source of a methodological error. It contributed to a wrong approach to the subject matter, a misguided procedure for understanding and grasping the object to be studied.

And what was this methodological error, this wrong approach, this misguided procedure? Marx continues,

First of all came what I was pleased to call the metaphysics of law, i.e., basic principles, reflections, definitions of concepts, divorced from all actual law and every actual form of law, as occurs in Fichte, only in my case it was more modern and shallower.[5]

Marx's view of the reality and unreality of the law is like his idealistic formulation of his love. The law is real in that there are actual laws which punish, coerce, or regulate human behavior; it is unreal in that the principles that ground these laws seem to be divorced, far removed, and distant from them. What is consists of actual laws, with no underlying principles; what ought to be consists of metaphysical principles that seem to have little relation to the actual laws. The only way to overcome this opposition, it appears, is to put forward arbitrary divisions of the subject matter such that the principles correlate in some way with the actual laws.

Marx insists that this attempt to overcome the is/ought opposition in the philosophy of law is inadequate. Its major fault is that it does not permit the subject matter "to take shape as something living and developing in a many-sided way." He claims,

. . . in the concrete expression of a living world of ideas, as exemplified by law, the state, nature, and philosophy as a whole, the object itself must be studied in its development; arbitrary divisions must not be introduced, *the rational character of the object itself must develop as something imbued with contradictions in itself and find its unity in itself.*[6]

This is a pivotal formulation of Marx's emerging conception of ethics. To be sure, it remains extremely vague, unexplained, and suggestive. But it contains his first attempt to search for a way to overcome the is/ought opposition, to minimize arbitrariness in rationally determining norms.

This first attempt to grapple with the is/ought opposition appeals to the development of the subject matter. This development is assumed, not demonstrated, to be rational, intelligible, capable of being understood. The development of the subject matter (or object) is rational and intelligible in that it consists of contradictions which ultimately are reconciled and unified.

Marx says that in his three hundred page work on the philosophy of law he examined the development of ideas in positive Roman law. He distinguished between the theory of formal law (form of the legal system) and the theory of material law (content of the legal system). He made this distinction in order to show how the form becomes embodied in its content. But he is not satisfied with this approach.

> This mistake lay in my belief that matter and form can and must develop separately from each other, and so I obtained not a real form, but something like a desk with drawers into which I then poured sand.[7]

He then states,

> The concept is indeed the mediating link between form and content. In a philosophical treatment of law, therefore, the one must arise in the other; indeed, the form should only be the continuation of the content.[8]

Again, we have only vague suggestions, little elaboration and discussion. But his attempt to come up with an acceptable and adequate philosophy of law continues.

> Thus I arrived at a division of the material such as could be devised by its author for at most an easy and shallow classification, but in which the spirit and truth of law disappeared. All law was divided into contractual and non-contractual.[9]

Marx disappointedly notes that at the end of the section on material private law and the beginning of the public law section which connects the law to the public good,

> . . . I saw the falsity of the whole thing, the basic plan of which borders on that of Kant, but deviates wholly from it in the execution, and again it became clear to me that there could be no headway without philosophy.[10]

Marx writes another large work. This time it is purely philosophic, based on a new system of metaphysical principles. He soon becomes disillusioned with it. This disillusionment forces him back to literary writing (e.g., plays, dramas, novels) and produces physical illness. Emerging from this illness, which requires a doctor-ordered stay in the country, he boldly announces:

> A curtain had fallen, my holies of holies was rent asunder, and new gods had to be installed.
>
> From the idealism which, by the way, I had compared and nourished with the idealism of Kant and Fichte, *I arrived at the point of seeking the idea in reality itself.* If previously the gods had dwelt above the earth, now they became its centre.
>
> I had read fragments of Hegel's philosophy, the grotesque craggy melody of which did not appeal to me. Once more I wanted to dive into

the sea, but with the definite intention of establishing that the nature of the mind is just as necessary, concrete and firmly based as the nature of the body. My aim was no longer to practice tricks of swordsmanship, but to bring genuine pearls into the light of day.[11]

After having been under the influence of Kant and Fichte, he now rejects them. His conception of ethics moves from being hard objectivist, idealist, and metaphysical (Kantian) to being soft objectivist, developmental, and immanentist ("idea in reality itself"). The new viewpoint closely resembles Hegel's dialectical perspective, a perspective he had resisted.

I wrote a dialogue of about 24 pages: "Cleanthes, or the Starting Point and Necessary Continuation of Philosophy." Here art and science, which had become completely divorced from each other, were to some extent united, and like a vigorous traveller I set about the task itself, a philosophical-dialectical account of divinity, as it manifests itself as the idea-in-itself, as religion, as nature, and as history. My last proposition was the beginning of the Hegelian system . . . this work, my dearest child, reared by moonlight, like a false siren delivers me into the arms of the enemy.[12]

Again physical sickness sets in, during which time he reads Hegel from "beginning to end" with disciples of Hegel, namely university lecturers and others who constitute the famous Doctor's Club (commonly known as the Left Hegelians). Marx throws himself into the embrace of Hegelian philosophy, dissecting it, scrutinizing it, and struggling not to swallow it whole. It appears to him that Hegel's philosophy is capable of overcoming the opposition between is and ought, form and content, with a methodology (and ontology) having something to do with the turn from the "ideal in itself" to the "idea in reality itself." Marx remarks,

. . . I became ever more firmly bound to the modern world philosophy from which I had thought to escape.[13]

The Dissertation

Marx's first attempt to come to terms with the is/ought opposition in a Hegelian way, to pursue the development of the "rational character of the object itself" is his doctoral dissertation. This work, entitled "Difference between the Democritean and Epicurean Philosophy of Nature," primarily attempts to examine the notions of contradiction and reconciliation in a world of process and development in light of a rational ideal immanent in this world. His enthusiastic extolling of philosophy and Epicurus can be seen as his endorsement of Hegel's anti-transcendental, this-worldly though soft objectivist, approach to ethics.

The basic aim of Marx's interpretation of Epicurus' philosophy of nature is to examine the contradiction in the Epicurean atom between its existence and essence, reality and ideality, content and form, matter and concept, isness and oughtness. With the Epicurean atom, Marx is able to grapple with the world in process wrought with contradiction yet containing an immanent ideal moving toward rational reconciliation.

Epicurus conceives the atom as *arche* and *stoicheia,* as beginning principle and element (or material substratum), as different determinations and revelatory moments of the same atom. (The resemblance to Hegel is obvious here.) These two roles constitute poles between which the atom moves, swinging like a pendulum from an alienated state to a state of wholeness and reconciliation.

> The contradiction between existence and essence, between matter and form, which is inherent in the concept of the atom, emerges in the individual atom itself once it is endowed with qualities. Through the quality the atom is alienated from its concept, but at the same time is perfected in its construction. It is from repulsion and the ensuing conglomerations of the qualified atoms that the world of appearance now emerges.[14]

At this point, Marx begins to struggle with the intelligibility of the contradiction in the atom. How can the atom be both endowed with qualities and real yet negate these qualities and be ideal? How can it exist alienated from its concept yet also be perfected? Under the guise of grasping Epicurean physics, he is grappling with the is/ought opposition. He is trying to come to terms with the way in which the ideal relates to the real, form to content, concept to matter, such that the "latter takes shape as something living and developing in a many-sided way" and that "the rational character of the object itself develops as something imbued with contradictions in itself and finds its unity in itself." His effort to arrive at a satisfactory conclusion goes as follows:

The atoms are, it is true, the substance of nature, out of which everything emerges, into which everything dissolves; but the continuous annihilation of the world of appearance comes to no result. New appearances are formed; but the atom itself always remains at the bottom as the foundation. Thus insofar as the atom is considered as pure concept, its existence is empty space, annihilated nature. Insofar as it proceeds to reality, it sinks down to the material basis which, as the bearer of a world of manifold relations, never exists but in forms which are indifferent and external to it. This is a necessary consequence, since the atom, presupposed as abstractly individual and complete, cannot actualise itself as the idealising and pervading power of this manifold.[15]

Marx's explication is similar to Plato's treatment of the beautiful and its relation to beautiful things. For Marx here, the pure concept of the atom and the matter of the atom, its ideality and reality, form and content, are connected by the self-presentation of the former in a variety of modes in the latter. The ideality, form, and concept of the atom have no independent status. They are known only insofar as they are revealed in the reality, content, and matter of the atom. Yet the two realms are not identical.

Plato tries to secure this relation with his concept of participation *(methexis);* Marx attempts to do so by assuming activity on behalf of the atom. This activity consists of the tiny swerve of the atom. This swerve is a constant move of the atom between absence and presence, concealment and revealment. In contrast to his earlier formulation of the is/ought opposition in the letter to his father, Marx now associates what is with presence and what ought to be with absence. By shifting his perspective from "the ideal in itself" to "the idea in reality itself," ideality and oughtness become hidden, absent, mere potentiality within reality. They are revealed only within a reality (and isness) in process and development. Ideality and oughtness constitute activity in reality which actualizes hidden potentialities. This activity is generated by contradiction in reality or in this case in the atom.

For Marx, the sphere of absence of the atom constitutes the ideality of the atom, the negation of the atom, the lack of any qualities. The real, material, quality-endowed atoms represent concrete determinations of atoms, determinations which are self-presentations of the ideality of atoms. In short, it is the atom as *arche* revealed as *stoicheia*. This seems to be what Marx means when he writes:

Abstract individuality is freedom from being, not freedom in being. It cannot shine in the light of being. This is an element in which this individuality loses its character and becomes material. For this reason the atom does not enter into the daylight of appearance or it sinks down to the material basis when it does enter it. The atom as such only exists in the void.[16]

The void is the realm of absence and concealment, the view of the atom as *arche;* appearance is the realm of presence and revealment, the view of the atom as *stoicheia.*

At this point, Marx's conception of ethics seems to be that ideals and norms can be known and discerned only insofar as they are manifest in the real world. Just as Plato claims that we know the beautiful solely by its making itself visible in beautiful things, Marx holds that we know ideality by its activity in reality, actualizing particular potentialities and specifically the motion, repulsion, or contradiction in the atom. Just as the beautiful, for Plato, is not reducible to beautiful things, so, for Marx, ideality of the atom is not reducible to the reality of the atom. *Arche* is never identical with *stoicheia.* Both constitute different modes of being, mediated by activity. Marx's embrace of a Hegelian solution to the is/ought opposition is quite evident here. Ideals exist in another realm (the idealist premise), but they take on significance only when they make their appearance in the world (the immanentist claim). It is their "activity" that warrants our attention, not their status independent of this "activity."

Marx goes on to claim that the opposition between is and ought, reality and ideality, existence and essence, content and form, matter and concept, in the Epicurean atom is overcome in the permanence and stability of the heavenly bodies. The heavenly bodies are the atoms made whole. The activity that mediates between the *arche* and *stoicheia,* ideal and real, essence and existence, ought and is, poles of the atom leads to a reconciliation in rationally necessary and universal Archimedian entities, immutable and invariable heavenly bodies—an appropriate Hegelian solution.

The heavenly bodies are eternal and unchangeable; they have their center of gravity in, not outside, themselves. Their only action is motion, and, separated by empty space, they swerve from the straight line, and form a system of repulsion and attraction while at the same time preserving their own independence and also, finally, generating time out of themselves as the form of their appearance. *The heavenly bodies are therefore the atoms become real.* In them matter has received in itself individuality.[17]

Marx continues,

Indeed, we have seen how the whole Epicurean philosophy of nature is pervaded with the contradiction between essence and existence, between form and matter. *But this contradiction is resolved in the heavenly bodies;* the conflicting moments are reconciled. In the celestial system matter has received form into itself, has taken up the individuality into itself and has thus achieved its independence . . . matter has reconciled itself with the form and has been rendered self-sufficient, individual self-consciousness emerges from its pupation, proclaims itself the true principle and opposes nature, which has become independent.

All this can also be expressed from another point of view in the following way: *Matter,* having received into itself individuality, form as is the case with the heavenly bodies, *has ceased to be abstract individuality; it has become concrete individuality, universality.*[18]

Marx's preoccupation with the is/ought opposition and his Hegelian resolution of it can be seen in his moralistic conception of philosophy in the sixth of his notebooks for the dissertation. Philosophy—in the form of critique—becomes the rational guiding element in that activity which mediates between reality and ideality, existence and essence, what is and what ought to be.

. . . the *practice* of philosophy is itself *theoretical.* It is the *critique* that measures the individual existence by the essence, the particular reality by the Idea. But this *immediate realisation* of philosophy is in its deepest essence afflicted with contradictions, and thus its essence takes form in the appearance and imprints its seal upon it.[19]

Philosophy must be conceived as an activity, a critical activity which opposes the actual world as an act of moral judgment upon it. Philosophy and the world form an intimate relationship, like two young lovers, each reaching out to fulfill the other.

What was inner light has become consuming flame turning outwards. The result is that as the world becomes philosophical, philosophy also becomes worldly, that its realisation is also its loss, that what it struggles against on the outside is its own inner deficiency, that in the very struggle it falls precisely into those defects which it fights as defects in the opposite camp, and that it can only overcome these defects by falling into them. That which opposes it and that which it fights is always the same as itself, only with factors inverted.[20]

At this fork in the road, philosophy can travel one of two paths. It can either turn toward the real world and promote the "turn about of philosophy, its transubstantiation into flesh and blood," or it can further distance itself from the world, harking back to a transcendental, even religious position.

> This duality of philosophical self-consciousness appears finally as a double trend, each side utterly opposed to the other. One side, the *liberal* party, as we may call it in general, maintains as its main determination the concept and the principle of philosophy; the other side, its *non-concept,* the moment of reality. This second side is *positive philosophy.* The act of the first side is critique, hence precisely that turning-towards-the-outside of philosophy; the act of the second is the attempt to philosophize, hence the turning-in-towards-itself of philosophy. This second side knows that the inadequacy is immanent in philosophy, while the first understands it as inadequacy of the world which has to be made philosophical.[21]

Marx's extolment of philosophy, and its role as a critical activity that impinges upon the world in the form of a moral judgment, puts ethics at its core. The standard or criterion of the critical moral judgment remains vague, e.g., essence, Idea. Marx seems to opt here for a moral ideal which is found within reality, embedded within the process and development of that which it criticizes. His inquiry into the "idea in reality itself" yields an ideal implanted within reality, an ideal inseparable but not identical with what is. He remains a soft objectivist, with a this-worldly, immanentist thrust.

Journalistic Articles: Rational Moral Criticism

Marx's journalistic articles in the *Rheinische Zeitung* contain some of his most explicit reflections about the issues of objectivity and validity in ethics. On the one hand, these articles represent a deepening of his commitment to the Hegelian resolution of the is/ought opposition and to the moralistic conception of philosophy as the rational guiding element in activity that mediates between what is and what ought to be, philosophy as moral judgment on the evolving present. On the other hand, his later articles reveal an uneasiness with the Hegelian position, owing to his exposure to the mundane world of politics and power.

In the first article I will consider, entitled "The Philosophical Manifesto of the Historical School of Law" (written between March 1842 and August 1842), Marx attempts to reveal the skepticism of Gustav Hugo, the founder of the Historical School of Law. What upsets Marx about Hugo's "historicism" is that it seems to preclude the possibility of objectivity and validity in ethics. Hugo's skepticism—or his extreme moral nihilist viewpoint—cuts at the very foundations of Marx's moralistic conception of philosophy. So in this article we see Marx implicitly defending objectivism, in his Hegelian way, against Hugo's extreme nihilism.

> He is a *sceptic* as regards the *necessary essence* of things, so as to be *courtier* as regards their *accidental appearance*. Therefore, he by no means tries to prove that the *positive* is *rational;* he tries to prove that the *positive* is *irrational*. With self-satisfied zeal he adduces arguments from everywhere to provide additional evidence that no rational necessity is inherent in the positive institutions, e.g., property, the state constitution, marriage, etc., that they are even *contrary* to reason, and at most allow of idle *chatter* for and against.[22]

It is Hugo's reduction of moral reasoning to "idle chatter for and against" that disturbs Marx. This reduction also results in a wide schism between reason and history. For Hugo, the idea of a rational process in history (at this point already one of Marx's cherished beliefs) is nonsense. Marx notes,

> Hugo, therefore, *profanes* all that the just, moral, political man regards as holy, but he smashes these holy things only to be able to honour them as *historical relics;* he desecrates them in the *eyes of reason* in order afterwards to make them honourable in the *eyes of history* and at the same time to make the eyes of the *historical school* honourable.[23]

Marx's critique of Hugo does not put forward a more coherent and convincing positive position. Rather, it consists of presenting the objectionable relativist consequences of Hugo's view. For example, he claims,

Even when Hugo weighs up the force of the arguments, he finds with an unerring sure instinct that what is rational and moral in institutions is *doubtful* for reason. Only *what is animal* seems to *his reason* to be *indubitable*.[24]

Marx then proceeds to castigate Hugo's amoral, functionalist view of marriage (Marx is engaged to Jenny at the time).

But the sanctification of the sexual instinct by *exclusiveness,* the bridling of this instinct through laws, the *moral beauty* which idealises the bidding of nature and makes it an element of spiritual union, *the spiritual essence* of marriage, that is precisely what Herr Hugo finds *dubious* in marriage.[25]

Despite this castigation, Hugo's view is not unacceptable to Marx primarily because it yields unpopular pronouncements on current institutions. Rather it is objectionable because it results in a strong relativism. In short, Marx's basic criticism of Hugo is a philosophic one.

Hugo's *reasoning,* like his *principle,* is *positive* i.e., uncritical. He knows no *distinctions*. Eveything *existing* scares him as an *authority*, every authority serves him as an *argument* . . . according to Hugo, the *Siamese,* who considers it an eternal law of nature that his king should have the mouths of chatterers sewn up and the mouth of a clumsy orator slit to the ears, is just as *positive* as the *Englishman,* who would consider it a political anomaly if his king were autocratically to impose even a penny tax. The shameless *Conci,* who runs about naked and at most covers himself with mud, is as positive as the *Frenchman,* who not only dresses, but dresses elegantly. The *German,* who brings up his daughter as the jewel of the family, is not more positive than the Rajput, who kills his daughter to save himself the trouble of feeding her. In short, *a rash is just as positive as the skin itself.*

In one place, one thing is positive, in another something else; the one is as irrational as the other. Submit yourself to what is positive in your own home.[26]

Lurking under Marx's deep dissatisfaction with Hugo's view is the haunting question Marx poses,

Has not Hugo proved that man can cast off even the last fetter of *freedom,* namely, that of being a *rational being?*[27]

Marx's reply—a critical one, as we shall see in later articles—is to link such skepticism and relativism to *the unjustified "right of arbitrary power.*" Like Plato and a good objectivist, Marx holds that without objectivity and validity in moral deliberation, we are stuck with Thracymachus: might makes right. And this view must be opposed at all costs, lest there be no room for critical activity, or for moral judgment on the present. In short, no role for philosophy.

At this stage of his thinking Marx is grappling with two crucial issues: What is the relationship between ethics and the critical function of philosophy? And what is the status of philosophy? The status of philosophy is a more pressing problem for him because he subordinates the status of ethics to the matter of philosophy's relation to the world. Up to this point, Marx has held that philosophy's relation to the world is a moralistic one; that is, the task of philosophy is to provide rational moral guidance or to pinpoint desirable potentialities within the evolving present. This task still assumes, as we saw in the Hugo article, that philosophy and hence ethics is in need of necessary grounds or universal foundations; yet philosophy also attempts to be "the critical activity of reason" in the actual world.

Marx's most explicit reflections on the critical function of philosophy during this period occur in his piece, "The Leading Article in No. 179 of *Kolnische Zeitung*" (written and published in June–July 1842). In this article Marx admits that philosophy has a reputation for being esoteric, isolated, and unpractical, hence apparently unrelated to the business of the world.

He vehemently opposes this view.

> However, philosophers do not spring up like mushrooms out of the ground; they are products of their time, of their nation, whose most subtle, valuable and invisible juices flow in the ideas of philosophy. The same spirit that constructs railways with the hands of workers, constructs philosophical systems in the brains of philosophers. Philosophy does not exist outside the world, any more than the brain exists outside man because it is not situated in the stomach.[28]

Marx then proceeds to put forward the same conception of philosophy that we saw earlier in his dissertation, at times almost word for word. I quote at length.

> Since every true philosophy is the intellectual quintessence of its time, the time must come when philosophy not only internally by its content, but also externally through its form, comes into contact and interaction

with the real world of its day. Philosophy then ceases to be a particular system in relation to other particular systems, it becomes philosophy in general in relation to the world, it becomes the philosophy of the contemporary world. The external forms which confirm that philosophy has attained this significance, that it is the living soul of culture, that philosophy has become worldly and the world has become philosophical, have been the same in all ages . . . Philosophy comes into the world amid the loud cries of its enemies, who betray their inner infection by wild shouts for help against the fiery ardour of ideas. This cry of its enemies has the same significance for philosophy as the first cry of the newborn babe has for the anxiously listening ear of the mother: it is the cry testifying to the life of its ideas, which have burst the orderly hieroglyphic husk of the system and become citizens of the world.[29]

Philosophy must encounter the real world, the mundane world of everydayness. It must pierce through the veils of illusion, pettiness, and irrelevancy dangled by journalists. Philosophy is, as he writes, the "action of free reason" in the contemporary world.

For a long time philosophy had remained silent in the face of the self-satisfied superficiality which boasted that by means of a few hackneyed newspaper phrases it would blow away like soap-bubbles the long years of study by genius, the hard-won fruits of self-sacrificing solitude, the results of the unseen but slowly exhausting struggles of contemplative thought: Philosophy had even *protested against the newspapers* as an unsuitable arena, but finally it had to break its silence; it became a newspaper correspondent, and then—unheard-of diversion!—it suddenly occurred to the loquacious purveyors of newspapers that philosophy was not a fitting pabulum for their readers.[30]

Despite this praise of a "worldly philosophy," Marx is quite aware of its limitation, namely that it cannot move the world, only rationally inform and possibly convince the public. Marx is clear about this.

And, in truth, philosophy has enough knowledge of the world to realise that its results do not flatter the pleasure-seeking and egoism of either the heavenly or the earthly world. But *the public,* which loves truth and knowledge for their own sakes, will be well able to measure its judgment and morality against the judgment and morality of ignorant, servile, inconsistent and venal scribblers.[31]

We should note briefly Marx's idea of "the public" in this passage. Regardless of his possible idealizing of "the public" Marx here makes it clear that publicity is a crucial element in the critical function of philosophy. That is, the rational moral judgments on the evolving present put forward by philosophy ought to be available to all or the possible possession of everyone.

In his text, "Debates on the Law on Theft of Wood" (written and published in October–November 1842), Marx deepens his understanding of this notion of publicity, and links it to his embryonic conception of ideology as public deception. Publicity is now seen as the bringing to light of private interests that are disguised as public interests in political affairs. This notion of publicity forces him to rethink his approach to ethics, renders the status of ethics more ambiguous, and opens the door to a more aggressive view of philosophy. His rethinking leads toward a slight shift from his Hegelian-like view to a form of moral naturalism (grounding norms in certain needs and interests of people). This shift renders the status of ethics more ambiguous by making him aware of some of the *social* determinants in moral deliberation and opens the door to a more aggressive view of philosophy by forcing him to question seriously the efficacy of rational moral criticism.

This essay contains a different emphasis than the earlier works we have examined. For the first time in his writings, Marx openly sides with "the poor, politically and socially propertyless many" against the rich. This shift is significant in that it occurs when he makes a connection between the needs of the poor, who are forced to gather pieces of fallen wood for heat in the cold, and the moral desirability of satisfying these needs, of gathering this wood.

Marx begins by noting that the whole issue of the status of customary rights *(Gewohnheitsrechte)* is problematic. Customary rights arise when there is ambiguity in the law, when the imprecision is such that it unable to say unequivocally what the law is at a certain point or on a particular issue. In regard to the specific case of the gathering of pieces of fallen wood, it is not clear who owns the wood and, therefore, is entitled to it. Hence,

> Customary right as a *separate domain* alongside legal right is therefore rational only where it exists *alongside* and *in addition to law,* where custom is the *anticipation* of a legal right.[32]

When the poor exercise their customary rights in this case, they not only satisfy their needs, but do so on moral grounds since their actions promote a legal tendency, an anticipation of a legal right.

> It will be found that the customs which are customs of the entire poor class are based with a sure instinct on the *indeterminate* aspect of property; it will be found not only that this class feels an urge to satisfy a natural need, but equally that it feels the need to satisfy a rightful urge.[33]

The actions of the poor in this case anticipate a legal right because they point to a larger problem, namely, the position of the poor themselves, who, like the pieces of fallen wood that have no place in nature, have no dignified status in society.

> In these customs of the poor class, therefore, there is an instinctive sense of right; their roots are positive and legitimate, and the form of *customary right* here conforms all the more to nature because up to now the *existence of the poor class itself* has been a *mere custom* of civil society, a custom which has not found an appropriate place in the conscious organisation of the state.[34]

Marx then asks, if the state stoops low enough to allow itself to be used as a tool by the private forest owners to persecute the poor for gathering pieces of fallen wood, do not such private interests set the limits wherein the public sphere acts? Doesn't the state become a fraud, parading around as embodying the interests of all while, in reality, being controlled by private interests? Marx answers these questions affirmatively.

> This logic, which turns the servant of the forest owner into a state authority, *turns the authority of the state into a servant of the forest owner.* The state structure, the purpose of the individual administrative authorities, everything must get out of hand so that everything is degraded into an instrument of the forest owner and his interest operates as the soul governing the entire mechanism. All the organs of the state become ears, eyes, arms, legs, by means of which the interest of the forest owners hears, observes, appraises, protects, reaches out, and runs.[35]

At this point, Marx seems to display a sense of despondency, a kind of skepticism about the possibility of action-determining moral reasons in political deliberation. He suggests that the situation he is examining seems

> to prove what little meaning "noble deeds" can have in our debate, if the whole debate did not prove that moral and humane reasons occur here merely as phrases. But interest is miserly even with phrases. It invents

them only in case of need, when the results are of considerable advantage.[36]

Marx then begins to pursue the theme of deception and the need for public knowledge of it; he explores the idea of dangling principles before others with no intention of taking them seriously. And he could not have picked a better case to frustrate his moral idealism. The connection in this case between outright self-interest and disguised moral ideals is quite evident.

> We see that selfishness has a double set of weights and measures for weighing and measuring people, and two world outlooks, two pairs of spectacles, one showing everything black and the other in rosy tints . . .
> We do not intend to argue with the world outlook of selfishness, but we want to compel it to be consistent. We do not want it to reserve all worldly wisdom for itself and leave only fantasies for others. We want to make the sophistical spirit of private interest abide for a moment by its own conclusions.[37]

When the private forest owners heighten the debate, moving from mere persecution of the poor wood gatherers to fining them, with the fine compensating the private forest owner (instead of the state), Marx throws up his arms in moral despair.

> If, in the absence of a rightful claim to do so, I make the criminal act of a third person an independent source of income for myself, do I not thus become his accomplice? Or am I any less his accomplice because to him falls the punishment and to me the fruit of the crime? The guilt is not attenuated by a private person abusing his status as a legislator to arrogate to himself rights belonging to the state because of a crime committed by a third person. The embezzling of public, state funds is a crime against the state, and is not the money from fines public money belonging to the state?[38]

Marx notes that now the private forest owners have thrown off their masks of disguised moral posture, no longer even attempting to conceal their self-interest in this matter. He quips,

> We are only surprised that the forest owner is not allowed to heat his stove with the wood thieves.[39]

Then he seriously states,

At this point the method of the deception stands out in sharp and undisguised relief, indeed in self-confessed clarity, for there is no longer any hesitation to proclaim it as a principle.[40]

This essay is a pivotal one in Marx's writings in that it first reveals Marx's awareness of some kind of relationship between private interests, private property, and the state (public sphere). This awareness occurs about the same time that he moves toward naturalism in ethics and first sides with the poor in philosophic discussions of political matters. This awareness further blossoms in the last text we shall consider in this section, "Justification of the Correspondent from the Mosel" (written and published January 1843).

Marx's central aim in this text is to prove that the need for a free press arises from the specific character of the state of distress in the Mosel region. In short, the oppressive conditions of the Mosel vinegrowers demand rational moral criticism.

Marx begins this inquiry with a methodological consideration. This consideration extends and expands his approach in the previous essay, stressing the way in which structural relations between property owners and the state shed light on human behavior in social disputes and political debates. I quote at length.

> In investigating a situation *concerning the state* one is all too easily tempted to overlook the *objective nature of the circumstances* and to explain everything by the *will* of the persons concerned. However, there are *circumstances* which determine the actions of private persons and individual authorities, and which are as independent of them as the method of breathing. If from the outset we adopt this objective standpoint, we shall not assume good or evil will, exclusively on one side or on the other, but we shall see the effect of circumstances where at first glance only individuals seem to be acting. Once it is proved that a phenomenon is made *necessary* by circumstances, it will not longer be difficult to ascertain the *external* circumstances in which it must *actually* be produced and those in which it could not be produced, although the need for it already existed. This can be established with approximately the same certainty with which the chemist determines the *external* conditions under which substances having affinity are bound to form a compound. Hence we believe that by our proof "that the *necessity* for a free press follows from the *specific character* of the state of distress in the Mosel region" we give our exposition a basis that goes far beyond anything personal.[41]

This crucial passage represents Marx's new understanding of the "nature of things" or the development of the "object in itself." In the texts we have examined so far, we have seen that these phrases have remained abstract. Now Marx relates them to politics and society. He now talks not simply about the inherent laws of reality, but rather the objective nature of circumstances, and specifically, political and social circumstances that directly affect human action and reflection. This new understanding shifts the focus from the intentions of people to the necessary limits wherein people behave.

Marx applies this mode of analysis to the dispute between the administration and the Mosel vinegrowers.

> *Not intentionally*, but *necessarily*, the individual official who is in closest contact with the vinegrower sees the state of things as better or other than it actually is. He thinks that the question whether things are all right in his region amounts to the question whether *he* administers the region correctly. Whether the administrative principles and institutions are good or not is a question that lies outside his sphere, for that can only be judged in *higher* quarters where a wider and deeper *knowledge* of the *official* nature of things, i.e., of their connection with the state as a whole, prevails.[42]

The political disagreement between the Mosel vinegrowers and the public administration rests upon conflicting moral judgments. The administration interprets the complaints of the vinegrowers as antagonistic criticisms of their policies; the vinegrowers view the few public gestures to deal with their problems as inadequate and insufficient.

Marx claims this situation "signifies a contradiction between reality and administrative principles." This contradiction consists of an apparently irresolvable conflict required by the objective nature of the circumstances within which both parties find themselves. Both sides, despite possible good intentions, are unable to transcend the situation which limits their viewpoints.

This dilemma is a moral one, with important political consequences. On the one hand,

> the administrative authorities, even *with the best intentions*, the most zealous humanity and the most powerful intellect, *can* find no solution for a conflict that is more than momentary or transient, the constant conflict between reality and the principles of administration, for it is not their official task, nor would it be possible, despite the best intentions, to make

a breach in an *essential relation* or, if you like, *fate*. This *essential relation* is the *bureaucratic* one . . .[43]

On the other hand,

the private vine-grower can no more deny that *his* judgment may be affected, intentionally or unintentionally, by *private interest,* and therefore the correctness of his judgment cannot be assumed absolutely.[44]

How is this moral dispute to be adjudicated? How is this ethical disagreement to be resolved? How does one transcend the bureaucratic outlook of the public administration and the private interest of the vinegrower? Marx replies to these queries by appealing to a third party, an impartial, rational judge who can possibly transform conflicts between particular interests into a resolution in the interest of all, and possibly unite the legitimate concerns of the public administration with the needs of the vinegrowers. This third party or impartial, rational judge is the free press.

In order to solve this difficulty, therefore, the rulers and the ruled alike are in need of a *third* element, which would be *political* without being official, hence not based on bureaucratic premises, an element which would be of a civil nature without being bound up with private interests and their pressing need. This supplementary element with the *head of a citizen of the state* and the *heart of a citizen* is the *free press*. In the realm of the press, rulers and ruled alike have an opportunity of criticising their principles and demands, and no longer in a relation of subordination, but on terms of equality as *citizens of the state;* no longer as *individuals,* but as *intellectual forces,* as exponents of reason.[45]

Marx's conception of what the free press is becomes an important matter in relation to his changing view of the status of ethics in particular and the status of philosophic critical activity in general. First, he understands the free press to be truly *public* in that its task is precisely to bring to light the political realities and provide a *public* forum—equally accessible to all citizens—for discussions of these realities. Second, he sees the free press as possessing a *political* and *civil* character in that its function is to contribute to the common good, hence to stand above private and group interests. Third, he views the free press as providing the requisite sociopolitical conditions for the objective, impartial, and rational resolution of the matter agreeable to both the public administration and the Mosel vinegrowers.

This last article is crucial in the development of Marx's approach to ethics primarily because it shows how rational moral criticism or philosophy's critical "activity of reason" has become embodied or represented by an actual structural element, i.e., the free press, in society. A *moral* dispute or disagreement is transformed into an *objective* contradiction which is irresolvable within existing structural circumstances. This dispute can be resolved, the contradiction reconciled, only by appealing to an actual structural element in society which ultimately requires the creation of a new set of sociopolitical circumstances requisite for the resolution and reconciliation.

What is new and noteworthy in Marx's thinking here is that the relationship of philosophy's "critical activity of reason" to the world is no longer solely a *judgmental* one, but now also a *galvanizing* and *energizing* one, no longer simply a *moralistic* one, but now also in a weak sense, a *political* one. The free press, or the structural element in society he tries to galvanize and energize, is a public, civil, and political institution which, he claims, embodies ethical notions such as objectivity, impartiality, universality, and rationality.

Political Essays: Criticizing Rational Moral Criticisms

Marx's rational moral criticism, at this point, can be characterized in the following way. First, his criticism still is tied to philosophic conceptions of objectivity, impartiality, universality, and rationality. So his objectivism remains. Second, his criticism sides with "the poor, politically and socially propertyless many." And his interest in their conditions and circumstances increases. Third, his criticism is becoming more and more engaged in the mundane world of politics. Hence, he becomes more cognizant of considerations about power in society.

In his political essays, these three characteristics come together to create what I call Marx's *fecund criticism,* a criticism whose first and foremost aim is to give birth to societal alternatives based on discerning potentialities and possibilities in the existing order. This "fecund criticism" makes two requirements for itself. First, this criticism must neither merely condemn the present state of affairs nor endorse an ideal state of affairs. Rather, it must try to describe, explain, and analyze the present state of affairs in order to see what possible and desirable state of affairs can be realized. Second, this criticism must not only put forward moral judgments about the present or descriptions and explanations of the present. It also must become an integral part of the actual political movements in the present which can usher in a new future or activate a possible alternative to the present.

Marx's fecund criticism gives philosophy a more aggressive relationship with the world. His conception of philosophy's "critical activity of reason" becomes more political, activistic, engaged. Philosophy must now get its hands dirty in the actual world of power, politics, public policy. Any conception of philosophy which ignores this world makes a fetish of criticism and ultimately a fetish of philosophy itself.

Marx's aggressive view of philosophy's "critical activity of reason" is first put forward in his letter to Arnold Ruge, written in September 1843.

> Philosophy has become worldly, and the most striking proof for this is the fact that the philosophical consciousness itself is drawn into the torment of struggle, not only outwardly but inwardly as well. Even though the construction of the future and its completion for all times is not our task, what we have to accomplish at this time is all the more clear: *relentless criticism of all existing conditions,* relentless in the sense that the criticism is not afraid of its findings and just as little afraid of the conflict with the powers that be.[46]

The role of the philosopher is the role of the social critic. The task of this critic is to judge the present and discover how the ideals to which one appeals in this judgment can be realized in light of one's understanding of the present.

> The critic, therefore, can start with any form of theoretical and practical consciousness and develop the true actuality out of the forms *inherent* in existing actuality as its ought-to-be and goal. As far as actual life is concerned, the *political state* especially contains in all its *modern* forms the demands of reason, even where the political state is not yet conscious of socialistic demands . . . it everywhere gets into the contradiction between its ideal character and its real presuppositions.[47]

The philosopher is no longer a moralist, but now a social critic with a moral outlook and political concern. The task of philosophy is to bring to light the treasures which exist buried in the past and present, treasures that have been centuries in the making. These treasures consist of societal possibilities, results of human struggle down through the corridors of history.

> Nothing prevents us, therefore, from starting our criticism with criticism of politics, with taking sides in politics, hence with *actual* struggles, and identifying ourselves with them. Then we do not face the world in doctrinaire fashion with a new principle, declaring, "Here is truth, kneel here!" We develop new principles for the world out of the principles of the world. We do not tell the world, "Cease your struggles, they are stupid; we want to give you the true watchword of the struggle." We merely show the world why it actually struggles; and the awareness of this is something the world *must* acquire even if it does not want to.[48]

Societal possibilities can be realized only when the philosopher-critic digs for them. This digging consists of heightening people's awareness of the actual struggles they engage in. This awareness occurs when the philosopher-critic pierces through the prevailing veil of the present and reveals the actual forces that shape and mold the present.

> Our slogan, therefore, must be: Reform of consciousness, not through dogmas, but through analysis of the mystical consciousness that is unclear about itself, whether in religion or politics. It will be evident, then, that the world has long dreamed of something of which it only has to become conscious in order to possess it in actuality. It will be evident that there is not a big blank between the past and the future, but rather that it is a matter of *realizing* the thoughts of the past. It will be evident, finally, that mankind does not begin any *new* work but performs its old work consciously.[49]

The most significant point in this letter, the first characterization of his fecund criticism, is Marx's shift from *philosophic* language to *theoretic* language—that is, the move from terms such as "ideal," "moral judgment," and "external principles" to terms such as "actuality," "analysis" ("empirical analysis"), and "evolving principles." We saw in Chapter 1 that this shift indicates a move toward a radical historicist approach to ethics. And it seems that Marx's increasing political activism is primarily responsible for this shift. But what is important about Marx's approach to ethics at this point is that he more and more employs theoretic notions—"describe," "analyze," "explain," "role," "function"—yet he also remains tied to a left-Hegelian philosophic position, hence ultimately a form of objectivism.

In his political essays, we see two basic theoretical movements at work. On the one hand, Marx is concerned with setting his fecund criticism apart from other kinds of criticism (including earlier forms of his own). Therefore, he relentlessly engages in criticizing other critics. On the other hand, he is in search of a theoretical viewpoint regarding the status of philosophy and ethics that will "ease his philosophic conscience"; that is, he recognizes the tension between replacing philosophic language and aims with theoretic ones and remaining captive to an old vision of philosophy. Yet he remains unclear as to what this viewpoint can be. He does not arrive at this viewpoint—the radical historicist viewpoint—until his famous *Theses on Feuerbach,* written in March 1845, which we will examine in the next chapter.

The replacement of *philosophic* language and aims with *theoretic* ones becomes quite pronounced in Marx's famous essay "On the Jewish Question." In this penetrating critique of Bruno Bauer, he simply shows that Bauer's criticism of the "Christian" state and its discriminatory policy toward Jews does not cut deep enough or raise the fundamental issues precisely because Bauer is a weak theorist, and specifically a weak *social* theorist. Therefore, Bauer has no idea how structural relations in modern society impose constraints on human freedom—why and how political emancipation, the split between the state and civil society, public interest and private interest have debilitating effects on people.

This discovery of what modern society is doing to people, i.e., reinforcing egoism, even forces Marx to see that the left-Hegelian idea (i.e., formerly his own) of changing ideas without changing conditions or of merely attempting to "raise the consciousness" of people must be rethought and ultimately modified. Therefore philosophy and ethics must become self-consciously part of the powers and political forces in society. Marx's social-theoretic considerations lead him to conclude that

> Political emancipation is a reduction of man to a member of civil society, to an *egoistic independent* individual on the one hand and to a *citizen,* a moral person, on the other.
>
> Only when the actual, individual man has taken back into himself the abstract citizen and in his everyday life, his individual work, and his individual relationships has become a *species-being,* only when he has

recognized and organized his own powers as *social* powers so that social force is no longer separated from him as *political* power, only then is human emancipation complete.[50]

Marx's next essay, "Toward the Critique of Hegel's Philosophy of Law: Introduction" (written in Paris at the end of 1843), illustrates, more than any of the other fecund criticism texts, the new world that philosophy can help to usher in. In this piece, Marx for the first time identifies the proletariat as the revolutionary agent of history, as the means to actualize philosophy and achieve human emancipation.

As he pointed out in the "Notes on Epicurean Philosophy" for his dissertation, the deficiencies in philosophy could be overcome only by making the world more philosophical and the shortcomings of reality could be overcome only by philosophy becoming more worldly. Now for the first time, he unites philosophy and the world: the moral idealization (transformation) of reality and the realization (transcendence) of philosophy. This unity culminates in social revolution, a new worldly critical act described in Marx's texts.

Marx's grand claim about the actualization of philosophy and the transformation of the world or making philosophy worldly and the world philosophical has significant consequences for his conception of the status of ethics. First, philosophy's "critical activity of reason" no longer is merely embodied in the actual world as a political force, e.g., as a free press. This critical activity now galvanizes and energizes social forces and political powers that possess the capacity to fundamentally transform existing reality. Second, this transformed reality or world made "philosophical" signifies the end of philosophic notions such as criteria, grounds or foundations to judge states of affairs in the world. Philosophy is actualized only when its "critical activity of reason" is rendered obsolete, outmoded, superfluous, and only when its norms become realities.

He begins this famous essay with his now common theme: criticism. He states that "criticism of religion is the premise of all criticism" and notes with a sigh of relief that the criticism of religion is now exhausted, completed, done with in Germany.

For Marx, religion is to be considered a key to the shift from *philosophic* notions and aims (e.g., objectivity, validity, necessity, certainty) to *theoretic* ones (e.g., description, explanation, function, role). The completion of the criticism of religion indicates that the shift has occurred but only in relation to religion. The aim, at this point, is to broaden the *scope* of this shift by focusing on other alienated forms of theoretical activity, i.e., philosophic claims about society, politics, and history, still tied to the vision of philosophy as the quest for certainty, the search for foundations.

> Thus it is the *task of history*, once the *otherworldly* truth has disappeared, to establish the *truth of this world*. The immediate *task of philosophy* which is in the service of history is to unmask human self-alienation in its *unholy forms* now that it has been unmasked in its holy form. Thus the criticism of heaven turns into the criticism of the earth, the *criticism of religion* into the *criticism of law*, and the *criticism of theology* into the *criticism of politics*.[51]

What is novel about Marx's form of criticism is that the shift from philosophic to theoretic concerns deepens his sense of the intense engagement, even combat, that criticism is associated with and considered as. Marx stretches his conception of criticism (and philosophy) in order to make it fecund. He attempts to pack it with life juices so that it will not only judge but produce, not only measure but yield, not only condemn but give birth. This stretching and enriching ultimately leads him to employ militaristic imagery in relation to criticism.

> *War* on German conditions! By all means! They are *below the level of history, beneath all criticism,* but they are still an object of criticism just as the criminal below the level of humanity is still an object of the *executioner*. In its struggle against these conditions criticism is not a passion of the head but the head of passion. It is not a lancet, it is a weapon. Its object is an *enemy* it wants not to refute but to *destroy*. For the spirit of these conditions has already been refuted. In and for themselves they are objects not *worthy of thought* but *existences* as despicable as they are despised. Criticism itself does not even need to be concerned with this matter, for it is already clear about it. Criticism is no longer an *end in itself* but simply a *means*. Its essential pathos is *indignation*, its essential task, *denunciation*.[52]

And his critique of other critics continues: the target is the Young Hegelians, as a whole. As critics of philosophy they are suggestive, but they only adopt a critical philosophy (note the implicit self-criticism here). As negators of philosophy, they are acceptable, but they only arrive at a negative philosophy. They can never actualize their goals or fulfill their aims in the real world, only provide limited theoretical criticisms of it.

Hence, the *practical* political party in Germany rightly demands the *negation of philosophy*. It is wrong not in its demand but in stopping at the demand it neither seriously fulfills nor can fulfill. It supposes that it accomplishes that negation by turning its back on philosophy, looking aside, and muttering a few petulant and trite phrases about it. Because its outlook is so limited it does not even count philosophy as part of *German* actuality or even imagines it is *beneath* German practice and its theories. You demand starting from *actual germs of life* but forget that the actual life-germ of the German nation has so far sprouted only inside its *cranium*. In short: *you cannot transcend [aufheben] philosophy without actualizing it.*[53]

The main problem with the criticism of the Young Hegelians is that it is barren, it does not yield, produce or give birth to anything. It merely judges, measures and condemns. And, most importantly (and related to its other deficiencies), it fails to consider the means to actualize its ideals, namely praxis. Praxis is a crucial component of Marx's theoretic aims and concerns. For Marx, only his kind of criticism is fecund because it

> does not proceed in its own sphere but proceeds to *tasks* that can be solved by only one means—*practice [praxis]*.[54]

The acknowledgment of "tasks to be solved," moral ideals to actualize, social circumstances to transform, means criticism not only serves as a tool or instrument for "war on existing conditions." Criticism also galvanizes social forces or human collectivities, it activates radical and revolutionary action.

> The weapon of criticism obviously cannot replace the criticism of weapons. Material force must be overthrown by material force. But theory also becomes a material force once it has gripped the masses . . . The criticism of religion ends with the doctrine that *man is the highest being for man,* hence with the *categorical imperative to overthrow all condition* in which man is a degraded, enslaved, neglected, contemptible being . . .[55]

Social revolution can occur only when criticism (philosophy) energizes human needs, stimulates human wants, and arouses human desires. But it cannot be any arbitrary set of human needs, wants, and desires. It must be identifiable with that group of people which represents the universal interests of society and can actualize human freedom. This group must constitute a class of people that is compelled to overthrow the existing order and establish human emancipation "by its *immediate* condition, by *material* necessity, by its *very chains*." Marx then asks and answers:

> Where, then, is the *positive* possibility of German emancipation?
>
> *Answer:* In the formation of a class with *radical chains*, a class in civil society that is not of civil society, a class that is the dissolution of all classes, a sphere of society having a universal character because of its universal suffering and claiming no *particular* right because no *particular wrong* but *unqualified wrong* is perpetrated on it; a sphere that can invoke no *traditional* title but only a *human* title, which does not partially oppose the consequences but totally opposes the premises of the German political system; a sphere, finally, that cannot emancipate itself without emancipating itself from all the other spheres of society, thereby emancipating them; a sphere, in short, that is the *complete loss* of humanity and can only redeem itself through the *total redemption of humanity*. This dissolution of society as a particular class is the *proletariat*.[56]

Notice that Marx's move from philosophic concerns toward theoretic ones coincides with two crucial discoveries. On the one hand, he identifies the structural element in reality (or society) which, he believes, possesses the capacity to transform and emancipate this reality or society, that is, make it "philosophical." This structural element—the proletariat—is galvanized and energized by philosophy's "critical activity of reason." On the other hand, this critical activity culminates in revolutionary activity, that is, political praxis in which material force overthrows material force, political power overthrows political power. Marx's theoretic concerns about power in society have forced philosophy into the realm of actual political struggle and engagement, with revolutionary activity and aims.

> The only emancipation of Germany possible *in practice* is emancipation based on *the* theory proclaiming that man is the highest essence of man . . . The *head* of this emancipation is *philosophy*, its *heart* is the *proletariat*. Philosophy cannot be actualized without the transcendence [*Aufhebung*] of the proletariat, the proletariat cannot be transcended without the actualization of philosophy.[57]

The proletariat actualizes philosophy because only it can create social conditions which embody the ideals of philosophy, namely, human emancipation, social freedom, or the self-development of all. The human creation of such social conditions (by the proletariat) is revolutionary overthrow of the present order, a collective practice of indignation and denunciation, propelled by material necessity and social enslavement.

The "Alienation" Writings

Despite Marx's move from philosophic concerns toward theoretic ones, his discovery of the proletariat and his stress on revolutionary praxis, his basic thrust, at this point, remains a moral one. But it is moral in the broad sense of the word; that is, he appeals to moral sensibilities that tend to take for granted that human servitude and human suffering which can be avoided or overcome are wrong. For Marx, this belief continues to be a moral belief with philosophic foundations, i.e., humanistic Feuerbachian grounds.

Marx's humanistic viewpoint is still a philosophic one in that it is based on an essentialist conception of human beings. This conception of human beings separates essential qualities and characteristics from accidental, contingent ones. It rests upon fundamental philosophic distinctions—essence/accidental, necessary/contingent—crucial for the vision of philosophy as the quest for certainty, the search for foundations. The humanist viewpoint usually yields an objectivist (hard or soft) position since it views the essential qualities and characteristics of people as significant metaphysical, i.e., ahistorical, facts, which serve as the basis for generating philosophic criteria, grounds or foundations for moral principles.

This humanist, essentialist view of Marx's is found in his famous "alienation" writings or those writings in which alienation is a central theme. For Marx, alienation is a *theoretic* notion, a crucial term within the configuration of his theory of society. Generally, it refers to a particular kind of human domination and control, namely, that in which the dominated and controlled create the conditions for their own dehumanization or "thingification." Specifically, alienation (and its various forms) is the result of an objective social relation necessary for the working of modern capitalist societies in which workers produce products alien to them, products which are part of socioeconomic arrangements that dominate and control the producers. These products are owned (to be sold for profits) by nonproducers, i.e., capitalists, who possess the power and authority of hiring, firing, and paying wages to dependent producers, i.e., the proletariat.

But alienation is also a philosophic notion in that it is contrasted with a more desirable state of affairs which can be justified by appeals to essential qualities or characteristics, e.g., species-qualities, of human beings. At times, alienation becomes almost synonymous with inhumane, hence something morally undesirable.

My basic contention is that, for our purposes, there are two noteworthy theoretical movements in Marx's "alienation" writings. On the one hand, we see Marx move deeper into *theoretic* language, aims, and concerns. He is searching for a social theory that will bring to light the power dynamics of bourgeois capitalist society and the "social chains" of the proletariat. On the other hand, this search is intertwined with his attempt to liberate himself from the vision of philosophy as the quest for certainty, the search for foundations. His relatively smooth theoretic search ultimately lays the basis for his mature social theory. But his attempt to liberate himself from his old vision of philosophy is problematic—and remains so throughout his "alienation" writings.

It is commonly believed that Marx's first reflections about alienation are to be found in his famous *Economic and Philosophic Manuscripts*. This is not so. Marx first writes about alienation in the often overlooked "Excerpt-Notes of 1844" (written between March and the summer of 1844).

Marx first writes about alienation in relation to the whole system of credit, banking, and wage-labor. The common thread running throughout this system is the exchange of money. This exchange symbolizes, for Marx, what is fundamentally morally undesirable about the whole system: *it makes relations between human beings appear as relations between things*.

> The essence of money is not primarily that it externalizes property, but that the *mediating activity* or process—the *human* and social act in which man's products reciprocally complement one another—becomes *alienated* and takes on the quality of a *material thing*, money, external to man. By externalizing this mediating activity, man is active only as he is lost and dehumanized. The very *relationship* of things and the human dealings with them become an operation beyond and above man. Through this *alien mediation* man regards his will, his activity, and his relationships to others

as a power independent of himself and of them—instead of man himself being the mediator for man.[58]

This mediation represents the abstraction of a human relationship, the transformation of a human relationship into an exchange relation between private property, since money is private property. This exchange relation involves the exchange of value. Money, as private property, serves as the carrier or token of value. Money represents value only insofar as it can be exchanged and serves as the medium of exchange. Money that cannot be exchanged has no value, hence it is not money, only mere paper and metals.

> . . . the *actual* value of things, after all, is their *exchange value,* and the exchange value resides in money, just as money exists in precious metals. Money, therefore, is the *true* value of things and hence the most desirable thing.[59]

The most important aspect of this situation, for Marx, is that money soon becomes the standard against which people judge other people, especially other people's morality. For example, in the credit system, it is not money that is the medium of exchange, but people in the form of possible money. This makes possible "the *evaluation* of a man in terms of *money* as it takes place in the credit system." Man as the embodiment of material property, i.e., money and the medium of exchange, is alienated man.

> Within the credit relationship, money is not transcended in man, but man is transformed into *money,* and money is *incorporated* in him. *Human individuality* and human *morality* have become an article of trade and the *material* in which money exists. Instead of money and paper, my very personal existence, my flesh and blood, my social virtue and reputation is the matter and substance of the *monetary spirit.*[60]

In this credit system, people come to see their entire existence confirmed or denied by the capricious, calculating judgment of the wealthy creditor. This economic judgment, made in the interests of the wealthy creditor, takes on a moral character in regard to the debtor.

> *Credit* is the *economic* judgment of man's morality . . . Mutual dissimulation, hypocrisy, and sanctimoniousness are carried to the point that a moral judgment is added to the simple statement that a man without credit is poor, a judgment that he is untrustworthy and unworthy of

recognition, a social pariah and bad man. On top of suffering from his destitution the poor man suffers from having to make a debasing *plea* to the rich for credit.[61]

Marx claims that the nature of social bonds between people in a society determines the nature of the common life of that society. How a society goes about exchanging the products produced by people determines whether those people are able to form human rather than alienating bonds with one another. In a crucial yet rarely quoted passage Marx writes,

> As *human* nature is the *true common life* [*Gemeinwesen*] of man, men through the activation of their *nature create* and produce a human *common life*, a social essence which is no abstractly universal power opposed to the single individual, but is the essence or nature of every single individual, his own activity, his own life, his own spirit, his own wealth. *Authentic common life* arises not through reflection; rather it comes about from the *need* and *egoism* of individuals, that is, immediately from the activation of their very existence. It is not up to man whether this common life exists or not. However, so long as man does not recognize himself as man and does not organize the world humanly, this *common life* appears in the form of *alienation*, because its *subject*, man, is a being alienated from itself. Men as actual, living, particular individuals, not in an abstraction, *constitute* this common life. It is, therefore, *what* men are. To say that *man* alienates himself is the same as saying that the *society* of this alienated man is the caricature of his *actual common life*, of his true generic life. His activity, therefore, appears as torment, his own creation as a force alien to him, his wealth as poverty, the *essential bond* connecting him with other men as something unessential so that the separation from other men appears as his true existence.[62]

The chief problem with political economy (or bourgeois economics) is that it understands this common life in terms of exchange and commerce, as a series of multilateral exchanges (as does Destutt de Tracy) or as a commercial enterprise (as does Adam Smith). Therefore it becomes clear that "political economy *establishes* an *alienated* form of social intercourse as the *essential, original,* and definitive human form."[63]

Exchange relations reduce all labor to wage-labor. The laborers become laborers only in an act of exchange, in the creation of social exchange relations alien to them. Social exchange relations are alien to the laborers because their only source of subsistence is wages. Wages are obtained only through an exchange relation between the laborer and the owner of capital who hires and pays the laborer. Products produced by the laborer in social exchange relations become alien to the laborer, a source of domination and control.

> The complete domination of the alienated object *over* man is evident in *money* and the complete disregard of the nature of the material, the specific nature of private property as well as the personality of the proprietor.
>
> What formerly was the domination of one person over another has now become the general domination of the *thing* over the *person*, the domination of the product over the producer.[64]

In a section entitled "Free Human Production," Marx opposes an ideal situation to the alienated one, morally desirable social circumstances to the existing morally condemnable ones. In place of production for exchange, he proposes production for human needs. In place of the domination of the laborer by private owners of capital, he suggests the freedom of the laborer by mutual ownership of products.

> The ideal relationship to the mutual objects of our production is our mutual need. But the *real* and *truly effective* relationship is only the mutually *exclusive ownership* of mutual production. It is your *object*, the *equivalent* of my object, that gives your want for my object *value, dignity*, and *efficacy* for me. Our mutual product, therefore, is the *means*, the *intermediary*, the *instrument*, the *acknowledged power* of our mutual needs.[65]

In place of work as an alien activity of everyday drudgery in the service primarily of others, Marx wants "a free manifestation of life and an enjoyment of life."

> Furthermore, in my labor the *particularity* of my individuality would be affirmed because my *individual* life is affirmed. Labor then would be *true, active property*. Under the presupposition of private property my individuality is externalized to the point where I *hate* this *activity* and where it is a *torment* for me.[66]

In this text, Marx seems to appeal to human nature and social freedom as ideals which contrast sharply with alienation and dehumanization. But it is important to note that he understands human nature as the true common life of social persons created and produced by those persons. Alienation is an impediment for this true common life of people, a *de*humanization of this social intercourse and interaction of people. In this sense, Marx conceives human nature *as* social freedom and alienation *as* dehumanization, with the former morally desirable and the latter morally undesirable. Social freedom consists of the mutual ownership of products by producers; alienation consists of the private ownership of products by nonproducers.

Marx's search for a social theory and his attempt to liberate himself from his old vision of philosophy is best exemplified in his famous *Economic and Philosophic Manuscripts*. This text is exciting and fascinating precisely because he refuses to separate his emerging theory from his rejection of the old vision of philosophy. In the noteworthy preface to the work he writes:

> In the *Deutsch-Französische Jahrbücher* I announced a critique of juris-
> prudence and political science in the form of a critique of the *Hegelian*
> philosophy of law. Preparing this for publication, I found that the com-
> bination of criticism directed solely against speculation [philosophy and
> ethics] with criticism of various subjects would be quite unsuitable; it
> would impede the development of the argument and render comprehen-
> sion difficult . . . Therefore, I shall issue the critique of law, morals,
> politics, etc., in separate, independent brochures, and finally attempt to
> give in a separate work the unity of the whole, the relation of the separate
> parts, and eventually a critique of the speculative treatment of the mate-
> rial. Hence in the present work the relationships of political economy with
> the state, law, morals, civil life, etc., are touched upon only insofar as
> political economy itself, ex professo, deals with these subjects.[67]

Marx is still interested in criticizing inadequate rational moral critics, but at this point he is confronted with two sets of critics: philosophers, e.g., Hegelians, and political economists. The *Manuscripts* contain critical formulations against these two sets of critics, attempting to show the limitations of both.

We are concerned primarily with his criticisms of the left-Hegelians and their implications for his understanding of philosophy and ethics. In order to see clearly these criticisms it is best to begin with the last section of the *Manuscripts,* entitled "Critique of Hegel's Dialectic and Philosophy in General." Marx's shift from philosophic aims and language to theoretic ones and his search for a critique of philosophic aims and language is seen in his confrontation with Hegel's dialectic in this section.

Marx claims that the chief failure of the Young Hegelians is that they have not examined thoroughly the relation of the status of philosophy to Hegel's dialectic. Ludwig Feuerbach is the sole exception.

> *Feuerbach* is the only one who has a *serious, critical* relation to Hegel's dialectic, who has made genuine discoveries in this field, and who above all is the true conqueror of the old philosophy.[68]

And why is Feuerbach so important? Precisely because he provides Marx with a conception of philosophy (and ethics) which permits Marx to liberate himself from the vision of philosophy as the quest for certainty, the search for foundations. Marx writes:

> Feuerbach's great achievement is: (1) proof that philosophy is nothing more than religion brought to and developed in reflection, and thus is equally to be condemned as another form and more of the alienation of man's nature.[69]

Marx goes on to mention two other achievements—the establishment of true materialism and of real science—by focusing on the social practices of people and his opposition to Hegel's notion of the negation of the negation. But it is the first achievement that interests us here.

We saw earlier that for Marx the completion of the criticism of religion signifies that the concern with the objectivity, validity, and/or necessity of its claims and beliefs has been transformed into a concern with a description and explanation of the function and role of the beliefs—a shift from philosophic to theoretic concerns. We also saw Marx's concern to broaden the *scope* of this shift by focusing on other alienated forms of theoretical activity. Marx praises Feuerbach precisely because Feuerbach has shown that philosophy, like religion, is but an alienated form of theoretical activity. In other words, philosophic claims must no longer be scrutinized in terms of their objectivity, validity, or necessity, but rather described and explained in terms of their function and role in relation to groups, communities, societies, and history.

Marx does not say *how* Feuerbach has shown that philosophy is but an alienated form of theoretical activity. And Marx does not articulate this *how* until he arrives at his own theoretic position in *The German Ideology*. What is crucial to notice is that the advent of what Marx calls true materialism and real science—namely, the focus on the social practices of people, with their agreements and disagreements, conflicting aims, objectives, interests, prejudices, and biases—indicates that philosophy has the same status as religion. This means that just as people have moved from thinking of religion as having an autonomous status with a subject matter of its own to now viewing it principally in terms of a description and explanation of its complex and multiple functions and roles, so should we no longer think of philosophy as possessing an autonomous status with a subject matter of its own, so should we now view philosophy primarily in terms of a description and explanation of its functions and roles.

Hegel's dialectic is crucial to Marx because it highlights the *activity* of the *Weltgeist* (world spirit) within the everyday world of actual human beings. It stresses the dynamic self-development of the *Weltgeist* in the historical process. In short, Hegel understands the importance of labor as a self-formative activity which mediates between subjects and objects, the *Weltgeist* and history.

> The great thing in Hegel's *Phenomenology* and its final result—the dialectic of negativity as the moving and productive principle—is simply that Hegel grasps the self-development of man as a process, objectification as loss of the object, as alienation and transcendence of this alienation; that he thus grasps the nature of *labor* and comprehends objective man, authentic because actual, as the result of his *own labor*.[70]

Feuerbach's philosophic critique of Hegel's dialectic is crucial for Marx because it reveals the other-worldly character and idealistic content of Hegel's dialectic. Hegel may grasp the self-development of man, but man for him is equivalent to mere self-consciousness. He may grasp the nature of productive activity, but productive activity for him is only that of self-consciousness. He may grasp the nature of alienation, but alienation for him is but alienation of self-consciousness. Hegel's focus on labor is essential, but Feuerbach's "positive humanistic and naturalistic criticism" reveals Hegel's spiritual, religious substance.

> Hegel's standpoint is that of modern political economy. He views *labor* as the *essence*, the self-confirming essence of man; he sees only the positive side of labor, not its negative side. Labor is *man's coming-to-be for himself* within *externalization* or as *externalized* man. The only labor Hegel knows and recognizes is *abstract, mental* labor . . .
>
> For Hegel *human nature, man,* is equivalent to *self-consciousness.* All alienation of human nature is thus *nothing* but the *alienation of self-consciousness.* The alienation of self-consciousness is not taken to be an

expression of the *actual* alienation of human nature reflected in knowledge and thought. *Actual* alienation, that which appears real, is rather in its *innermost* and concealed character (which philosophy only brings to light) only the *appearance* of the alienation of actual human nature, of *self-consciousness.*[71]

Feuerbach's condemnation of philosophy, of, that is, its autonomous status and its concerns, and his critique of the idealistic content of Hegel's dialectic leads Marx to take seriously the alternative of abandoning philosophy and applying his theoretic concerns to labor as human productive activity, to labor as a human self-formative activity which mediates between human beings and nature and which appears in various forms in different historical moments or particular societal circumstances. In short, true materialism and real science are made possible by taking Hegel's dialectic seriously, robbing it of its idealistic content, understanding it in terms of human productive activity, and providing a persuasive historical description and social explanation of the forms this productive activity appears in and among human collectivities.

In the *Manuscripts,* Marx is concerned with the form in which productive activity appears under capitalist conditions, that is, under conditions of private property and the private ownership of the means of production. The particular form productive activity or human labor takes under capitalist conditions is what Marx calls alienated labor.

> We proceed from a *present* fact of political economy.
> The worker becomes poorer the more wealth he produces, the more his production increases in power and extent. The worker becomes a cheaper commodity the more commodities he produces. The *increase in value* of the world of things is directly proportional to the *decrease in value* of the human world. Labor not only produces commodities. It also produces itself and the worker as a *commodity,* and indeed in the same proportion as it produces commodities in general.
> This fact simply indicates that the object which labor produces, its product, stands opposed to it as an *alien thing,* as a *power independent* of the producer.[72]

The neglect of this alienated labor by other political economists, for Marx, reveals the prejudice and partiality of political economy, making it a "science" which stresses the viewpoint of the privileged in society. Marx's starting point—beginning with alienated human labor—yields a different viewpoint, hence a new way of looking at private property and its consequences. The political economists believe these consequences to be inevitable or unavoidable, and they thereby manage to skirt questions about the morality of the human misery resulting from the institutions of capitalist production. Therefore the viewpoint of these political economists conceals and hence ultimately justifies the alienated character of human labor in capitalist society.

> *Political economy conceals the alienation in the nature of labor by ignoring the direct relationship between the worker* (labor) *and production.* To be sure, labor produces marvels for the wealthy but it produces deprivation for the worker. It produces palaces, but hovels for the worker. It produces beauty, but mutilation for the worker. It displaces labor through machines, but it throws some workers back into barbarous labor and turns others into machines. It produces intelligence, but for the worker it produces imbecility and cretinism.[73]

After considering alienated labor in the form of products being alien to the labor (product-alienation), Marx examines three other forms: process-alienation in which the worker is alienated from himself in the very act of production; species-alienation in which the worker is alienated from his own species-life, his actual and objective existence as a member of the species; and neighbor-alienation in which the worker is alienated from his neighbor or other people. These forms result from social realities in the real world.

> The means whereby the alienation proceeds is *practical* means. Through alienated labor man thus not only produces his relationship to the object and to the act of production as an alien man at enmity with him. He also creates the relation in which other men stand to his production and product, and the relation in which he stands to these other men. Just as he begets his own production as loss of his reality, as his punishment; just as he begets his own product as a loss, a product not belonging to him, so he begets the domination of the nonproducer over production and over product. As he alienates his own activity from himself, he confers upon the stranger an activity which is not his own.[74]

This nonproducer, stranger, or capitalist owns and possesses the product produced by the laborer. The product is alien and independent of the laborer owing to this ownership and possession by one who does not labor.

If a man is related to the product of his labor, to his objectified labor, as to an *alien*, hostile, powerful object independent of him, he is so related that another alien, hostile, powerful man independent of him is the lord of this object. If he is unfree in relation to his own activity, he is related to it as bonded activity, activity under domination, coercion, and yoke of another man.[75]

And, of course, in a full-blown capitalist system, there is not one man but a class of men whose authority and power rest upon their ownership and possession of products produced by a class of workers. These products become the private property of those who own and possess them.

The implications for ethics of Marx's philosophic to theoretic shift and his search, à la Feuerbach, for a critique of philosophic aims and concerns are twofold. First, he no longer sees ethics as a philosophic discipline. His rejection of philosophy as an autonomous discipline entails the rejection of philosophic ethics. Instead of focusing on issues such as objectivity or validity in ethics, he begins to accent the role and function that ethical beliefs, values, or sensibilities play *within* particular theories—and especially those theories put forward by bourgeois political economists. Second, he is forced to acknowledge the role and function of ethical beliefs, values and sensibilities within *his own* embryonic theory and how (or whether) he can justify them without engaging in a quest for philosophic certainty or search for philosophic foundations. Let us begin by examining the first implication.

Marx's attempt to disclose the role and function that ethical beliefs, values, or sensibilities play within theories put forward by bourgeois political economists begins by showing how these ethical beliefs are, in a complex way, related to the basic need of the capitalist system of production.

Every man speculates upon creating a *new* need in another in order to force him to a new sacrifice, to place him in a new dependence, and to entice him into a new kind of pleasure and thereby into economic ruin. Everyone tries to establish over others an alien power in order to find there the satisfaction of his own egoistic need. With the increasing mass of objects therefore, the realm of alien entities to which man is subjected also increases. Every new product is a new *potentiality* of mutual deceit and robbery. Man becomes increasingly poor as a man, he has increasing need of *money* in order to take possession of the hostile being. The power of his *money* diminishes directly with the growth of the quantity of production, i.e. his need increases with the increasing *power* of money. The need for money, is therefore, the real need created by the modern economic system, and the only need which it creates.[76]

This need for money—and the capitalists' need for profits—sets the limits within which the dominant ethical beliefs, values, and sensibilities of persons in bourgeois capitalist society flourish. More importantly, this limit is viewed as an intractable, inevitable limit—the unquestioned given for bourgeois political economists. Therefore ethical beliefs must be adjusted to this limit, they must fit within this limit. Since all human productive activity is subordinated to the need for money, the need for profits, human moral activity will likewise be subordinated to this fundamental need. For the worker, this subordination means that he or she must live the most impoverished life, since the more impoverished (without becoming unfit for work) the producer, the more products, hence more money and profits, produced. So for the political economist,

> . . . all working class *luxury* seems to him blameworthy, and everything which goes beyond the most abstract need (whether it be a passive enjoyment or a manifestation of personal activity) is regarded as a *luxury*. Political economy, the science of *wealth,* is, therefore, at the same time, the science of renunciation, of privation, and of saving, which actually succeeds in depriving man of fresh *air* and of physical *activity*. This science of a marvellous industry is at the same time the science of *asceticism*. Its true ideal is the *ascetic* but *usurious* miser and the *ascetic* but *productive* slave . . . Thus, despite its worldly—and pleasure-seeking appearance, it is a truly moral science, and the most moral of all sciences. Its principal thesis is the renunciation of life and of human needs.[77]

Marx's grand claim that political economy is "the most moral of all sciences" means that it contains a deep moral element—ethical beliefs, values, and sensibilities—*within* its theories. This moral element presupposes the inevitable limit, the need for money and profits, and, therefore, articulates, implicitly and explicitly, justifications for ways of life which promote and encourage the satisfaction of this need of the capitalist system of production.

The less you eat, drink, buy books, go to the theatre or to balls, or to the public house, and the less you think, love, theorize, sing, paint, fence etc. the more you will be able to save and the *greater* will become your treasure which neither moth nor dust will corrupt—your *capital*. The less you *are*, the less you express your life, the more you *have*, the greater is your *alienated* life and the greater is the saving of your alienated being. Everything which the economist takes from you in the way of life and humanity, he restores to you in the form of *money* and *wealth*.[78]

Marx noted that some bourgeois economists advocate luxury and condemn saving whereas others advocate saving and condemn luxury. But the former—economists such as Lauderdale and Malthus—advocate luxury because they believe such consumption of the rich will create work, hence more products and more money and profits. The latter—economists such as Ricardo and Say—advocate saving because they believe such saving is needed in order to create wealth.

Marx digs deeper into the relation of morality and the fundamental need, i.e., profits, of the capitalist system of production by probing into what he calls "economic morality," or that human behavior directly regulated by this fundamental need of the capitalist system of production.

Suppose I ask the economist: Am I acting in accordance with economic laws if I earn money by the sale of my body, by prostituting it to another person's lust (in France, the factory workers call the prostitution of their wives and daughters the nth hour of work, which is literally true); or if I sell my friend to the Moroccans (and the direct sale of men occurs in the form of the trade in conscripts)? He will reply: You are not acting contrary to my laws, but you must take into account what Cousin Morality and Cousin Religion have to say. My *economic* morality and religion have no objection to make, but . . .[79]

In this passage, Marx is highlighting the *discrepancy* which exists between human behavior directly regulated by the fundamental need of the capitalist system of production, which justifies prostitution and slavery, and human behavior regulated by moral (or religious) principles. Two verdicts can be inferred from this example. First, one can say that if the moral principles clash with the economic laws, then these laws must not be moral. Therefore the economist is rendering a self-indictment and acknowledging his own immorality. Second, one can say that moral principles, for the most part, conform to and are usually compatible with the economic laws. Therefore these moral principles legitimate and justify the economic laws. But whatever verdict one chooses, the important point to note is that Marx's notion of "economic morality" signifies his attempt to understand the historical and societal limits wherever human behavior occurs, whether it be deemed moral or immoral.

In light of this observation, we can look briefly at Marx's discussion of the dehumanizing effects of money in capitalist society. As in his earlier discussion of money in the "Excerpt-Notes of 1844," Marx tries to show how the possession of money becomes the prerequisite for one to be human, to possess human properties and faculties. Since "money is the *pander* between need and object, between human life and the means of subsistence,"[80] to have no money is to not be human—or literally to not be alive. Money determines not only existence but the quality of existence. It is the "ontological" ground of being.

> That which exists for me through the medium of *money,* that which I can pay for (i.e., which money can buy), that *I am,* the possessor of the money . . . what I *am* and *can do* is, therefore, not at all determined by my individuality . . . money is the highest good, and so its possessor is good.[81]

For Marx, in capitalist society, not only does money have dehumanizing effects on individuals. It also distorts all natural and human properties and qualities. Money determines value, embodies value, and therefore appears to be synonymous with human value.

> Since money, as the existing and active concept of value, confounds and exchanges everything, it is the universal *confusion and transposition* of all things, the inverted world, the confusion and transposition of all natural and human qualities.[82]

It is obvious that Marx's notions of alienation and dehumanization presuppose some standard of wholeness (or "nonalienation") and the human. An acknowledgment of this standard brings us to an examination of the ethical beliefs, values, and sensibilities embedded *within* Marx's own embryonic theory and how (or whether) he can justify them without engaging in a quest for philosophic certainty or search for philosophic foundations.

Despite Marx's philosophic to theoretic shift and his condemnation of philosophy as an autonomous discipline, he remains partly captive of the old vision of philosophy, of its quest for certainty and search for foundations. He does so because he tends to defend his standard of wholeness and the human by appealing to a "human essence" or essential human activity. Following Feuerbach, Marx conceives of human beings as possessing essential qualities or as engaged in essential activity separated from their so-called accidental qualities or alienated activity. This humanist view permits the essential qualities or activity to serve as metaphysical facts about people which then form the basis for generating timeless criteria, necessary grounds, or universal foundations against which to measure moral principles and action.

Marx does not explicitly engage in the usual philosophic activity of specifying his criteria and justifying his ethical beliefs by appealing to the criteria. In this sense, he already has rejected certain aspects of the old vision of philosophy. But within the confines of his theoretic concerns and aims, he employs essentialist, i.e., philosophic, language which *implicitly* serves as a standard against which to measure certain kinds of qualities and activities.

This essentialist language takes the form of phrases such as "species-life" *(Gattungsleben)* and "species-being" *(Gattungswesen)*. These phrases employed by Marx come directly from the writings of Feuerbach. They express the fissure Feuerbach perceives between animals and human beings. Feuerbach claims that human beings are distinguished from animals by their possession of a consciousness that they are members of the human species. This consciousness assures or posits that there must be a fundamental human essence, e.g., this consciousness itself or engagement in a particular activity which accounts for this common membership in the species.

This essentialist viewpoint seems to have been understood by Marx in terms of his conception of human nature as social freedom, which we examined earlier in the discussion of the "Excerpt-Notes of 1844." Marx uses the Feuerbachian terms, species-life and species-being, as roughly synonymous with a certain kind of social life and social being, a life characterized by a particular kind of interaction with others, a person's being within a particular kind of community.

So, on the one hand, we see Marx making the Feuerbachian distinction between human beings and animals as in the following passage:

The animal is one with its life activity. It does not distinguish the activity from itself. It is *its activity*. But man makes his life activity itself an object of his will and consciousness. He has a conscious life activity. It is not a determination with which he is completely identified. Conscious life activity distinguishes man from the life activity of animals. Only for this reason is he a species-being. Or rather, he is only a self-conscious being, i.e. his own life is an object for him, because he is a species being. Only for this reason is his activity free activity.[83]

Yet, on the other hand, Marx conceives species-being in relation to a particular kind of productive activity or labor which is inextricable from a certain kind of social arrangement or community.

It is just in his work upon the objective world that man really proves himself as a *species-being*. This production is his active species-life. By means of it nature appears as *his* work and reality. The object of labor is, therefore, the *objectification* of *man's species-life;* for he no longer re-produces himself merely intellectually, as in consciousness, but actively and in a real sense, and he sees his own reflection in a world which he has constructed.[84]

Marx goes on to accent the social character of this species life, this productive activity which shapes the world.

The individual *is* the *social being*. The manifestation of his life—even when it does not appear directly in the form of a communal manifestation, accomplished in association with other men—is, therefore, a manifesta-tion and affirmation of *social-life*. Individual human life and species-life are not different things, even though the mode of existence of individual life is necessarily either a more *specific* or a more *general* mode of species-life, or that of species-life, a *specific* or more *general* mode of individual life.

In his *species-consciousness* man confirms his real *social-life*, and reproduces his real existence in thought, while conversely, species-life, confirms itself in species-consciousness and exists for itself in its universality as a thinking being. Though man is a unique individual—and it is just his particularity which makes him an individual, a really *individual* communal being—he is equally the *whole*, the ideal whole, the subjective existence of society as thought and experienced. He exists in reality both as the representation and the actual satisfaction of social existence and as the whole of human manifestations of life.[85]

My chief point of quoting at length the above passages is to show how the Feuerbachian terms that Marx employs are fused with meaning derived from his own earlier formulation of human nature as social freedom. In this way, Marx's conception of the standard of wholeness and the human becomes a standard of a certain kind of society and community, or more basically, a particular kind of productive activity of persons which makes a certain kind of society and community possible.

As we saw in his earlier discussion in the "Excerpt-Notes of 1844," Marx wants to replace production for exchange with production for human needs. Instead of the domination of the workers by private owners of their products, Marx promotes the freedom of the workers by mutual ownership of their products. This replacement must take the form of political struggle and ultimately revolutionary activity:

> From the relation of alienated labor to private property it follows further that the emancipation of society from private property, etc., from servitude, is expressed in its *political* form as the *emancipation of workers,* not as though it is only a question of their emancipation but because in their emancipation is contained universal human emancipation. It is contained in their emancipation because the whole of human servitude is involved in the relation of worker to production, and all relations of servitude are only modifications and consequences of the worker's relation to production.[86]

Marx pursues the nature and consequences of this emancipation in the section entitled, "Private Property and Communism." He distinguishes this emancipation from four other kinds: crude communism (Proudhon), democratic communism (Cabet), despotic communism (Babeuf), and stateless communism (Dezamy). What separates Marx's own brand of emancipation from the others is that his communism rests upon the kind of human productive activity which promotes social freedom, that is, satisfies evolving human needs and permits the expression of human properties and faculties. The expression of human properties and faculties takes the form of engaging in the process of self-development and self-formation in relation to others or in community.

> . . . in place of the *wealth* and *poverty* of political economy, we have the *wealthy* man and the plentitude of *human* need. The wealthy man is at the same time one who *needs* a complex of human manifestations of life, and whose own self-realization exists as an inner necessity, a *need*. Not only the

wealth but also the *poverty* of man acquires, in a socialist perspective, a *human* and thus a social meaning. Poverty is the passive bond which leads man to experience a need for the greatest wealth, the *other* person.[87]

Notice that, for Marx, to evoke the standard "human" is to relate activity and relations of and among people, i.e., social activity and social relations, which are no longer mediated by money and cash-exchange but rather by one's own human properties and faculties.

> Let us assume *man* to be *man,* and his relation to the world to be a human one. Then love can only be exchanged for love, trust for trust, etc. If you wish to enjoy art you must be an artistically cultivated person; if you wish to influence other people you must be a person who really has a stimulating and encouraging effect on others. Every one of your relations to man and to nature must be a *specific expression,* corresponding to the object of your will, of your *real individual* life. If you love without evoking love in return, i.e., if you are not able, by the manifestation of yourself, as a loving person, to make yourself a *beloved person,* then your love is impotent and a misfortune.[88]

Therefore, for Marx, communism "is not itself the goal of human development" but rather a means, a stage, "a real and necessary factor in the emancipation and rehabilitation of man."[89] The emancipation and rehabilitation of humankind means the self-realization of each and every unique individual within a community in which the products produced by producers are mutually owned, i.e., are the common good, of the community. Such productive activity by people is not alienated activity but rather essential activity or species-activity in the sense that it does not reduce human relations (especially in the productive powers) to money-exchange relations and thus does not have dehumanizing effects on people. Instead, this productive activity promotes a communal life which encourages and permits the self-development of individuals.

> *Communism* is the *positive* overcoming of *private property,* of *human self-alienation,* and thus the actual *appropriation* of the *human* essence through and for man. It is therefore, the complete and conscious restoration of man to himself within the total wealth of previous development, the restoration of man as a *social,* that is really human, being.[90]

Marx's social understanding of Feuerbach's essentialist language can be viewed in two ways. First, one can say, as does Louis Althusser, that Marx was at this stage in his thinking a Feuerbachian tied to serious talk about a "human essence" or "human nature." and Marx's next published work, *The Holy Family* (written in the fall-winter of 1844), indeed explicitly endorses Feuerbach's "real humanism." Second, one can say that Marx is praising Feuerbach yet simultaneously going beyond Feuerbach. He is praising Feuerbach because Feuerbach's formulations permit Marx to grasp the importance of Hegel's dialectic (and its link to labor, as we saw earlier) and reject the idealistic content of Hegel's dialectic. Yet Marx goes beyond Feuerbach because he continues to take Hegel's dialectic seriously *after* Feuerbach's materialistic critique of it. In this way, Marx remains preoccupied with activity—human productive activity—and thus understands Feuerbach's "human essence" or "species-life" in a social and dynamic way, i.e., in terms of human labor.

My previous readings of Marx's texts point toward the second way of looking at Marx's employment of essentialist language. Marx surely is using Feuerbachian language, but when we looked carefully at his textual practice we saw that he was engaged in something quite different from talking about a static "human essence" or "human nature." Yet, in my reading of Marx, this discrepancy between his Feuerbachian language and his un-Feuerbachian textual practice creates confusion—on the part of interpreters of his texts and on the part of Marx himself. This confusion consists primarily of his struggling to express his theoretic aims and concerns within philosophic language—a language in which the essential/accidental distinction is central—even while his social understanding of essentialistic terminology is making the employment of the philosophic language more and more problematic.

Marx's struggle can be seen clearly in his attempt to embed ethical elements within particular theories of political economy, including his own (as we saw earlier in this section). On the one hand, he shows clearly the particular moral element within theoretic formulations. On the other hand, in his own embryonic theory, we saw him talk about the moral elements in philosophic, i.e., essentialist, language, even though he understood the language in a dynamic, social way.

This tension is best illustrated by Marx's brief discussion of the relation of morals and political economy. He begins with Chevalier's criticism of Ricardo and then goes on to make comments—ambiguous comments—of his own.

> Thus M. Michel Chevalier reproaches Ricardo with leaving morals out of account. But Ricardo lets political economy speak its own language; he is not to blame if this language is not that of morals. M. Chevalier ignores political economy in so far as he concerns himself with morals, but he really and necessarily ignores morals when he is concerned with political economy: for the bearing of political economy upon morals is either arbitrary and accidental and thus lacking any scientific basis or character, is a mere *sham* or else it is *essential* and can then only be a relation between economic laws and morals. If there is no such relation, can Ricardo be held responsible? Moreover, the antithesis between morals and political economy is itself only *apparent;* there is an antithesis and equally no antithesis. Political economy expresses, *in its own fashion,* the moral laws.[91]

In the next section we shall see how Marx attempts to resolve this tension between his theoretic aims and his philosophic language, between political economy as a theoretic activity and morals as a philosophic activity, between evolving social practices, communities, societies, and talk of a "human essence" or "human nature."

◇ 3 ◇

Marx's Adoption
of Radical Historicism

Marx adopts the radical historicist conception of philosophy and thus the radical historicist approach to ethics for the first time in his famous *Theses on Feuerbach* (written in March 1845). Marx's criticisms of Feuerbach are, in many ways, criticisms of aspects of his own past positions. Rightly called by Engels "the first document in which the brilliant kernel of the new worldview is revealed," and justly advanced by Marxist thinkers as a turning point in the history of philosophy, this text represents Marx's arrival at the radical historicist viewpoint.

In light of our discussion of the radical historicist viewpoint in Chapter 1, I shall briefly examine six crucial theses from his eleven theses on Feuerbach.

(1)

The chief defect of all previous materialism (including Feuerbach's) is that the object, actuality, sensuousness is conceived only in the form of the *object of perception [Anschauung]*, but not as *sensuous human activity, practice [Praxis]*, not subjectively. Hence in opposition to materialism the *active* side was developed by idealism—but only abstractly since idealism naturally does not know actual, sensuous activity as such. Feuerbach wants sensuous objects actually different from thought objects: but he does not comprehend human activity itself as *objective*. Hence in *The Essence of Christianity* he regards only the theoretical attitude as the truly human attitude, while practice is understood and fixed only in its dirty Jewish form of appearance. Consequently, he does not comprehend the significance of "revolutionary," of "practical critical" activity.[1]

This first thesis makes two separate claims. First, that all materialists,

63

presumably from Democritus to Feuerbach have failed to take seriously the activity or practices of human beings. Second, that this activity or practice consists of agreed-upon social conventions erected by people in order principally to facilitate the satisfaction of certain perceived needs and interests. Feuerbach's main fault is that he overlooks this activity or practice.

Materialists have tended to ignore the activity or practices of human beings because their mechanistic (and often deterministic) models of causation assumed the human mind to be merely passive, to be solely the receptor of outside stimuli. It was left to the idealists, e.g., Kant, Fichte, Reinhold, Hegel, to stress the activity of the mind, the human contribution to knowing. Armed with its own set of anticipations, assumptions, categories, and aims, the mind, for the idealist, transforms and transcends that which is 'given' to it or that which it confronts. Knowing is a struggle between the obstinate object and active subject. But the idealists conceive human beings solely as subjects of knowing, mere bearers of self-consciousness. They ignore the material side of people, their natural needs and social interest.

Feuerbach's contribution is to expose the material content of idealism, to point out that the activity of the subject (or self-consciousness) in idealism is but the activity of actual people; his mistake is to view the activity of actual people in an abstract way, unrelated to the broad matrix of natural needs, social interests, and political power. For Feuerbach, the central task was merely to liberate people from the alienated power their own mental creations, e.g., God, have over them. Hence, he understood the human attitude to be a theoretical, contemplative one. In this way, he put forward a critique of idealism that results in an incomplete materialism, a view which begins with people's religious needs, transforms these needs into human ones, yet ignores the social conditions and historical circumstances that may possibly generate such needs. Consequently, Feuerbach cannot see the importance of a form of social activity, a way of knowing and living and wielding political power, that calls for the radical transformation of such conditions and circumstances in order to satisfy certain needs and interests of people.

(2)

The question whether human thinking can reach objective truth—is not a question of theory but a *practical* question. In practice man must prove the truth, that is, actuality and power, this-sidedness of his thinking. The dispute about the actuality or nonactuality of thinking—thinking isolated from practice—is a purely *scholastic* question.[2]

Marx holds at arm's length the traditional theories of truth in philosophy, namely, the correspondence and coherence theories of truth. The doctrine of an idea corresponding or agreeing with its object presupposes a clear understanding of correspondence, or what it means for an idea to "correspond" or "agree" with an object. The doctrine of ideas cohering with other ideas, e.g., being logically consistent, theoretically intelligible, makes sense but surely such coherence could hold with it being unrelated to reality, or independent of empirical evidence.

For Marx, the question of whether human thinking can reach objective truth is a practical question for two basic reasons. First, it is a practical question in the trivial sense, namely, that whatever "objective truth" is, it is arrived at by particular social practices and human activities, e.g., "scientific" practices and activities. Second, it is a practical question in a deep sense, namely, that "objective truth" should not be associated with *copying* the world, but rather with *coping* in the world, that "objective truth" should not be associated with representations *agreeing with* objects in the world, but rather *with people transforming* circumstances and conditions in the world. In short, truth-searching is not a quest for necessary and universal forms, essences, substances, categories, or grounds, but rather a perennial activity of solving problems, responding to dilemmas, or overcoming quagmires. Marx's philosophic to theoretic shift leads him to conclude that philosophic discussions on the nature of truth, independent of theoretical activity related to concrete problems or pressing social circumstances, are mere playthings for "scholastics."

(3)

The materialist doctrine that men are products of circumstances and upbringing, and that, therefore, changed men are products of other circumstances and changed upbringing, forgets that it is men who change circumstances and that the educator must himself be educated. Hence, this doctrine is bound to divide society into two parts, one of which is superior to society (in Robert Owen, for example).

The coincidence of the changing of circumstances and of human activity can be conceived and rationally understood only as a revolutionising practice.[3]

This thesis is a criticism of abstract moralism, and especially of Utopian socialists, who adhere to a materialist view of nature yet remain tied to hard objectivism (or moral idealism). Despite similar goals, Marx differs sharply with Utopian socialists in regard to their views of history and the status of their ideals. And their views of history and hard objectivism are interrelated. For Marx, the Utopian socialists have an inadequate understanding of history, which is best reflected in their failure to account for the sources and status of their own moral and political stances. They ignore the antecedent social realities that, in some sense, determine their own ideals and circumstances. Consequently, they come to believe that they, unlike other people whose ideals are determined by history and society, are above such determinants and hence objective, rational, viewing things *sub specie aeternitatis*.

This view of themselves and their ideals leads them away from realistic conceptions of political power and historical possibilities for structural social change. Ideals unrelated to such conceptions and possibilities are, for Marx, mere abstract moral claims, beliefs, or formulas. Ethical considerations or deliberations independent of an adequate theory of history and society constitute either misguided strategies or barren academicism.

(6)

Feuerbach resolves the essence of religion into the essence of man. But the essence of man is no abstraction inherent in each single individual. In its reality it is the ensemble of the social relations.

Feurbach, who does not enter upon a criticism of this real essence, is hence obliged:

1. To abstract from the historical process and to define the religious sentiment [*Gemut*] regarded by itself, and to presuppose an abstract— *isolated*—human individual.

2. The essence of man, therefore, can with him be regarded only as "species," as an inner, mute, general character which unites the many individuals only *in a natural way*.[4]

(7)

Feuerbach, consequently, does not see that the "religious sentiment" is itself a *social product,* and that the abstract individual which he analyses belongs in reality to a particular form of society.[5]

These two theses constitute Marx's celebrated rejection of the doctrine of essentialism we examined earlier. We have seen Marx himself employ such language in earlier texts. The mistake Feuerbach makes is to substitute one essence for another: the religious essence for the human essence. Marx views "essencemaking" as elevating particular human characteristics within a specific social arrangement to an abstraction with transhistorical status. In short, the idea of a particular essence of humankind results from a historical expression of a human trait and the notion of the abstract individual to whom this essence is attributed is a product of a certain kind of society.

Just as for Feuerbach theological reflections about the religious essence of people are transformed into philosophic formulations about the human essence of people, for Marx these philosophic formulations are dissolved into theoretic ones which probe the socioeconomic circumstances out of which the theological and philosophic claims come. For Feuerbach, anthropology or philosophy of abstract man is the secret of theology; for Marx, a theory of history and a social analysis is the secret of anthropology.

These two theses are the most important ones Marx puts forward because they express more than any of the others his radical historicist viewpoint. His move from philosophic aims and language to theoretic ones is now *fully* complete. This means that fundamental distinctions such as objectivism/relativism, necessary/arbitrary, or essential/accidental will no longer be viewed through a *philosophic* lens. That is, no longer will one be concerned with arriving at the timeless criteria, necessary grounds, or universal foundations for philosophic objectivity, necessity, or essentiality. Instead, any talk about objectivity, necessity, or essentiality must be under-a-description, hence historically located, socially situated and "a product" of revisable, agreed-upon human conventions which reflect particular personal needs, social interests, and political powers at a specific moment in history. The task at hand then becomes a *theoretic* one, namely, providing a concrete social analysis which shows how these needs, interests, and powers shape and hold particular human conventions and in which ways these conventions can be transformed.

(11)

> The philosophers have only *interpreted* the world in various ways; the
> point, however, is to *change* it.[6]

This last—and most famous—thesis signifies the *metaphilosophical
implications* of Marx's radical historicist viewpoint, that is, it indicates
the *consequences* for the task of philosophy once one adopts a radical
historicist perspective. In this thesis, Marx explicitly separates himself
from the dominant philosophical tradition in the West—the tradition,
from Plato through Hegel, which embarks on quests for philosophic
certainty and searches for philosophic foundations. This tradition has
provided a variety of profound and penetrating interpretations of the
world, reality, truth, knowledge, and the self, and it has offered complex and fascinating arguments to show why particular interpretations
are acceptable. But this tradition, for the most part, has limited philosophic activity merely to putting forward such interpretations and their
philosophic justifications.

The crucial role of social practices and conventions revealed to Marx
by his political activism and the importance of historical consciousness—hence stressing the dynamic character of these practices
and conventions (derived from Hegel's dialectic)—leads Marx to go
beyond the dominant tradition in the West, to transgress its boundaries
and step over its limits. Marx's radical historicist viewpoint assumes
that the heightened awareness of the limitations of traditional philosophy will soon render that philosophy barren, a mere blind and empty
will-to-nothingness. In its place will thrive a theory of history and
society, able to account for its own appearance and status, aware of the
paradoxes it cannot solve, grounded in ever changing personal needs
and social interests, and beckoning for action in order to overcome
certain conditions and realize new conditions. In this way, the radical
historicist viewpoint enables Marx to make the philosophic to theoretic
shift without bothering his philosophic conscience. It liberates him
fully from the old vision of philosophy and frees him to pursue his
theoretic concerns and aims.

Marx's radical historicist viewpoint is not a rejection of rational
dialogue, discourse, or discussion, nor is it a call for blind activism.
Rather it is a recognition of a much-needed transformation of philosophy, a transformation required by the theoretic activity philosophy

itself made possible, especially historical and social theoretic activity. For a radical historicist—be it Pascal, Kierkegaard, Marx, or Wittgenstein—the aim of philosophy is not to interpret the world but to change it. For the philosophically inclined radical historicist who, like Wittgenstein, shies away from theoretic activity, this means to first and foremost change the dominant conception of philosophy, to change philosophy by making clear where and how it goes wrong. For a highly theoretically inclined radical historicist, like Marx, this means to leave the confines of philosophic discourse and the reform of philosophy and plunge eagerly into full-fledged theory construction.

In Marx's next text, *The German Ideology* (written between November 1845 and August 1846), Marx says his last good-bye to the old vision of philosophy (and ethics) and, for the first time, puts forward his famous theory of history. But before we examine this text, I think it is essential to look briefly at the impact on Marx of Max Stirner's *The Ego and Its Own* (1844), especially in light of the fact that over 400 pages (or about three-fifths) of *The German Ideology* is devoted to Stirner's book. In my view, Stirner's book is the straw that broke the camel's back, and hence partly responsible for the culmination of Marx's farewell to the old vision of philosophy and ethics.

Stirner's Radical Psychologism: A Challenge to Marx

Stirner's book—read by Marx in November 1844, hence *prior* to his *Theses on Feuerbach*—is primarily concerned with the same issues bothering Marx: the status of philosophy and ethics and the philosophic to theoretic shift. Stirner makes a daring critique of philosophy and ethics and ultimately opts for a radical psychologism. That is, he calls into question the possibility of *philosophic* criteria, grounds, or foundations and rests his views on the fleeting states of mind—and specifically, the egoistic ideas—of the individual.

We are concerned primarily with two elements in Stirner's book: first, his trenchant critique of the essentialist language found in the writings of Feuerbach, Marx (especially in *The Holy Family*), and other Young Hegelians; second, his radical psychologism. Both of these elements are implicit in the first ebullient paragraph in Stirner's preface, entitled, "I Have Founded My Affair on Nothing" (borrowing from the first line of Goethe's poem, *Vanitas! Vanitatum Vanitas!*):

> What is not supposed to be my concern! First and foremost, the Good Cause, then God's cause, the cause of mankind, of truth, of freedom, of humanity, of justice; further, the cause of my people, my prince, my fatherland; finally, even the cause of Mind, and a thousand other causes. Only *my* cause is never to be my concern. "Shame on the egoist who thinks only of himself!"[7]

In this passage, Stirner lumps the idea of God with moral ideals and opposes them both to his egoism. These two themes will be his chief focus: one, the illusory status of the idea of God, moral ideals, and philosophic abstractions, and two, the uniqueness of the self.

Just as Feuerbach claims that God is an illusion that contains a truth, namely, man's essential nature conceived as existing separately from man, so Stirner holds that Feuerbach's account of man's essential nature is itself an illusion, a mere secular residue of religious superstition. For Stirner, the idea of God, moral ideals, and philosophic abstractions are all mere fetishes that dominate and control people. Therefore he rejects any talk about God, ideals, or truths which are binding on people. He responds in the following passage in particular to Feuerbach:

> Haven't we the priest again there? Who is his God? Man with a capital M! What is the divine? The human! Then the predicate has indeed only been changed into the subject, and, instead of the sentence, "God is love," they say "love is divine"; instead of "God has become man," "Man has become God," etc. It is nothing more or less than a new—*religion*. "All moral relations are ethical, are cultivated with a moral mind, only where of themselves (without religious consecration by the priest's blessing) they are counted *religious*." Feuerbach's proposition, "Theology is anthropology," means only "religion must be ethics; ethics alone is religion."[8]

For Stirner, the doctrine of essentialism is inseparable from theology, philosophy, and morality. This doctrine presupposes the existence of a fixed idea or static ideal to which people must submit or which they must allow to regulate their behavior. In his provocative section, entitled "Bats in the Belfry," he writes,

Man, your head is haunted; you have bats in your belfry! You imagine great things, and depict to yourself a whole world of gods that has an existence for you, a spirit-realm to which you suppose yourself to be called, an ideal that beckons to you. You have a fixed idea!

Do not think that I am jesting or speaking figuratively when I regard those persons who cling to the Higher, and (because the vast majority belongs under this head) almost the whole of men, as veritable fools, fools in a madhouse. What is it, then, that is called a "fixed idea"? An idea that has subjected the man to itself.[9]

These "fools," Stirner claims, are possessed, controlled by a sacred idea, a moral ideal, or a philosophic abstraction. Thus so-called atheists are usually as possessed or religious as Christians, in that both cherish certain ideals the violation of which terrifies them.

Take notice how a "moral man" behaves, who today often thinks he is through with God and throws off Christianity as a bygone thing. If you ask him whether he has ever doubted that the copulation of brother and sister is incest, that monogamy is the truth of marriage, that filial piety is a sacred duty, then a moral shudder will come over him at the conception of one's being allowed to touch his sister as wife also. And whence this shudder? Because he *believes* in those moral commandments. This moral *faith* is deeply rooted in his breast. Much as he rages against the *pious* Christians, he himself has nevertheless as thoroughly remained a Christian—to wit, a *moral* Christian. In the form of morality Christianity holds him a prisoner, and a prisoner under *faith*.[10]

Stirner then launches into a tirade against objectivity in morality, against attempts to achieve an Archimedean point, a *sub specie aeternitatis* perspective. He views these attempts as the mere unsatisfiable wishes of theologians and philosophers who want to provide philosophic foundations for their fixed ideas, to secure philosophic validity and objectivity for their sacred ideas, moral ideals, or philosophic abstractions.

The fixed idea may also be perceived as "maxim," "principle," "standpoint" and the like. Archimedes, to move the earth, asked for a standpoint *outside* it. Men sought continually for this standpoint, and every one seized upon it as well as he was able. This foreign standpoint is the *world of mind,* of ideas, thoughts, concepts, essences; it is heaven. Heaven is the "standpoint" from which the earth is moved, earthly doings surveyed and—

despised. To assure to themselves heaven, to occupy the heavenly stand-point firmly and for ever—how painfully and tirelessly humanity struggled for this![11]

Stirner extends this viewpoint into the political sphere, attacking socialist and communist ideals. Such ideals, no matter how radical or revolutionary, have the same illusory status as the theologians' "God" or Feuerbach's "Man." They are mere fetishes that bind, dominate, and control people.

> As the communists first declare free activity to be man's essence, they like all workday dispositions, need a Sunday; like all material endeavours, they need a God, an uplifting and edification alongside their witless "labour."
>
> That the communist sees in you the man, the brother, is only the Sunday side of communism. According to the workday side he does not by any means take you as man simply, but as human labourer or labouring man. The first view has in it the liberal principle; in the second, illiberality is concealed. If you were a "lazybones," he would not indeed fail to recognize the man in you, but would endeavour to cleanse him as a "lazy man" from laziness and to convert you to the *faith* that labour is man's "destiny and calling."[12]

This attack is aimed at the German socialist thinker Wilhelm Christian Weitling (who had written a book entitled *Mankind As It Is and As It Ought to Be*) and at those such as Moses Hess and Marx whom he considered Feuerbachian disciples. For Stirner, these thinkers merely replace the present ideal of individualistic competition with cooperative labor, obligating people to overcome their egoism in order to establish a society of laborers.

> The beautiful dream of a "social duty" still continues to be dreamed. People think again that society gives what we need, and we are *under obligations* to it on that account, owe it everything. They are still at the point of wanting to *serve* a "supreme giver of all good" . . . imprisoned in the religious principle, and zealously aspire after—a sacred society, such as the State was hitherto.
>
> Society, from which we have everything, is a new master, a new spook, a new "supreme being," which "takes us into its service and allegiance"![13]

Stirner opposes essentialism, "spookism" or "possession," with his egoistic doctrine. His program of radical psychologism, directed against theology, philosophy, and morality, results in doing away with all sacred ideas, abstractions, and ideals. In their place, he heralds a unique, irreplaceable ego and defends the phenomena of *owness,* of one's ownership of what one has in one's power or what one controls. He distinguishes this *owness* from freedom.

> Think that over well, and decide whether you will place on your banner the dream of "freedom" or the resolution of "egoism," of "owness." "Freedom" awakens your *rage* against everything that is not you; "ego-ism" calls you to *joy* over yourselves, to self-enjoyment; "freedom" is and remains a *longing,* a romantic plaint, a Christian hope for unearthliness and futurity; "owness" is a reality, which *of itself* removes just so much unfreedom as by barring your own way hinders you.[14]

One denies one's owness when one submits to fixed ideas, binding oneself to them. One can acquire an authentic freedom only through one's *owness,* by one's might.

> My freedom becomes complete only when it is my—*might;* but by this I cease to be a merely free man, and become an own man. Why is the freedom of the peoples a hollow word? Because the people have no might![15]

Stirner thus overthrows morality and unequivocally endorses Thracymachus' view: might makes right. For him, right is might (or values are brute power) transformed into a ghost, a spook, an illusory ideal. Stirner laughs at the communists who throw moral arguments at the existing order but show no signs of might or force. He concludes that they have not realized that morality is "a bat in the belfry" with no power against entrenched realities like a social order.

> The polemic against privilege forms a characteristic feature of liber-alism, which fumes against "privilege" because it itself appeals to "right." Further than to fuming it cannot carry this; for privileges do not fall before might falls, as they are only forms of right. But right falls apart into its nothingness when it is swallowed up by might, when one understands what is meant by "Might goes before right." All right explains itself then as privilege, and privilege itself as power, as—*superior* power.[16]

The aim for Stirner is to increase one's might, extend one's spheres of *owness.* One does this by utilizing other things or people for one's own enjoyment and happiness. He goes so far as to claim that he writes his book, not in order to satisfy some philosophic abstraction (such as truth) or promote a worthy cause (such as learning, enlightenment), but in order to procure his thoughts existence in the world and to find some enjoyment by using his readers.

> But not only not for your sake, not even for truth's sake either do I speak out what I think. No—
>
> > I sing as sings the bird
> > That perches on the bough;
> > The song that wells from me
> > Is pay enough for now.
>
> I sing because—I am a singer. But I *use* you for it because I—need ears.
>
> Where the world comes in my way—and it comes in my way everywhere—I consume it to quiet the hunger of my egoism. For me you are nothing but—my food, even as I too am fed upon and turned to use by you. We have only one relation to each other, that of *usableness,* of utility, of use.[17]

Stirner's books represents the exhaustion of the Feuerbachian critique of Hegelian philosophy. He carries the profanization of Hegel's thought, best illustrated by Feuerbach, about as far as one can go. He reduces objectivity and validity to nonsense, theology and philosophy to ghost talk, morality to spookism. He rejects, in a radical way, the autonomy of philosophy—and of ethics.

The German Ideology:
Radical Historicist Critiques

I will examine *The German Ideology* in light of two basic concerns: Marx's radical historicist critiques of the essentialist language of Feuerbach, Bauer, Stirner, and the "true socialists" and the relation of Marx's own theoretic formulations of history to the status of philosophy and ethics. Although Marx's own theoretic formulations occur early in the text and most of his critiques appear later, I will begin with his critiques for the sake of continuity in this essay. (I will examine his theoretic formulations in the next section.)

Marx begins the preface of the work by claiming that the common denominator of contemporary German philosophy (as exemplified in the works of Feuerbach, Bauer, and Stirner) is the belief in the power of ideas to change the world, the ability of concepts to transform reality. This belief has produced misguided theories about who human beings are and misconceptions of what they should become. And, more importantly, this belief precludes attempts to overcome such misguided theories and misconceptions of moral ideals because it leaves out the only hope for rescue—the real world of human needs and interests, of social life and material production.

> Hitherto men have always formed wrong ideas about themselves, about what they are and what they ought to be. They have arranged their relations according to their ideas of God, of normal man, etc. The products of their brains have got out of their hands. They, the creators, have bowed down before their creations. Let us liberate them from the chimeras, the ideas, dogmas, imaginary beings under the yoke of which they are pining away. Let us revolt against this rule of concepts. Let us teach men, says one (Feuerbach) how to exchange these imaginations for thoughts which correspond to the essence of man; says another (Bauer), how to take up a critical attitude to them; says the third (Stirner), how to get them out of their heads; and existing reality will collapse.[18]

Marx claims that the aim of the work is to "ridicule and discredit the philosophic struggle with the shadow of reality."[19] He will try to lift German criticism out of the realm of philosophy and beyond the confines of philosophic reflection. His aim is to transform philosophy into a theory of history; he wants to view the discipline of philosophy, e.g., its concern with philosophic notions of justification and interpretation, as a set of conventions or social practices included in the variety of viewpoints, modes of rationality, sensibilities, norms, and values that are permitted, promoted, or given prominence in complex ways by requirements of the existing system of production.

> Since the Young Hegelians consider conceptions, thoughts, ideas, in fact all of the products of consciousness, to which they attribute an independent existence, as the real chains of men (just as the Old Hegelians declare them the true bonds of human society) it is evident that the Young Hegelians have to fight only against these illusions of consciousness. Since, according to their fantasy, the relations of men, all their doings, their fetters and their limitations are products of their consciousness, the Young Hegelians logically put to men the moral postulate of exchanging their present consciousness for human (Feuerbach), critical (Bauer) or egoistic (Stirner) consciousness, and thus of removing their limitations.

This demand to change consciousness amounts to a demand to interpret the existing world in a different way, i.e., to recognise it by means of a different interpretation.[20]

Contrary to the illusions and fantasies of the Young Hegelians, Marx turns to what he calls "the science of history." A central problem of contemporary German philosophy is that it is ahistorical. Only a science of history allows us to view contemporary German philosophy itself as a historical phenomenon and relate it to German society and history. Marx quips,

> It has not occurred to any one of these philosophers to inquire into the connection of German philosophy with German reality, the connection of their criticism with their own material surroundings.[21]

For Marx, the aim of a science of history or, even better, a theory of history, is to describe, explain, and project the active life-process of evolving productive systems and cultural formations. This task begins with the social practices of people, "their actual, empirically perceptible process of development under definite conditions." This approach goes beyond the dead facts of the empiricist historians and the imagined activity of fanciful subjects of the idealist historians. This theoretic task requires not only a rejection of the autonomous status of philosophy, it requires the virtual disappearance of philosophy.

> Where speculation ends, where real life starts, there consequently begins real, positive science, the expounding of the practical activity, of the practical process of development of men. Empty phrases about consciousness end, and real knowledge has to take their place. When reality is described, a self-sufficient philosophy [*die selbständige Philosophie*] loses its medium of existence. At the best its place can only be taken by a summing-up of the most general results, abstractions which are derived from the observation of the historical development of men. These abstractions in themselves, divorced from real history, have no value whatsoever. They can only serve to facilitate the arrangement of historical material, to indicate the sequence of its separate strata. But they by no means afford a recipe or schema, as does philosophy, for neatly trimming the epochs of history.[22]

In this passage, Marx's shift from any philosopic aims or language to theoretic ones is illustrated in a succinct manner. We shall see his explanation for this shift when we examine his theoretic formulations—

especially his notion of ideology—in the next section. The important point to note here is that this philosophic to theoretic shift results from taking history seriously, or more specifically, from focusing on the dynamic character of social practices and human agreements in evolving situations and circumstances.

This point is highlighted by Marx in his radical historicist critique of Feuerbach. Marx focuses first on Feuerbach because he considers Feuerbach the most sophisticated and progressive thinker of the Young Hegelians. But Feuerbach's basic shortcoming is his failure to take history seriously, his refusal to acknowledge the conventional, hence transient, character of the "grounds" for knowledge claims.

> He does not see that the sensuous world around him is not a thing given direct from all eternity, remaining ever the same, but the product of industry and of the state of society; and, indeed (a product) in the sense that it is an historical product, the result of the activity of a whole succession of generations, each standing on the shoulders of the preceding one, developing its industry and its intercourse, and modifying its social system according to the changed needs. Even the objects of the simplest "sensuous certainty" are only given him through social development, industry and commercial intercourse.[23]

Marx concludes that though Feuerbach stands above other materialists due to his conception of man as a sensuous object, he overlooks (as we saw Marx point out in his first thesis on Feuerbach) the practical activity of people. Feuerbach fails to acknowledge real, living individuals erecting conventions within their particular historical conditions and specific socioeconomic circumstances.

> As far as Feuerbach is a materialist he does not deal with history, and as far as he considers history he is not a materialist. With him materialism and history diverge completely.[24]

In his brief radical historicist critique of Bruno Bauer—in reply to Bauer's accusation that Marx is (in *The Holy Family*) but a "Feuerbachian dogmatist"—Marx views Bauer as an example of those German philosophers who "struggle with the shadows of reality." Bauer's chief shortcoming is that he overexaggerates the importance of philosophy, and that he therefore sees philosophic controversies as having monumental effects on the actual struggles being waged in the world of power and politics. In fact, Marx holds, Bauer ultimately confuses these philosophic controversies with the actual struggles. He engages in this confusion primarily because he tends to assume that one can change the world by merely changing ideas. Since Bauer posits a realm of thoughts and ideas, of philosophy, and of ethics that is independent and autonomous of (and the basis for) history and society, he regards transformation in this realm as constituting, in some crucial way, a transformation of history and society. In this way, Bauer exemplifies the misguided and impotent approach which attempts to change the world by employing philosophic concerns and aims.

> The specific peculiarity of Saint Bruno is that, unlike the authors of *Die heilige Familie,* he does not regard the question of the relation of self-consciousness to substance as "a point of controversy within Hegelian speculation," but as a world-historic, even an absolute question. This is the sole form in which he is capable of expressing the conflicts of the present day . . . for Bruno, along with all philosophers and ideologists, erroneously regards thoughts and ideas—the independent intellectual expression of the existing world—as the basis of this existing world. It is obvious that with these two abstractions, which have become senseless and empty, he can perform all kinds of tricks without knowing anything at all about real people and their relations.[25]

After Marx's rather brief radical historicist critiques of Feuerbach and Bauer, he confronts Max Stirner's radical psychologism viewpoint. What is distinctive of Stirner—and possibly the chief reason Marx spends over 400 pages replying to Stirner—is that he seems to have traveled a road to his radical psychogism view that is similar to the road Marx has traveled to his radical historicist view. Both Marx and Stirner reject the autonomous status of philosophy (and ethics) and both make a radical call for its disappearance. But what seems to upset Marx is how someone who shares his radical view of philosophy (and ethics) can differ so fundamentally on what the alternative is and ought to be. Stirner makes Marx aware of the can of worms he has opened by "overcoming" philosophy, his presence suggests that Marx will find himself among strange bedfellows unless he articulates clearly his radical historicist alternative. Therefore Marx's critique of Stirner exemplifies Marx engaged in a serious battle—a battle over what the alternative should be *after* one rejects the autonomous status of philosophy and calls for its disappearance, a battle over what form theoretic activity should take after Hegel and Feuerbach.

Marx's radical historicist critique of Stirner begins at the root: Stirner's radical psychologism. Marx does not try to show—as he did in the attacks on Feuerbach and Bauer—the limitations of being and remaining a philosopher. Instead Marx tries to illustrate the limitations of Stirner's alternative to philosophy. Marx acknowledges that Stirner accents—as does Marx's own radical historicist view—the dynamic character of human activities. But Marx then points out that by adopting a radical psychologism view Stirner holds that these human activities consist of dynamic, fleeting states of mind. The history of human beings is the history of their activities and the history of their activities is the history of their mental states, ideas, and thoughts.

> Stirner regards the various stages of life only as "self-discoveries" of the individual, and these "self-discoveries" are moreover always reduced to a definite relation of consciousness. Thus the variety of *consciousness* is here the life of the individual. The physical and social changes which take place in the individuals and produce an altered consciousness are, of course, of no concern to Stirner.[26]

Instead of overcoming Cartesian dualism and undermining the Ego's initial captivity in the Cartesian veil of consciousness—the central philosophic paradigm extolling the autonomy of philosophy—Stirner's radical psychologism accepts and reinforces it. Similar to Berkeley's radical idealism, but much cruder, Stirner's radical psychologism merely accepts the world within the veil of consciousness—as being, in fact, the world. This leaves philosophy with little to do since its basic distinctions—reality/appearance, objectivism/relativism, essential/accidental, etc.—have been called into question. Stirner toys with the extreme moral nihilist implications of his move, but then goes on to opt for his own pleasant states of consciousness (i.e., for egoism) as the standard for moral action.

One would expect Marx to question what the status of this standard is—is it a normative claim or a descriptive one? If it is a normative claim, an ought-statement, then it falls victim to Stirner's own tirades against such claims or statements—that they are mere fetishes that control and dominate people. If it is a descriptive claim, an empirical statement, where is the evidence? But Marx will have none of this neat philosophic classifying of claims and statements. Instead Marx understands Stirner's notions of the unique ego and "ownness" as theoretic notions, and specifically notions sedimented with personal needs, social interests, and cultural biases. In short, Marx considers Stirner's claims, statements, and notions as being *ideological*.

For Marx, Stirner's theoretic notions of the unique ego and "own-ness" are rooted in the pervasive perceptions and behavior of a par-ticular group in society, and specifically Stirner's group, the petit bourgeoisie.

> Since Saint Max pays no attention to the physical and social "life" of the individual, and says nothing at all about "life," he quite consistently abstracts from historical epochs, nationalities, classes, etc., or, which is the *same thing*, he inflates the *consciousness* predominant in the class nearest to him in his immediate environment into the normal consciousness of "a man's life."[27]

This comment regarding Stirner's notions should not be read as a vulgar reductionist treatment of them. Rather Marx is applying his own theoretic formulations to Stirner's theoretic notions. Marx attempts to unmask Stirner's notions, to historically locate and socially situate these notions and ultimately describe and explain their role and function.

Marx's radical historicist viewpoint differs from Stirner's radical psy-chologism as an alternative to philosophy in two ways. First, Marx understands dynamic human activities as ever changing social practices of people, their particular agreements or disagreements on conventions and their behavior which is often regulated by these conventions. As we saw earlier, Stirner understands dynamic human activities as fleeting mental states of people. Second, Marx rejects the fundamental *philo-sophic* distinctions of reality/appearance, objectivism/relativism, essen-tial/accidental in order to discard the aim of providing philosophic criteria, grounds, and foundations for reality, objectivity, or essen-tiality. These distinctions may be employed for theoretic aims, i.e., under-a-description, but they then are to be understood in a completely different way, having a different status and viewed as an instance of a dynamic human social practice. We will examine this claim more care-fully in the next section. Stirner also rejects these fundamental phi-losophic distinctions, but he remains in the veil of consciousness owing to his understanding of dynamic human activities as mental activities. From within this veil, he proceeds to put forward theoretic formula-tions which consist roughly of preaching egoism. Marx is insistent on this second difference because his own theoretic formulations preclude preaching any sort of morality. As we noted earlier, Marx's theoretic formulation *contain* moral elements, e.g., self-realization of the individual in community, but he does not put forward purely moral rhetoric to defend these elements or his theory.

Consequently, Marx asserts that Stirner misunderstands the communist movement when Stirner claims that it is tied to an essentialism, obligated to a fixed idea or static moral ideal. Marx writes,

> *Communism* is quite incomprehensible to our saint because the communists do not oppose egoism to selflessness or selflessness to egoism, nor do they express this contradiction theoretically either in its sentimental or in its highflown ideological form; they rather demonstrate its material source, with which it disappears of itself. The communists do not preach *morality* at all, as Stirner does so extensively. They do not put to people the moral demand: love one another, do not be egoists, etc.; on the contrary, they are very well aware that egoism, just as much as selflessness, *is* in definite circumstances a necessary form of the self-assertion of individuals.[28]

In the next section, we shall examine what Marx means when he claims that communists show how such a moral opposition "disappears of itself."

Marx's radical historicist critiques of proponents of "true socialism" (in Volume Two of *The German Ideology*) point essentially to the refusal of those thinkers to make the philosophic to theoretic shift. Because they do not make the shift they regard socialism as "a question of the 'most reasonable' social order and not the needs of a particular class and a particular time."[29] They detach socialist ideals from the proletarian movement and turn to "humanity," appealing to the universal love of humankind. Like the Young Hegelians, "true socialists" fail to adequately analyze historical and social phenomena.

> The German ideology, in the grip of which these "true socialists" remain, prevents them from examining the real state of affairs. Their activity in face of the "unscientific" French and English consists primarily in holding up the superficiality and the "crude" empiricism of these foreigners to the scorn of the German public, in eulogising "German science" and declaring that its mission is to reveal for the first time the *truth* of communism and socialism, the absolute, true socialism.[30]

In short, the "true socialists," like the Young Hegelians, remain idealistic and ahistorical in their moral deliberations about socialist norms. Since they assume the autonomous status of philosophy and ethics, they engage in abstract, "objective" determinations of these norms while ignoring the transient historical bases for such determinations.

> They detach the communist system, critical and polemical writings from the real movement, of which they are but the expression, and force them into an arbitrary connection with German philosophy. They detach the consciousness of certain historically conditioned spheres of life from these spheres and evaluate it in terms of true, absolute, i.e., German philosophical consciousness. With perfect consistency they transform the relations of these particular individuals into relations of "Man"; they interpret the thoughts of these particular individuals concerning their own relations as thoughts about "Man." In so doing, they have abandoned the real historical basis and returned to that of ideology, and since they are ignorant of the real connection, they can without difficulty construct some fantastic relationship with the help of the "absolute" or some other ideological method.[31]

Marx begins by examining an article by Hermann Semmig, which is more concerned with grasping the essence of socialism than understanding the evolution of concrete social conditions that allow for the possibility of socialism. In complete opposition to Marx's view, Semmig asserts that Germans ought to be proud that they judge everything *sub specie aeternitatis* whereas foreigners do so from the standpoint of actual existing people and circumstances. For Marx, this view yields the following kind of unempirical, philosophical reasoning:

> It is a fact that proletarians exist and that they work mechanically. Why are proletarians driven to "mechanical labour?" Because the rentiers "allow their own essence to decay." Why is it that the rentiers allow their own essence to decay? Because "our present-day society has relapsed into savagery to such an extent." Why has it relapsed into savagery? Ask thy maker.[32]

This leads Marx to conclude that,

> German philosophy in it socialist disguise appears, of course, to investigate "crude reality," but it always keeps at a respectable distance and, in hysterical irritation, cries: *noli me tangere*! (Touch me not!)[33]

Contrary to this kind of ahistorical, unscientific approach, Marx stresses the role and function of communist ideals, their close ties to the proletarian movement and their unequivocal opposition to the existing order. Sentimental appeals or claims about the love of humankind, the "essence" of socialism or the "truth" of property only obscure and dilute the fundamental social conflict between capitalists and proletariat, owners and workers.

> In reality: the actual property-owners stand on one side and the propertyless communist proletarians on the other. This opposition becomes keener day by day and is rapidly driving to a crisis. If, then, the theoretical representatives of the proletariat wish their literary activity to have any practical effect, they must first and foremost insist that all phrases are dropped which tend to dim the realisation of the sharpness of this opposition, all phrases which tend to conceal this opposition and may even give the bourgeois a chance to approach the communists for safety's sake on the strength of their philanthropic enthusiasms. All these bad qualities are, however, to be found in the catchwords of the true socialists . . .[34]

Rudolph Matthai argues in the second article Marx examines that the standard for the good society or the "most reasonable" social order is nature. Just as the individual plant demands the soil, warmth, sun, air, and rain in order to grow and flourish, so people desire a society which permits the all-round development and satisfaction of their needs and capacities. Matthai's strategy is to impute the ideas of individuality and universality to nature which he would like to see realized in society. He then demands that present society conform to his ideal.

Marx replies that it is unclear why society should not always have been a true image of nature since Matthai does not touch on the historical development of present society. And it is difficult for Matthai to defend the harmonious character of nature if society does not naturally conform to such harmony. And if it doesn't why not? Has it ever? If so, why the Fall?

Marx next attacks the very criterion of nature, claiming that plants do not "demand" the conditions of existence as stated by Matthai. Rather plants depend completely on the actual conditions of existence. If a plant does not find them already present, it remains a grain of seed and never becomes a plant. In this way, Matthai's moral ideal rests upon a static conception of the "natural."

We should be only too pleased to believe that "all the social virtues" of our true socialist are based "upon the feeling of natural human affinity and unity," even though feudal bondage, slavery and all the social inequalities of every age have also been based upon this "natural affinity." Incidentally, "natural human affinity" is an historical product which is daily changed at the hands of men; it has always been perfectly natural, however inhuman and contrary to nature it may seem, not only in the judgment of "Man," but also of a later revolutionary generation.[35]

His moral ideal represents an ahistorical idealism.

The socialist opposes a present-day society, which is "based upon external compulsion," the ideal of true society, which is based upon the "consciousness of man's *inward* nature, i.e., upon reason." It is based, that is, upon the consciousness of consciousness, upon the thought of thought. The true socialist does not differ from the philosophers even in his choice of terms. He forgets that the "inward nature" of men, as well as their "consciousness" of it, i.e., their "reason," has at all times been an historical product and that even when, as he believes, the society of men was based "upon external compulsion," their "inward nature" correspond to this "external compulsion."[36]

Karl Grün, the most influential "true socialist," is the author of the last essay Marx considers in the second volume of *The German Ideology*. Marx's basic criticism of Grün is what we have now come to expect: that Grün knows nothing about what he morally judges, that he possesses no understanding of what he morally condemns. Thus Grün takes refuge in the protective arms of normative discourse, specifically of talk about human essence, "the last hiding-place of the true socialist." Marx remarks,

All he has to do is to hunt everywhere for the words "Man" and "human" and condemn when he cannot find them.[37]

Marx is not saying that taking a moral position results from an ignorance of what one is evaluating, but rather that moralism as a political stance and philosophic viewpoint constitutes an escape from reality (from analyzing and explaining it) and forces one to presuppose an inadequate conception of history to justify this moralistic stance and viewpoint.

So Herr Grün declares that the real living conditions of men are *manifestations*, whereas religion and politics are the *basis and the roots* of these manifestations. This threadbare statement shows that the true socialists put forward the ideological phrases of German philosophy as truths superior to the real expositions of the French socialists; it shows at the same time that they try to link the true object of their own investigations, human essence, to the results of French social criticism. If one assumes religion and politics to be the basis of material living conditions, then it is only natural that everything should amount in the last instance to an investigation of human essence, i.e., of man's consciousness of himself.[38]

Marx's radical historicist critiques of Feuerbach, Bauer, Stirner, and the "true socialists" raises questions as to what precisely constitutes his own *positive* viewpoint.[39] What are his theoretic formulations after his move away from philosophic concerns and aims? We have seen that, for Marx, philosophy disappears after the shift to theoretic concerns and aims, but does anything take its place?

The German Ideology: Theoretic Formulations

In this section, I will examine briefly the theoretic formulations of history that follow, Marx believes, from his radical historicist viewpoint. I will focus specifically on the relation of these formulations to the disappearance of philosophy and on the central role of his notion of ideology.

For Marx, the radical historicist perspective, with its stress on the dynamic character of social practices and the groundlessness of philosophic claims, entails an inquiry into the beginnings of certain social practices and, for our purposes, into the emergence of the conception of the autonomy of philosophy.

Marx's theoretic formulations amount roughly to a theory of historical limits. On the one hand, he is concerned with circumscribing the boundaries within which each new generation must struggle to survive. This includes acknowledging the particular kind of system of production each new generation inherits (and at what stage of development it is), and it includes acknowledging the evolving beliefs, views, and sensibilities crystallized in the existing cultural lifestyles and political and social institutions. On the other hand, Marx's aim is to point out how these boundaries are transient, the results of human activities and social practices which can be transformed.

> History is nothing but the succession of the separate generations, each of which uses of the materials, the capital funds, the productive forces handed down to it by all preceding generations, and thus, on the one hand, continues the traditional activity in completely changed circumstances and, on the other, modifies the old circumstances with a completely changed activity.[40]

Marx's particular theory of historical limits is a materialist theory in that it begins with the productive activity of people, with how people produce their means of subsistence and create systems of production to insure their survival. But human productive activity is not only the starting point of Marx's materialist theory of history; it also is the major factor in comprehending, explaining, describing, and tracing (these are all theoretic activities) the links to evolving beliefs, values, and sensibilities crystallized in the existing cultural lifestyles and political and social institutions. Since Marx includes philosophy (and ethics) in this evolution of beliefs, values, and sensibilities, it can be expected that his theoretic formulations will provide an explanation and description of the perceived status of philosophy in different epochs. In his most lucid and succinct summary of his theory of history—and for this reason I quote at length—Marx writes,

> This conception of history thus relies on expounding the real process of production—starting from the material production of life itself—and comprehending the form of intercourse connected with and created by this mode of production, i.e. civil society in its various stages, as the basis of all history; describing it in its action as the state, and also explaining how all the different theoretical products and forms of consciousness, religion, philosophy, morality, etc., arise from it, and tracing the process of their formation from that basis, thus the whole thing can, of course, be depicted in its totality (and therefore, too, the reciprocal action of these various sides on one another). It has not, like the idealist view of history, to look for a category in every period, but remains constantly on the real *ground* of history: it does not explain practice from the idea but explains the formation of ideas from material practice, and accordingly it comes to

the conclusion that all forms and products of consciousness cannot be dissolved by mental criticism . . . But only by the practical overthrow of the actual social relations which gave rise to this idealistic humbug; that not criticism but revolution is the driving force of history, also of religion, of philosophy, and all other kinds of theory.[41]

Marx's materialist conception of history is supported by his radical historicist viewpoint in that both focus on the dynamic social practices of people. The materialist theory holds that a certain kind of social practices (i.e., those directly linked to material production for sustenance) serves as the ground for history (i.e., as the dominant factor in historical explanation and description); and the radical historicist perspective claims that these (as well as other) dynamic social practices are revisable human conventions which cannot serve as immutable, invariable grounds, criteria, or foundations for philosophic validity or objectivity. Marx's attempt to replace philosophic grounds with dynamic and social practices, or to replace philosophic concerns with historical, explanatory (i.e., theoretic) aims, is illustrated rhetorically in the following passage:

This sum of productive forces, capital funds and social forms of intercourse, which every individual and every generation finds in existence as something given, is the real basis of what the philosophers have conceived as "substance" and "essence of man," and what they have deified and attacked: a real basis which is not in the least disturbed, in its effect and influence on the development of men, by the fact that these philosophers revolt against it as "self-consciousness" and the "unique." These conditions of life, which different generations find in existence, determine also whether or not the revolutionary convulsion periodically recurring in history will be strong enough to overthrow the basis of everything that exists.[42]

Marx's materialist conception of history, aided by his radical historicist perspective, leaves philosophy no space to exist. As we saw in a passage quoted earlier, "a self-sufficient philosophy loses its medium of existence." In fact, Marx goes on to say,

Incidentally, when things are seen in this way, as they really are and happened, every profound philosophical problem is resolved . . . quite simply into an empirical fact.[43]

And by "empirical fact" Marx means a reality (or set of realities) in process, as understood within the interpretive schema of his materialist conception of history.

Marx suggests that philosophy is viewed as self-sufficient, autonomous (or bound-to-certainty, tied-to-necessity, or linked-to-universality), primarily owing to its role and function in specific societies. The autonomy of philosophy is assumed primarily to promote a particular cultural description of truth, reality, and knowledge which appears unrelated to or independent of the social practices (or conventions) of people. The function of this assumption is to hide and conceal the particularity of this cultural description and hence to blind people to the possible ulterior aims or sinister motives (conscious or unconscious) of its proponents.

With the advent of a division of material and mental labor in human history arises the distinction between two classes of people—one group which manually labors and materially produces and another group which consumes without materially producing, survives without manually laboring.

> From this moment onwards consciousness *can* really flatter itself that it is something other than consciousness of existing practice, that it *really* represents something without representing something real; from now on consciousness is in a position to emancipate itself from the world and to proceed to the formation of "pure" theory, theology, philosophy, morality, etc.[44]

Marx connects this division of labor—manual vs. mental labor—to his notion of a ruling class, specifically that class which consumes without materially producing and survives (and thrives) without manually laboring. This ruling class owns and controls the means of material production and directs and guides the ideas, beliefs, and sensibilities crystallized in cultural lifestyles and social and political institutions.

> The ideas of the ruling class are in every epoch the ruling ideas, i.e., the class which is the ruling *material* force of society is at the same time its ruling *intellectual* force. The class which has the means of material production at its disposal, consequently also controls the means of mental production, so that the ideas of those who lack the means of mental production are on the whole subject to it. The ruling ideas are nothing more than the ideal expression of the dominant material relations, the dominant material relations grasped as ideas; hence of the relations which make the one class the ruling one, therefore, the ideas of its dominance.

The individuals composing the ruling class possess among other things consciousness, and therefore think. Insofar, therefore, as they rule as a class and determine the extent and compass of an historical epoch, it is self-evident that they do this in its whole range, hence among other things rule also as thinkers, as producers of ideas, and regulate the production and distribution of the ideas of their age: Thus their ideas are the ruling ideas of the epoch.[45]

The ruling class is divided into two basic groups—those who inadvertently and unintentionally put forward illusory ideas about themselves and their conditions and those who are actively involved in owning, controlling and selling products produced by laborers. Opposition may occur between these two groups within the ruling class, but it is usually reconciled or overcome at any serious threat or conflict in which the ruling class as a whole is in danger.

Marx suggests that conceptions of the autonomy of philosophy constitute illusory ideas in the sense that such conceptions signify attempts by philosophers to make their cultural viewpoints appear objective and valid from *sub specie aeternitatis*. These conceptions are illusory (i.e., demonstrably worthy of rejection) because the march of history reveals them to be neither timeless nor immutable. And theoretic concerns show that these conceptions perform particular roles and functions in regard to the existing system of production, political and social institutions, and cultural lifestyles. These particular roles and functions are *ideological* ones, that is, the primary role and function of the dominant ideas, values, beliefs, or sensibilities presented in the form of universality, necessity, or eternity is primarily to preserve and perpetuate, justify and legitimate the existing system of production, social and political arrangements, and cultural ways of life. This ideological function of such ideas, beliefs, values, or sensibilities cloaks particular interests behind the claim for universal interests, hides the contingency of conditions behind the claim for necessary conditions, conceals changeable circumstances behind the claim for unavoidable circumstances.

> For each new class which puts itself in the place of one ruling before it is compelled, merely in order to carry through its aim, to present its interest as the common interest of all members of society, that is, expressed in ideal form: it has to give its ideas the form of universality, and present them as the only rational universally valid ones.[46]

The illusory idea of philosophy's autonomy is promoted and encouraged by historians who uncritically accept what past ruling class thinkers imagined themselves to be saying and claiming. This uncritical acceptance of each ruling class's self-conception and self-image leads historians to believe in the autonomy of ideas, values, beliefs, and sensibilities—and of philosophy—and to understand them as existing in a realm of their own. By accepting the illusions of past epochs, these historians preoccupied with the realm of ideas, values, beliefs, and sensibilities come to share the illusion of their own epoch.

> Once the ruling ideas have been separated from the ruling individuals and, above all, from the relations which result from a given stage of the mode of production, and in this way the conclusion has been reached that history is always under the sway of ideas, it is very easy to abstract from these various ideas, "the Idea," the thought, etc., as the dominant force in history, and thus to consider all these separate ideas and concepts as "forms of self-determination" of the Concept developing in history. It follows then naturally, too, that all the relations of men can be derived from the concept of man, man as conceived, the essence of man. This has been done by speculative philosophy.[47]

Marx's materialist conception of history is able to reveal this deception, for two basic reasons. First, it stresses the ideological function of past and present ideas, values, beliefs, and sensibilities. This emphasis permits his theory to locate and situate the real ground or basis of history, namely, the dynamic social practices and the constellation of institutions erected thereon by human beings. Second, Marx's materialist conception of history has no interest in perpetuating the illusion of its own (capitalist) epoch. Its theoretic aim is to unmask the deception concealed by current historians and philosophers.

The important implication for ethics of Marx's materialist conception of history is a radical distinction between moral practices and moral ideals. Moral ideals are to be treated like any other ideas, namely, in terms of their ideological role and function, while moral practices are to be understood like any other social practice, namely, in light of the particular limits circumscribed by the existing system of production, social and political institutions, and cultural ways of life.

For Marx, the demythologizing of the autonomy of ethics consists first, roughly, of disclosing the ideological function of moral ideals, and hence their conventional status; and second, the demythologizing consists of demonstrating the *discrepancy* between moral ideals and moral practices, a discrepancy resulting primarily from the requirements of the existing system of production—which precludes overcoming the discrepancy.

> Thus, society has hitherto always developed within the framework of a contradiction—in antiquity the contradiction between free men and slaves, in the middle ages that between nobility and serfs, in modern times that between the bourgeoisie and the proletariat. This explains, on the one hand, the abnormal, "inhuman" way in which the oppressed class satisfies its needs, and, on the other hand, the narrow limits within which inter-course, and, with it the whole ruling class, develops. Hence this restricted character of development consists not only in the exclusion of one class from development, but also in the narrowmindedness of the excluding class, and the "inhuman" is to be found also within the ruling class. This so-called "inhuman" is just as much a product of presentday relations as the "human" is; it is their negative aspect, the rebellion—which is not based on any new revolutionary productive force—against the prevailing relations brought about by the existing productive forces, and against the way of satisfying needs that corresponds to these relations. The positive expression "human" corresponds to the definite relations *predominant* at a certain stage of production and to the way of satisfying needs determined by them, just as the negative expression "inhuman" corresponds to the attempt to negate these predominant relations and the way of satisfying needs prevailing under them without changing the existing mode of production, an attempt that this stage of production daily engenders afresh.[48]

For Marx, moral language is the means by which human beings articulate and legitimate either their struggle to preserve the existing order, hence control and contain oppositional values, beliefs, and sen-sibilities in culture and society, *or* their struggle to overcome the existing order, hence negate and undermine the dominant values, be-liefs, and sensibilities in culture and society. When Marx claims that "communists do not preach morality at all" he does not mean that communists do not employ moral language. Rather he means that this employment is unavoidable but never a sufficient means for social change. Therefore, it is crucial not to confuse changing people's moral ideals—sometimes a result of employing moral language—with chang-ing societal circumstances, or even patterns of moral practices.

If there is a fundamental problem in ethics for Marx, it consists of the discrepancy between moral ideals and moral practices—or more specifically, the way in which systems of production have hitherto seemed to require a discrepancy between particular interests of a specific class and the claims of universal interests by ideologues of that class. Hitherto ideology has been required to hide and conceal this discrepancy. Marx believes quite optimistically that communists have a solution to this problem—for it is a problem that must be understood in a historical way and resolved only in a practical way. In other words, the problem should be viewed as the many manifestations of *the discrepancy between the rhetoric of universal interests and the reality of particular class interests* within the limits circumscribed by particular systems of production and the boundaries of the concomitant social and political institutions and cultural ways of life. The problem can be solved only when the rhetoric/ reality discrepancy is overcome, that is, when a particular system of production is established which permits the coincidence of the universal interests of society with the particular interests of a class, and when the concomitant social and political institutions and cultural lifestyles promote and encourage this coincidence. This coincidence results for Marx in the self-realization and self-development of *all* individuals within a society: this outcome has truly become the common good.

> Theoretical communists, the only comunists who have time to devote to the study of history, are distinguished precisely by the fact that they alone have *discovered* that throughout history the "general interest" is created by individuals who are defined as "private persons." They know that this contradiction is only a *seeming* one because one side of it, what is called the "general interest," is constantly being produced by the other side, private interest, and in relation to the latter it is by no means an independent force with an independent history—so that this contradiction is in practice constantly destroyed and reproduced.[49]

Conditions of abundance, primarily owing to technological innovation, and the maldistribution of the abundance, due to the private ownership of production and private appropriation of profits, become so destructive of human lives that the producers, united as a class, are compelled to abolish private property and the class division of labor. This abolition constitutes proletarian revolution. This revolution can usher in a new society that permits and makes possible the self-realization and self-development of individuals, since private property can be abolished only on condition of an all-round development of individuals, precisely because the existing form of intercourse and the existing productive forces are all-embracing and only individuals that are developing in an all-round fashion can appropriate them, i.e., can turn them in free manifestations of their lives.[50]

Proletarian abolition of private property can produce a society in which nobody has an exclusive sphere of activity, a society in which everyone can develop in a many-sided way, a society thereby creative of harmonious personalities and lives of wholeness.

This society, Marx claims, is communist society,

the only society in which the genuine and free development of individuals ceases to be a mere phrase, this development is determined precisely by the connection of individuals, a connection which consists partly in the economic prerequisites and partly in the necessary solidarity of the free development of all, and, finally, in the universal character of the activity of individuals on the basis of the existing productive forces. We are, therefore, here concerned with individuals at a definite stage of development and by no means merely individuals chosen at random, even disregarding the indispensable communist revolution, which itself is a general condition for their free development. The individuals' consciousness of their mutual relations will, of course, likewise be completely changed, and, therefore, will no more be the "principle of love" or *dévouement* than it will be egoism.[51]

As we noted earlier, Marx insists upon the *practical* overcoming of the rhetoric/reality discrepancy in history, an overcoming which will ultimately render ideology useless and permit the realization of the coincidence and transparency, i.e., publicity, of particular class interests and universal societal interests. Therefore, to employ moral language without understanding the rhetoric/reality discrepancy in history and hence to preclude any practical way of overcoming this discrepancy is, in essence, to engage in rhetoric, to fall prey to ideology, and ultimately to impede the practical overcoming of this discrepancy. So Marx states,

Communism is for us not a state of affairs which is to be established, an *ideal* to which reality (will) have to adjust itself. We call communism the *real* movement which abolishes the present state of things.[52]

For Marx, the communist movement is privileged in the sense that only it has the potential of overcoming the rhetoric/reality discrepancy in history. This is so not because of the moral ideals, e.g., self-realization, self-development, that it espouses—for many movements in the past and present espouse these ideals—but rather because of the *historical timing* of the movement, that is, when it appears in history, what it has at its disposal (e.g., technology, values of freedom and equality) due to this appearance, and how it intends to put to use what it has at its disposal (i.e., to promote and permit individuality within community under conditions of abundance and participatory democracy).

> Communism differs from all previous movements in that it overturns the basis of all earlier relations of production and intercourse, and for the first time consciously treats all naturally evolved premises as the creations of hitherto existing men, strips them of their natural character and subjugates them to the power of the united individuals. Its organization is, therefore, essentially economic, the material production of the conditions of this unity; it turns existing conditions into conditions of unity. The reality which communism creates is precisely the true basis for rendering it impossible that anything should exist independently of individuals, insofar as reality is nevertheless only a product of the preceding intercourse of individuals.[53]

Further Theoretic Formulations

Since this essay is primarily concerned with providing an in-house discussion of the historicist approach to ethics in the Marxist tradition, I have focused principally on Marx's radical historicist critique and rejection of philosophic ethics, rather than putting forward in any detailed manner Marx's own theoretic alternative. So in this section, I shall briefly examine Marx's own distinction between science and ideology, and specifically the status of his own critique of political economy; I shall also examine his theoretic understanding of ethics, and specifically the status of moral notions such as "right" or "just."

I contend that the chief enabling factor behind Marx's radical historicist approach to ethics was his radical historicist view of science and epistemology. By calling into question the idea of philosophic foundations, grounds, or bases, he simultaneously was calling into question the philosophic foundations, grounds, or bases of science and knowledge. As we saw earlier, the only "foundations," "grounds," or "bases"—for science or ethics—available to radical historicists are the contingent, dynamic, community-specific agreements people make in relation to particular aims, goals, and objectives.

Indeed, to summarize Marx's critique of political economy, he sees the bourgeois economists as mistaking the contingent features of the capitalist system of production for necessary, inevitable, and unavoidable characteristics, while they mistake a system that is historically transient for one that is ahistorically external. But the important question confronting us now is how does Marx understand the status of his own critique of political economy?

Marx surely believes his theory of history and capitalist society refers to realities of past societies and realities of the capitalist societies of his day. But he does not believe that the justification for the truth of his theory is a philosophic affair, or that the truth of his theory is determined by a correspondence or coherence theory of truth, by a criterion of accurate or cohering representations independent of or isolated from his theory. Yet Marx does believe that the theories of bourgeois economists are, in some important sense, wrong. How then does he defend his own theory?

This crucial query leads us directly to Marx's distinction between science and ideology and why he believes his theoretic formulations are not merely ideological formulations. Let us first be clear that Marx understands ideology not (as do many modern Marxists influenced by Louis Althusser) as ideas which reflect class interests, but rather as a set of ideas which distort reality, impede a clear understanding of reality, and conceal the biases and prejudices of its proponents. For Marx, to be scientific is to pierce the veil of appearance, to disclose, unearth, and reveal what has hitherto been concealed.

> But all science would be superfluous if the outward appearance and the essence of things directly coincided.[54]

The significance of this distinction between appearance and reality, between what seems to be and what is, is theoretic rather than philosophic. Marx is not concerned with the philosophic foundations, grounds, or bases for this distinction; rather, he is concerned with the concrete problems that promote such discrepancies between what people perceive about societies and what is missing from their perceptions.

For Marx, the motivating factor for highlighting appearance/reality or seems/is distinctions is criticism and transformation of existing reality. Since his radical historicist viewpoint leads him to acknowledge and accent the dynamic character of reality, the crucial issue for Marx is how inevitable crises can be best responded to or how stages of development can be best dealt with. As he states in his preface to the first German edition of *Capital,*

> And even when a society has got upon the right track for the discovery of the natural laws of its movement—and it is the ultimate aim of this work, to lay bare the economic law of motion of modern society—it can neither clear by bold leaps, nor remove by legal enactments, the obstacles offered by the successive phases of its normal development. But it can shorten and lessen the birth-pangs.[55]

For Marx, the task of the scientific theorist is to overcome appearance/reality or seems/is distinctions, because his basic analytic approach, namely, the dialectical approach,

> . . . includes in its comprehension and affirmative recognition of the existing state of things, at the same time also, the recognition of the negation of that state, of its inevitable breaking up; because it regards every historically developed social form as in fluid movement, and therefore takes into account its transient nature not less than its momentary existence; because it lets nothing impose upon it, and is in its essence critical and revolutionary.[56]

As I noted earlier, Marx's theoretic concerns are motivated by concrete problems, impending crises and degenerating social forms of life. Marx's dialectical approach insists that there is something deeply wrong with any theorist who defends a state of affairs either by rendering it difficult to call this state of affairs into question or by refusing to acknowledge that this state of affairs is being called into question. Marx believes this lack of a genuinely critical posture holds for bourgeois economists principally because the very nature of capitalist society itself is deceptive owing to the mystical character of its basic units, namely, commodities.

> A commodity appears, at first sight, a very trivial thing, and easily understood. Its analysis shows that it is, in reality, a very queer thing, abounding in metaphysical subtleties and theological niceties. So far as it is a value in use, there is nothing mysterious about it . . . but, so soon as it

steps forth as a commodity, it is changed into something transcendent . . .

A commodity is therefore a mysterious thing, simply because in it the social character of men's labour appears to them as an objective character stamped upon the product of that labour; because the relation of the producers of the sum total of their own labour is presented to them as a social relation, not between themselves, but between the products of their labour.[57]

Therefore Marx believes that capitalist society can be understood only by an analytical approach which embodies a "hermeneutics of suspicion," that is, a dialectical approach whose aim is primarily that of demystification. This analytical act of demystifying is carried out best by scrutinizing capitalist society in its most developed form.

In this work I have to examine the capitalist mode of production, and the conditions of production and exchange corresponding to that mode. Up to the present time, their classic ground is England. That is the reason why England is used as the chief illustration in the development of my theoretical ideas.[58]

This idea of focusing on the most advanced industrial capitalist society of the day is noteworthy in that it acknowledges the importance of historical timing (and geographic setting) in regard to theoretic formulations. Historical timing is important for Marx's theoretic formulations because, coming after the formulations of Adam Smith and David Ricardo, Marx is able to benefit from these pioneers of political economy as well as grasp retrospectively why they perceived what they did and why they may have been mystified in regard to certain aspects of capitalist society. This advantage of retrospection, of reflecting back on the beginnings of political economy (as a developing discipline) and capitalist society, should not be overlooked, for it enables Marx to put forward his understanding of capitalist society in light of the dynamic changes in the discipline and the society. Coming as he does after Smith and Ricardo and after the accumulation of capital and the intensification of labor in highly industrial England, Marx must now incorporate and *account for* the dynamic changes in the discipline and the society.

Despite his advantage over Smith and Ricardo, Marx's major defense of his theory against the bourgeois economists of his day is that his theory provides the most thought-provoking and ultimately devastating self-criticism of the discipline. And it does this primarily because his theory is a response to and gives priority to problems and impending crises either ignored or downplayed by bourgeois economists. It is precisely Marx's historical consciousness and his political concern for the exploited working class—along with his mastery of his discipline—which leads him to call into question crucial assumptions of political economy and to open a new arena of self-criticism for the discipline. In fact, this augmenting or enlarging of the conversation among political economists, coupled with an augmenting or enlarging of the awareness of concrete problems or impending crises, signifies that this theory is "scientific," "objective," and not mere ideology.

For Marx—and radical historicists—the scientific or objective status of theories is not linked to philosophic notions of verification or of correct correspondence relations (e.g., idea/object, words/things, propositions/states of affairs); rather, the status of the theories depends on the sensitivity expressed toward pressing problems, the solutions offered for urgent dilemmas, and openings made into new areas of self-criticism. Note carefully how Marx closely relates "objective understanding" to self-criticism in the following passage from the renowned section on "The Method of Political Economy" in the introduction to the *Grundrisse:*

> The so-called historical presentation of development is founded, as a rule, on the fact that the latest form regards the previous ones as steps leading up to itself, and, since it is only rarely and only under quite specific conditions able to criticize itself—leaving aside, of course, the historical periods which appear to themselves as times of decadence—it always conceives them one-sidedly. The Christian religion was able to be of assistance in reaching an *objective understanding* of earlier mythologies only when its own self-criticism had been accomplished to a certain desire, so to speak, dynamai. Likewise, bourgeois political economy arrived at an [objective] *understanding* of feudal, ancient, oriental economics only after the self-criticism of bourgeois society had begun.[59]

Marx's radical historicist understanding of the "scientific" or "objective" status of theories informs his theoretic understanding of ethics, and specifically the status of moral notions such as "right" or "just." Marx's theoretic understanding of ethics focuses on explaining and describing the role and function of ethical principles, beliefs, judgments, and practices in the actual history of society. He is interested in how such principles, beliefs, judgments, and practices relate to power in society. In this sense, he stresses the political status of ethics in society.

For Marx, an adequate theoretic account of ethical notions, e.g., "just" or "right," must understand them as human conventional attempts to regulate social practices in accordance with the requirements of a specific system of production. These dynamic requirements set the limits wherein the content of ethical notions such as "just" or "right" is ever changing. Therefore, the question as to what is a just distribution of goods and services is not a philosophic question. That is, it should not solicit an answer which puts forward philosophic foundations, bases, or grounds which justify a particular distribution of goods and services in an abstract manner. Rather, this question demands a theoretic response, namely, an attempt to understand the specific needs and requirements of the existing system of production, how these needs and requirements set the boundaries in which current realizable "just" distributions are articulated, why moral justifications of "just" distributions often hide and conceal these boundaries, and what the possibilities are for overcoming these boundaries and transgressing these limits, not in an abstract philosophic way but rather a concrete politically practical way.

In response to the Eisenachers' Lassallean (or moralistic) viewpoint regarding notions such as "just" or "right," Marx says the following in his brief letter entitled *Critique of the Gotha Program:*

> What is a "fair distribution"? Do not the bourgeois assert that the present-day distribution is "fair"? And is it not, in fact, the only "fair" distribution on the basis of the present-day mode of production? Are economic relations regulated by legal conceptions or do not, on the contrary, legal relations arise from economic ones? Have not also the socialist sectarians the most varied notions about "fair distribution"? . . .
>
> What we have to deal with here is a communist society, not as it has *developed* on its own foundations, but on the contrary, just as it *emerges* from capitalist society; which is thus in every respect, economically, morally, and intellectually, still stamped with the birth marks of the old society from whose womb it emerges . . . Right can never be higher than the economic structure of society and its cultural development conditioned thereby.[60]

In these passages, Marx is saying not that there is no particular kind of distribution of goods and services which is morally desirable, but rather that the issue of what kind of distribution is morally desirable is not one of putting forward philosophic criteria. Instead, the issue is one of practically creating circumstances in which people can arrive at consensus or collectively agree upon a particular kind of distribution. Of course, this latter option incorporates a moral conviction or attitude. But this conviction or attitude, e.g., self-realization of individuals in community, comes inextricably united and integrally related to theoretic formulations as to how the moral conviction can be realized, the moral attitude actualized.

In fact, Marx believes that the moral preoccupation with a "fair distribution" results from a theoretic failure, namely, the failure to see the all-important background conditions of production which constitute the "stage setting" for any moral talk about a "fair distribution." In his critique of Utopian socialists, Marx argued that philosophic yearnings for abstract moral criteria for a fair distribution signify theoretic deficiences regarding the relation of distribution and production. Here he writes:

> Quite apart from the analysis so far given, it was in general a mistake to make a fuss about so-called *distribution* and put the principal stress on it.
>
> Any distribution whatever of the means of consumption is only a consequence of the distribution of the conditions of production themselves. The latter distribution, however, is a feature of the mode of production itself. The capitalist mode of production, for example, rests on the fact that the material conditions of production are in the hands of non-workers in the form of property in capital and land, while the masses are only owners of the personal condition of production, or labour power. If the elements of production are so distributed, then the present-day distribution of the means of consumption results automatically. If the material conditions of production are the co-operative property of the workers themselves, then there likewise results a distribution of the means of consumption different from the present one. Vulgar socialism has taken over from the bourgeois economists the consideration and treatment of distribution as independent of the mode of production and hence the presentation of socialism as turning principally on distribution. After the real relation has long been made clear, why retrogress again.[61]

For Marx, in this passage, to retrogress is to not merely treat distribution independent of production but also to put forward philosophic bases or grounds for a "fair distribution" and hence ultimately to remain captive of the vision of philosophy as the quest for certainty, the search for foundations; to progress is to not merely integrally relate distribution to production, but also to acknowledge the important and indispensable role of theoretic formulations regarding moral notions and hence ultimately to join the ranks of radical historicists.

◇ 4 ◇

The Classical Marxist Position: Engels' Teleological Quest

The major Marxist approaches to ethics bear the historicist stamp. They deny the existence of an Archimedian point from which to adjudicate rival ethical judgments, they accent the fleeting character of moral views, and they thereby preclude traditional foundationalist justifications of moral positions.

Yet despite this historicist orientation, the major Marxist thinkers who have been concerned with ethical matters have engaged in the philosophic quest for objectivity, the search for foundations. I shall try to show that the three major texts which represent the three chief approaches to ethical matters in the Marxist tradition—Frederick Engels' *Anti-Dühring* (1878), Karl Kautsky's *Ethics and the Materialist Conception of History* (1907), and Georg Lukács' *History and Class Consciousness* (1923)—put forward different versions of the *moderate* historicist viewpoint.

These three Marxist texts reveal a deep uneasiness about the charge of relativism. And they each try to reply to such a charge. There are two basic reasons why Engels, Kautsky, and Lukács engage in the philosophic quest for objectivity. First, because their epistemology is itself foundationalist. Therefore they find it difficult to reconcile the anti-foundationalist, historicist view in ethical matters with their own particular brands of foundationalism in epistemological matters. Second, and this reason is closely related to the first one, they all assume a foundationalist conception of science, be it based on hard positivistic "facts" or unalterable "dialectics." So they find it difficult to bring together a foundationalist view of science and an anti-foundationalist view of ethics. I will try to show that this is the primary reason why

102

none of the three are able to adopt a *radical* historicist position in ethics.

I shall call the view of Engels the *teleological* quest because it attempts to ground moral objectivity in the ever broadening intersubjective agreement which shall occur at the end of history (or, in Marxist terminology, at the end of prehistory and the beginning of history). In my reconstruction of his arguments, his perspective resembles a Peircian move to preserve the notion of moral objectivity by claiming that it amounts to what moral agents will converge to or agree upon in the long run.

I will call Kautsky's view the *naturalist* quest because it tries to hold all metaphysics at arm's length and promote an evolutionary naturalism which ensures that moral progress and technological progress go hand in hand. It is a crude kind of Deweyan move that tries to translate norms-talk into needs-talk (or, more specifically, instincts-talk) in order to sidestep strong relativism. Lastly, I shall call Lukács' view the *ontological* quest because it tries to ground moral objectivity in the "dialectics" inherent in the nature of reality, in the development of history. It is a sophisticated Hegelian move to overcome traditional foundationalist epistemology and ethics, only to resurrect an untraditional foundationalism in ontological garb. I shall conclude that all three Marxist thinkers remain moderate historicists, that they put forward unsuccessful attempts to secure moral objectivity and therefore diverge from Marx's own radical historicist viewpoint.

The chapters on morality in Engels' *Anti-Dühring* provide the most extensive discussion on ethical matters within the classical Marxist corpus. They present what I shall call the classical Marxist position on moral objectivity. I use the word "classical" not in the sense of being most authentic or true but rather in the sense of representing the first and most detailed discussion of the position in the Marxist tradition.

The crucial role Frederick Engels played in shaping and molding the Marxist tradition is often downplayed. He is often portrayed as Marx's mediocre sidekick, a personal confidante and financial supporter. To many Marxist scholars, he is the grand vulgarizer of the sophisticated Marxist theory of history and capitalist society. It is undeniable—as Engels himself said repeatedly—that Marx was the major talent of the two. But being less talented than Marx hardly makes one mediocre. And putting forward one's own viewpoint as a Marxist thinker hardly makes one the grand vulgarizer of Marx's own views.

Therefore we should not assume that Marx and Engels were in agreement on how to approach ethical matters. It is significant that Engels differed from Marx on many important issues, e.g., the scope of the dialectical method, the usefulness of the work of Lewis Henry Morgan and Charles Darwin, the kind of authority in factories, etc. Marx presumably assisted in the writing of the first edition of *Anti-Dühring*. It is unclear precisely how he assisted Engels in this matter. Yet even this "assistance" does not necessarily entail that Marx agreed with Engels' ethical viewpoint in the book. It only insures that Marx was knowledgeable of what Engels was putting forward under his own name.

Like a good Marxist, Engels does not separate ethics from the historical process. But like a good moderate historicist, he does try to provide acceptable *philosophic* criteria with which to rationally justify socialist norms. Engels seems to make this move principally owing to the criticisms of Prof. Dühring, a moralistic socialist who claimed among other things that the Marxist ethical position was untenable and that it made socialist norms look arbitrary and capricious.

This charge of strong relativism appears to have prompted Engels to show that the philosophic validity and objectivity of socialist norms could be defended. It is interesting to note that Engels does not mention Marx's own conception of ethics, he only points out what a justification of socialist norms would look like in light of Marx's theory of history.

Progress in Morality

Engels writes the following passage in *Anti-Dühring*:

We therefore reject every attempt to impose on us any moral dogma whatsoever as an eternal, ultimate and forever immutable moral law on the pretext that the moral world too has its permanent principles which transcend history and the differences between nations. We maintain on the contrary that all former moral theories are the product, in the last analysis, of the economic stage which society had reached at that particular epoch. And as society has hitherto moved in class antagonism, morality was always a class morality; it has either justified the domination and the interests of the ruling class, or, as soon as the oppressed class has become powerful enough, it has represented the revolt against this domination and the future interests of the oppressed.[1]

In this passage, Engels unequivocally rejects moral absolutism and endorses some form of relativism by refusing to posit a timeless, transhistorical standard against which to judge rival ethical judgments. Yet it is clear that he does not find class morality desirable. The basic reason for this seems to be that, for him, any morality which is a product of a class-ridden society is undesirable. Therefore, it is reasonable to infer that, for Engels, a desirable morality will not reflect class cleavages; that is, desirable morality reflects a classless society, or class equality, or a socialist mode of production. So the move from the present class morality to a socialist morality constitutes progress in morality.

That in this process there has on the whole been progress in morality, as in all other branches of human knowledge, cannot be doubted. But we have not yet passed beyond class morality. A really human morality which transcends class antagonisms and their legacies in thought becomes possible only at a stage of society which has not only overcome class contradictions but has even forgotten them in practical life.[2]

And as to why a "really human morality" is better or preferable over other moralities, besides their class character, he writes,

What morality is preached to us today? There is first Christian-feudal morality, inherited from past periods of faith; and this again has two main subdivisions, Catholic and Protestant moralities . . . Alongside of these we find the modern bourgeois morality and with it too the proletarian morality of the future, so that in the most advanced European countries alone the past, present and future provide three great groups of moral theories which are in force simultaneously and alongside of one another. Which is then the true one? Not one of them, in the sense of having absolute validity; but certainly that morality which contains the maximum of durable elements is the one which, in the present, represents the overthrow of the present, represents the future: that is, the proletarian.[3]

Let us examine these two quotes briefly. First, Engels' talk about morality as a branch of knowledge must be taken seriously. He is claiming that the moral beliefs of people progress, that there is a discernible pattern in the history of moral beliefs which rules out purely random change. He considers such progress in morality to be similar to progress in the sciences, e.g., biology, physics, chemistry, etc. All such progress has enriched human understanding and awareness of the determinants at work in each discipline.

When Engels talks about progress in morality he is not only referring to progress in the way in which we account for the moral beliefs people hold, but more importantly, progress in the particular moral beliefs people have come to hold over time. Certain moral beliefs have been appropriate for particular historical epochs, but the shifts in the systems of morality over time represent progress in morality. In short, certain historical shifts in moral beliefs constitute shifts to *better*, or more desirable, moral beliefs.

And what is the standard against which such progress is measured? This standard, on my interpretation of his view, is best understood as the ever-broadening intersubjective agreement and convergence among people that a classless society is desirable. Progress in morality is the enlarging of the pool of people who agree that class equality is preferable. Such progress in morality takes the form of a highly *critical* disposition toward the present society and its dominant moral beliefs.

For Engels, Marx's theory of history explains why there has been limited agreement in morality and predicts what particular social conditions are necessary for this agreement to broaden. The class character of human societies restricts human agreement in morality and prohibits convergence among people on the desirability of a classless society.

Engels identifies a desirable morality with the proletarian future revolution because, following Marx's social theory, broad agreement on the desirability of a classless society is possible only after successful transfer of power from the capitalist class to the proletariat. And this transfer of power can be achieved only by revolution. In this way, the substance of proletarian morality at the present time is critical revolutionary activity, bringing about the conditions requisite for broad agreement on class equality.

Justifying Broad Moral Agreement Without Vicious Circularity

Engels' conception of broad moral agreement on class equality is grounded within the historical process; that is, such agreement would reflect a particular mode of production at a specific time in history. He assumes that Marx's theory of history has shown that class antagonisms are the most fundamental conflicts in society as well as being principally responsible for conflicting moralities or for systematic moral disagreement in society. The lack of broad moral agreement, the presence of systematic moral disagreement, on class equality presupposes the existence of class struggle. For Engels, since any class-ridden society is never free of class antagonisms and since broad moral agreement on class equality is possible only in a society free of class antagonisms, broad moral agreement is possible only in a classless society. In this way, broad moral agreement on class equality and the actual existence of a classless society are inseparable.

Two central questions arise at this point. First, the *empirical* question as to whether it is true that class antagonisms are the chief cause of systematic moral disagreement in society. Since we are not particularly interested in this controversy at this moment, we shall give Engels the benefit of the doubt and grant that it is true. The second question, more pertinent for us, is a philosophic one, namely, how can Engels justify broad moral agreement on class equality by claiming that it will be arrived at only under conditions of class equality? Isn't this vicious circular reasoning? Can class equality be the object of collective choice and the actual conditions under which such a choice is made without such vicious circular reasoning?

It should be clear that Engels is not claiming that no one will choose class equality unless historical conditions of class equality exist. For if he were making this claim, he would be forced to conclude that there would never be a socialist movement in a capitalist society. He also would not be able to explain his own preference for class equality. In fact, Engels explicity states that the demand for class equality is derived from a step above the bourgeois demand for legal equality.

And in the same way the bourgeois demand for equality was accompanied by the proletarian demand for equality. From the moment when the bourgeois demand for the abolition of class *privileges* was put forward, alongside of it appeared the proletarian demand for the abolition of the *classes* themselves—at first in religious form basing itself on primitive Christianity, and later drawing support from the bourgeois equalitarian theories themselves. The proletarians took the bourgeoisie at their word: equality must not be merely apparent, must not apply merely to the sphere of the state, but must also be real, must be extended to the social and economic sphere . . . the proletarian demand for equality has arisen as the reaction against the bourgeois demand for equality, drawing more or less correct and more far-reaching demands from this bourgeois demand, and serving as an agitational means in order to rouse the workers against the capitalists on the basis of the capitalists' own assertions. . .[4]

Engels seems to be making three basic claims in this important passage. First, he is saying that the rising (or parvenu) bourgeoisie have put forward a general and acceptable claim about equality. Second, he further holds that the bourgeoisie have restricted its application, owing to the class structure of bourgeois society and their acceptance of this structure. Third, he is saying that the proletariat shows that the restrictions are arbitrary, i.e., based on class interests, and that only the proletarian demand for class equality takes the idea of equality seriously in a concrete way.

A crucial question facing Engels, which gets us back to the issue of alleged vicious circularity, is why the proletarian demand for class equality is not just as arbitrary as the bourgeois demand for restrictions of equality (or for class inequality). He cannot appeal to broad moral agreement on class equality as a criterion for a morally desirable state of affairs because this agreement presupposes the very state of affairs we are asking justification for.

There are only two ways out of this dilemma. One way is to adopt a radical historicist view which claims that class equality is desirable owing to its capacity to allow for the development of the potentialities and capacities of individuals, or at least, more so than a class-ridden society. On this view, the objectivity of this moral belief is not the main concern; rather what is crucial is to bring about class equality by persuading those whose values and interests motivate them to realize class equality and by struggling against those whose values and interests motivate them to prevent this realization. The key is to link preferable values and interests to the largest possible community capable of making the collective moral choice of class equality.

The second way out of Engel's dilemma is to initiate a philosophic quest for objectivity. This quest would involve adopting a moderate historicist view which holds that there are two kinds of human preferences. Certain preferences represent who and what we really are; they correspond to deep metaphysical facts about us. Other preferences represent who and what we really are not; they correspond to accidental and contingent facts about us. On this view, the philosophic quest for (soft) objectivity amounts to trying to ground our moral choices upon the deep metaphysical facts about us and then turning to Marxist theory to see whether the objective laws in history ensure the realization of these moral choices.

A Historicized Rational Preference Model: Essential vs. Accidental Preferences

On my interpretation of Engel's view, he opts for the second alternative. I believe that he tends to waver between the two alternatives, but he ultimately leans toward the latter. That is, he tacitly assumes a metaphysical view of rational human preferences when it comes to justifying the desirability of broad moral agreement on class equality. This assumption is directly related to the distinction between essential preferences—those preferences that represent deep metaphysical facts about us—and accidental preferences—those preferences that represent contingent facts about us.

Like a radical historicist, Engels relates rational human preferences to people's interests, but he seems more concerned about how these interests would be perceived under not-yet-arrived-at, i.e., ideal historical circumstances. As a moderate historicist, Engels is interested in preserving a threadbare notion of moral objectivity. And it seems he is able to do this by positing ideal historical choice-conditions, i.e., conditions of class equality, then asking whether such conditions correspond to the deep metaphysical facts about us, thereby yielding a justification of the essential preferences which are made under such ideal historical choice-conditions.

On my interpretation, Engels' view resembles a historicized Rawlsian Original Position within the historical process. This "Original Position" consists of not-yet-arrived-at historical circumstances of class equality which serve as ideal choice-conditions for actual broad moral agreement. Essential preferences result from who and what human beings really are, namely, rational social creatures who cherish order, freedom, and equality. This is why, he seems to believe, human beings prefer to live in a society of class equality, rational control, and social freedom. And accidental preferences result from the prevailing ideological distortions which breed choices of irrationality, servitude, and inequality. That is, people don't prefer a classless society now primarily because their essential preferences have been distorted by the predominant ideology of the day.

By staking the objective status of socialist norms on broad moral agreement, Engels is forced to correlate them with essential preferences while correlating the subjective status of other norms, e.g., capitalist ones, with accidental preferences. Since he wants to take history seriously, he cannot afford to do as Rawls does and simply strip persons of their contingent facts, e.g., sex, race, class position, and put them in an Original Position in order to generate broad moral agreement. Instead, Engels locates his situation for such agreement under not-yet-arrived-at historical conditions. In this way, his persons, unlike those of Rawls, remain full human beings (with both their metaphysical and contingent facts); yet, as with Rawls, these persons make essential preferences that reflect only their metaphysical facts under Engels' ideal historical choice-conditions.

Engels seems to believe that under ideal historical choice-conditions people would just prefer freedom over servitude and class equality over class inequality. Putting aside the alleged vicious circularity for a moment, Engels' belief still seems to rest upon an optimistic trust in the correspondence between human nature (as it evolves) and goodness, human history (as it develops) and the realization of reasonable human values. How can we ever be sure that people *really* prefer rationality, freedom, and equality? Does it help at all to get involved in such *really*-searches, such quests for objectivity and foundations in regard to human preferences? Doesn't any view of this kind assume some preconceived ideal of human preferences and impose it upon human nature? Isn't this project but a metaphysical one which requires that one be coaxed into believing that this ideal of human preferences can be justified by the historical process? Surely, any hope in such a justification constitutes a "leap of faith," a deep abiding but groundless trust in the ultimate harmony of human existence and human history. My main point here is not that Engels' view is necessarily wrong, but rather that it is at bottom a metaphysical view devoid of philosophic foundations and that it cannot be substantiated by an empirical investigation or historical inquiry. One may attempt to show that the historical process is developing in such a way that it will result in conditions requisite for the appearance of essential preferences, but these preferences are deemed essential by one's preconceived ideal of human preferences. Of course, there is no harm in hoping that such a result will occur. Nor is there anything objectionable about using such a hope as the basis for action. But this hope cannot serve any grander function, such as providing the bedrock for ethical objectivity or the foundation of broad moral agreement. In short, Engels leaves us with an inadequate historicized metaphysics of socialist morals.[5]

Engels and Radical Historicism

As I noted earlier, Engels puts forward a moderate historicist approach to ethics. And based on my interpretation, he struggles to retain this view by embarking on a philosophic quest for objectivity or search for foundations. An important question to be asked at this point is why he is so concerned about objectivity or philosophic foundations? In other words, why isn't he a radical historicist?

The major obstacle preventing any moderate historicist from accepting a radical historicist position in ethics is a foundationalist conception of epistemology and science. That is, in a culture which extols science, if one believes that science rests upon secure philosophic foundations, then more than likely one will believe (like the soft objectivist or moderate historicist) that ethics ought to rest upon philosophic foundations, or one will believe (like the moral nihilist) that ethics rests upon no philosophic foundations whatsoever. As we saw earlier, the radical historicist position—in ethics, epistemology, and science—differs from these positions in that it discards the obsession with the notion of philosophic foundations and hence the quest for objectivity.

The primary reason why Engels remains a moderate historicist rather than choosing to become a radical historicist is that he clings to the idea that there are such things as "hard" and "soft" sciences, or sciences with more philosophic foundations than others. Furthermore, he holds that the "harder" the science the better, thereby positing the "hard" sciences as the model of human knowledge in general. Let us examine briefly these claims in his text.

In regard to the division of the sciences and their relative degrees of hardness, Engels writes,

> Are there then nevertheless *eternal* truths, final and ultimate truths?
> Certainly there are. We can divide the whole realm of knowledge in the traditional way into three great departments. The first includes all sciences which are concerned with inanimate Nature and are to a greater or less degree susceptible of mathematical treatment: mathematics, astronomy, mechanics, physics, chemistry. If it gives anyone any pleasure to use mighty words for very simple things, it can be asserted that *certain* results obtained by these sciences are eternal truths, final and ultimate truths; for which reason these sciences are also known as the *exact* sciences. . .
> The second department of science is the one which covers the investigation of living organisms. In this field . . . the need for a systematic presentation of the interrelations make it necessary again and again to surround the final and ultimate truths with a luxuriant growth of hypotheses. . .
> But eternal truths are in an even worse plight in the third, the historical group of sciences. The subjects investigated by these in their historical sequences and in their present forms are the conditions of human life, social relationships, forms of law and the state, with their ideal superstructure of philosophy, religion, art etc.[6]

To be fair to Engels, we must acknowledge that he is engaged in polemic against Prof. Dühring's hard objectivist, absolutist, naive foundationalist position in science and ethics. Engels is highly critical of Prof. Dühring's obsession with eternal, immutable truths. What is interesting about Engels' reply is that he divides human knowledge into domains in terms of their capacity to generate eternal truths. In short, he adopts Prof. Dühring's criterion. Like a good moderate historicist, Engels is vehemently opposed to hard objectivism or naive foundationalism while remaining wed to the philosophic quest for objectivity.

At certain points, Engels employs the ammunition of radical historicism to attack Prof. Dühring's hard objectivism, even in regard to the "hard" sciences. For example, he writes,

With the introduction of variable magnitudes and the extension of their variability to the infinitely small and infinitely large, mathematics, in other respects so strictly moral, fell from grace; it ate of the tree of knowledge, which opened up to it a career of most colossal achievements, but at the same time a path of error. The virgin state of absolute validity and irrefutable certainty of everything mathematical was gone forever; mathematics entered the realm of controversy, and we have reached the point where most people differentiate and integrate not because they understand what they are doing but from pure faith, because up to now it has always come out right. Things are even worse with astronomy and mechanics, and in physics and chemistry we are surrounded by hypotheses as by a swam of bees. And it must of necessity be so. In physics we are dealing with the motion of molecules, in chemistry with the formation of molecules out of atoms, and if the interference of light waves is not a myth, we have absolutely no prospect of ever seeing these interesting objects with our own eyes. As time goes on, final and ultimate truths become remarkably rare in this field.[7]

This passage sounds like the rhetoric of a radical historicist in science, e.g., Kuhn. In place of Prof. Dühring's talk about secure foundations we have talk about "pure faith." Yet Engels refuses to make the radical historicist step. This step would consist of explaining the notion of the "pure faith" of mathematicians and scientists, without appealing to philosophic criteria. If he were a radical historicist, he would appeal to the social practices of mathematicians and scientists, e.g., the rules and interpretations of rules upon which they agree. Instead, he retains some idea of philosophic foundations linked to the presence of eternal truths. It is no surprise that when he comes to the sciences in the third department, namely the so-called historical sciences, he writes,

> Therefore, knowledge is here essentially relative, inasmuch as it is limited to the perception of relationships and consequences of certain social and state forms which exist only at a particular epoch and among particular people and are of their very nature transitory. Anyone therefore who sets out on this field to hunt down final and ultimate truths, truths which are pure and absolutely immutable, will bring home but little. . .[8]

What Engels fails to see is that this description of knowledge also roughly holds for the so-called hard sciences, especially if we take his radical historicist rhetoric seriously. And if we accept this, then the idea of knowledge being relative takes on a completely different sense than that put forward by a moderate historicist viewpoint. Such a viewpoint always understands "relative" against some philosophic criterion of objectivity. If the philosophic quest for objectivity is discarded, then the pejorative status of "relative" is undermined. The discarding of the philosophic quest for objectivity does not mean that we are left with mere capricious biases and unregulated prejudices. Rather it means that there is no philosophic criteria to adjudicate between rival positions. Instead, adjudication amounts to genuine conversation, critical dialogue and exchange under conditions of tolerance and/or intolerance.

But what philosophic criteria does Engels cling to? What impedes him from opting for radical historicism, what propels him to search for philosophic foundations? As I noted earlier, the move to radical historicism is metaphilosophical. That is, the move demands that one conceive of philosophy in such a way that it no longer is or ought to be engaged in grounding the eternal, immutable, invariable truths of science, ethics, etc. Engels makes hints in this direction, but instead of simply rejecting this traditional conception of philosophy he overcomes it, then replaces it with a surrogate, i.e., dialectics. He notes,

> . . . modern materialism is essentially dialectical, and no longer needs any philosophy standing above the other sciences. As soon as each separate science is required to get clarity as to its position in the great totality of things and of our knowledge of things, a special science dealing with this totality is superfluous. What still independently survives of all former philosophy is the science of thought and its laws—formal logic and dialectics. Everything else is merged in the positive science of Nature and history.[9]

What is important to note is not only that formal logic and dialectics replace philosophy, but more importantly that they preserve the only quest for eternal, immutable, invariable truths in nature and history. He explicitly admits,

> It goes without saying that my recapitulation of mathematics and the natural sciences was undertaken in order to convince myself in detail—of which in general I was not in doubt—that amid the welter of innumerable changes taking place in nature, the same dialectical laws of motion are in operation as those which in history govern the apparent fortuitousness of events; the same laws as those which similarly form the thread running through the history of the development of human thought and gradually

rise to consciousness in the mind of man; the laws which Hegel first developed in all-embracing but mystical form, and which we made it our aim to strip of this mystic form and to bring clearly before the mind in their complete simplicity and universality.[10]

Like a good moderate historicist, Engels holds that even dialectics provides no absolute guarantee for discerning eternal truths. But it should be clear that the old quest for objectivity and search for foundations is his regulative ideal. So despite his tirade against Prof. Dühring's hard objectivism in science and ethics, Engels ultimately remains tied to the same quest as Prof. Dühring, by putting new wine, e.g., dialectics, in old bottles.

Ethics and Science

At this point, we should be ready to see the way in which Engels' conception of science undergirds his moderate historicist metaphysics of socialist morals. The latter requires a teleological view of history in which the end of history (or some special moment in the historical process) yields ideal choices-conditions under which class equality will be chosen. As we noted earlier, this choice reflects the essential facts about people, namely, their fundamental desire for order, freedom, and equality.

Engels' conception of science leads him to think that the development of history is guided by dialectical laws—the same laws operating in human thought and nature. Only a scientific investigation into history can reveal these laws. And only by discerning these laws is one able to understand the development of history. The development of history culminates when people arrive at

. . . a state of society in which there are no longer class distinctions or anxiety over the means of subsistence for the individual, and in which for the first time there can be talk of real human freedom and of an existence in harmony with the established laws of Nature.[11]

On the one hand, this state of affairs constitutes the kind of society people would choose following their essential preferences. Therefore, for Engels, this society is morally desirable. On the other hand, this state of affairs constitutes the end or telos of history, as determined by a scientific investigation which discerns the dialectical laws governing the historical process. Therefore, for Engels, this society is historically necessary. This morally desirable and historically necessary state of affairs produces genuine freedom for the first time in human history.

> Freedom does not consist in the dream of independence of natural laws, but in the knowledge of these laws, and in the possibility this gives of systematically making them work towards definite ends. . . Freedom therefore consists in the control over ourselves and over external nature which is founded on knowledge of natural necessity; it is therefore necessarily a product of historical development.[12]

Engels makes an ingenious attempt to wed ethics and science, morality and history, dialectics and objectivity. But I hope it is clear that he fails. His case rests upon a moderate historicist viewpoint which is undergirded by two weak prongs: an untenable metaphysics of morals which falls short of objectively grounding socialist norms and an unsubstantiated foundationalist conception of science preoccupied with dialectical laws. And both prongs are guided by the traditional philosophic quest for objectivity and search for foundations, which is itself a highly questionable metaphilosophical vision.

◇ 5 ◇

The Positivist Marxist Position: Kautsky's Naturalist Quest

Kautsky's neglected book, *Ethics and the Materialist Conception of History* (1907), will serve as the second major philosophic quest for ethical objectivity in the Marxist tradition. His chief opponent and implicit object of criticism—Eduard Bernstein—had sketched a defense of socialist norms based on Kantian formulations.[1] The neo-Kantian milieu in German centers of learning at the turn of the century had profoundly influenced socialist thinkers such as Max Adler, Karl Vorlander, and others. This Kantianized socialist viewpoint took the form not only of diverse ahistorical metaphysics of morals but also of reformist politics. Kautsky intended to put a stop to such metaphysical and reformist tendencies. His aim was to weed out such alien elements and keep the Marxist tradition pure—that is, keep it scientific, this-worldly and revolutionary.

Kautsky's project is essentially a reductionist program. It is an attempt to reduce norms-talk to needs-talk, morals-talk to instincts-talk. He adopts an instrumentalist conception of morality. He stresses only what function norms and values have in society. He is an ethical naturalist in that he claims that moral facts are facts about nature and ought to be analyzed as facts about functions, roles, and interests in society. He is a moderate historicist in that he holds that his ethical naturalist position provides philosophic foundations for the objective status of socialist norms.

117

Positivism and the Scientific Method:
Marx and Darwin

The philosophic quest for objectivity and search for foundations rest upon the old Platonic distinctions between the world of being and the world of becoming, reality and appearance, knowledge and opinion. In order to acceptably ground claims about what really is, what is true, valid, or objective, they must be tested in some way. Positivism differs from other philosophic quests for objectivity or searches for foundations in that it deems the scientific method the only legitimate way in which knowledge claims about the self, the world, and God can be tested.

As there are many conceptions of what the scientific method is, so there are many versions of positivism. Kautsky's positivism conceives the scientific method to be a procedure which permits us to investigate and discover the general laws that ineluctably hold in nature and history. Science consists of a set of general laws that allow us to discern the inevitable behavior of phenomena in nature and history. Kautsky never explains what kind of procedure permits us to discover such laws or how one goes about using this procedure. But he is quite clear about the central role the notion of necessity plays in scientific aims and results. As he quips,

Science has only to do with the recognition of the necessary.[2]

For Kautsky, science detects what must happen, what cannot be avoided, what has to be accepted. This understanding of necessity is based on the mechanical cause-effect determinism espoused by the Newtonians of his day. It amounts to a machinelike necessity that governs phenomena independent of human will, consciousness, or choice.

Kautsky's position can be summarized in the following claims:
(1) The scientific method is the only acceptable procedure or testing mechanism for generating valid knowledge claims about the self, the world, society, nature, or God.
(2) The aim of this method is to discover and discern general laws that govern the necessary behavior or properties of phenomena.
(3) This method and this aim are best exemplified in the natural sciences.

Kautsky's enthusiasm for the scientific method and his own version of positivism leads him to attempt to wed Darwin and Marx, whom he considered the two great scientists of the nineteenth century. His attempt to bring these two giants together can be put in the following way:

(1) Inquiry in the social sciences ought to emulate inquiry in the natural sciences.

(2) Darwin's evolutionary theory, the most highly acclaimed and heralded scientific theory of his day, should be extended into the study of human societies and ethical matters.

(3) Marxist theory is the valid extension of Darwin's evolutionary theory into the study of human societies and ethical matters.

The unprecedented scientific achievements and undaunted prestige of the natural sciences at the turn of the century provided the historical background for Kautsky's outlook. And Engels' own praise of Darwin (often in Kautsky's presence) surely influenced Kautsky's attitude toward evolutionary theory.

The Historical Background: Idealism vs. Materialism

Kautsky believes that before one begins to extend scientific theory to the study of human societies and ethical matters, it is important to trace earlier attempts of such extensions. This historical account would presumably reveal the reasons why people opposed such extensions. By showing that this opposition rests upon illusions, he believes he will be able to put forward a convincing defense of his own extension. He also believes that by comparing the idealist and materialist approaches to ethics, he can show that the latter view can account for the source of morality, as well as explain why people take moral laws seriously.

Kautsky draws a line of demarcation between proponents and opponents of an earlier extension by tracing it back to idealist and materialist approaches to ethics in the postclassical world. He holds that the tempered hedonism of Epicurus represents the materialist approach. For Epicurus, the primary motive for human action is the pursuit of pleasure. Individuals rationally calculate between various kinds of pleasures, e.g., intellectual or bodily, taking into account the duration, intensity, and satisfiability of pleasures. Kautsky concludes that this approach closely resembles his own extension because it highlights the sense experience of people as the basis of calculating their pleasure. In short, the Epicurean viewpoint propagates a this-worldly, empirical, naturalist orientation. He writes,

This view of Ethics had the advantage that it appeared quite natural and it was very easy to reconcile it with the needs of those who desired to content themselves with the knowledge which our senses gives us of the knowable world as the real and to whom human evidence appeared only a part of this world. On the other hand, this view of ethics was bound to produce in its turn that materialist view of the world. Founding Ethics on the longing for the pleasure or happiness of the individual or on egoism and the materialist world concept, conditioned and lent each other mutual support. The connection of both elements comes most completely to expression in Epicurus (341–270 B.C.). His materialist philosophy of nature is founded with a directly ethical aim.[3]

Kautsky compares this materialist approach to the idealist approach. The latter arises, he claims, from a dissatisfaction with the former. Specifically, the idealist approach holds that the materialist approach does not explain or cannot account for the strong sense of obligation people feel toward the moral law, and especially in those cases where it seems highly unlikely that moral duties, such as self-sacrifice, come from rational self-interested hedonistic calculation. This dissatisfaction results in a contempt for the contingency and mutability of nature (including human nature) and yields a search for absolutes and timeless moral truths. This idealistic approach arrives at the view that the moral law is of supernatural origin; this approach then begins to work out a proof for the existence of a supernatural world. Kautsky notes,

Since they were unable to explain the moral law by natural means it became to them the surest and most unanswerable proof that man lived not only a natural life, but also outside of nature, that in him supernatural and non-natural forces work, that his spirit is something supernatural. Thus arose from this view the ethic of philosophic idealism and mono-theism, the new belief in God.[4]

Kautsky's brief and rather crude attempt to illustrate Epicurus' exten-sion program and the idealist opposition to it reveals his positivist bias against any ethical viewpoint based on metaphysics, religion, or the supernatural. He believes that the materialist approach is superior to the idealist approach because it does not posit illusory entities to account for why human beings take moral laws seriously. He also favors the materialist approach because it confines people to their sense experiences and claims that ethical matters should be restricted to the exercise of the natural faculties of people.

Kautsky's Ambiguity on Kant

Kautsky finds the materialist/idealist distinction a bit too rigid when applied to Kant's philosophical viewpoint. On the one hand, he considers Kant's epistemological breakthrough to be revolutionary. Regarding Kant's claim that the proper task of philosophy was to set the limits of our knowledge and to investigate our faculties of knowledge, Kautsky writes that "in this there is nothing contained that every materialist could not subscribe to."[5] As for the noumenal world, lying outside our experience and hence unknowable, Kautsky holds that this Kantian formulation supports "the fact that our knowledge of the world is always limited by the nature of our intellectual faculties, is always relative, that for us there can only be relative and no absolute truths, not a final and complete knowledge, but an endless process of knowing."[6] In this way, Kautsky implies that Kantian epistemology can undergird a materialist view of the world.

On the other hand, Kautsky derides Kant's moral philosophy because it falls into the idealist trap. That is, it attempts to escape from the natural world of pleasures and desires and posit a supersensuous world of reason and freedom outside of space and time.

> Kant assumed as his starting point that the world is really external to us and does not simply exist in our heads, and that knowledge about it is only to be attained through experience. His philosophical achievement was to be the examination of the conditions of experience, of the boundaries of our knowledge. But just this very examination became for him an incitement to surmount this barrier, and to discover an unknowable world, of which he actually knew that it was of quite another nature than the world

of appearances, that it was completely timeless and spaceless, and therefore causeless as well.[7]

Kautsky claims that Kant is forced to create or fancy a timeless, spaceless, unknowable world in order to justify his non-naturalistic view of ethics and, as with all idealist approaches, to provide an account for the obligatory power of moral laws.

Kautsky sees a crucial historical significance for the ambiguity he perceives in Kant. Kant's progressive epistemology represents the German bourgeoisie's tacit opposition to the old absolutist worldview of church and state; his idealist moral view represents the German bourgeoisie's fear of church and state.

> Kant's Critique of Pure Reason equally drives Christianity from out of the Temple; but the discovery of the origin of the moral law, which is brought about by the Critique of Practical Reason, opens for it again the door with all due respect. Thus through Kant, Philosophy became, instead of a weapon of the fight against the existing methods of thought and institutions, a means of reconciling the antagonisms.[8]

Yet, Katusky suggests, within the kernel of Kant's moral philosophy was a germ of protest. Kant's praise of the dignity of the autonomous individual was a "protest against the very concrete feudal society with its personal relations of dependency."[9]

The idealistic aim of the moral law is to free people from the world of appearances we can know, the world of deterministic causal laws, the world of bondage. The moral law is a self-legislated law based solely on the rationality, freedom, and equality of people *qua* noumenal selves. This law must be applicable to all other people *qua* noumenal selves who together constitute an ideal kingdom of ends. In short, the moral laws provide the moral preconditions and guidelines for a harmonious society or community of noumenal selves.

Kautsky holds that Kant does not allow pleasure, self-love, or happiness as the source of the moral laws primarily because such laws would result in or usher forth a disharmonious, conflict-ridden society. So Kautsky concludes that Kant's moral law is itself based on a particular human desire—or a concrete social need—namely, the desire for a harmonious society. Kant's positing of a supersensuous, spaceless, timeless world indicates that he believes such a harmonious society or community of noumenal selves was unrealizable under the prevailing social and historical circumstances.

> The Kantian moral law assumes thus, in the first place, a harmonious society as desirable and possible. But it also assumes that the moral law is the means to create such a society, that this result can be achieved through a rule which the individual sets to himself. We see how thoroughly Kant was deceived, when he thought that his moral law was independent from all conditions pertaining to the world of sense, and that it formed thus a principle which would apply to all timeless and spaceless spirits, including God Almighty himself.[10]

Kautsky commends Kant for confronting the issue of free will, but rejects Kant's positing of two worlds—the noumenal and phenomenal, supersensuous and sensuous worlds—to deal with this issue. In place of this two-worlds view, Kautsky proposes that the one real world be viewed from two perspectives—the retrospective and prospective views. The former view is regulated by causal determinism and cause-effect mechanism; the latter, by freedom and moral action.

> The world of freedom and of the moral law is thus certainly another than that of recognized necessity, but it is no timeless and spaceless and no super-sensual world, but a particular portion of the world of sense seen from a particular point of view. It is the world as seen in its approach to us, the world on which we have to work, which we have to rearrange . . .[11]

Kautsky wants to maintain the distinction between human freedom and determinism. His dilemma, of course, is that without the former there would be no moral action, hence no ethics. And without the latter there would be no science. His attempt to grapple with this dilemma roughly amounts to Hans Vaihinger's solution—that one should act as if one were free, though in hindsight one must admit that one has no free will, no real choice. In short, Kautsky preserves the deterministic world of science along with an illusion of moral freedom. This illusion is requisite, he suggests, for people to act meaningfully in the present.

> Certainly I can extend the experience of the past into the future, certainly I can conclude that these will be even so necessarily determined as those, but even if I can only recognize the world on the assumption of necessity, yet I shall only be able to act in it on the assumption of a certain

Freedom . . . For action the feeling of freedom is an indispensable psychological necessity, which is not to be got rid of by any degree of knowledge.[12]

Kautsky's ambiguous attitude toward Kant is important because it will play a significant role in his metaphilosophical views and his foundationalist conception of science. It also illustrates that, despite his polemics against the socialist neo-Kantians, Kant remains for him a central figure.

Scientific Progress, Technical Progress, and Moral Progress

In this section, I shall define the central terms in Kautsky's argument for the objective status of socialist norms. As I noted earlier, Kautsky holds an instrumentalist conception of morality; that is, morality has little status or interest apart from the particular use or end it serves. And, for Kautsky, this use or end is technical (or technological) progress.

Technical progress is the mastery of nature for the aims of human beings. It is closely tied to scientific progress. Scientific progress is the discovery of more and more reliable general laws that discern necessity in natural and historical phenomena. Scientific progress promotes technical progress in that the discovery of such laws makes possible the creation of technical instrumentalities which broaden the human capacity for control and mastery over nature and society.

Moral progress is subordinate to technical progress in that it refers to a state of affairs which is compatible with and promotes the augmentation of the human capacity to control and master the natural environment and socioeconomic circumstances. Moral progress is a dependent variable within the historical process; that is, a morality is desirable to the degree to which it contributes to technical progress.

Kautsky's central terms can be defined in the following way:

(1) *Scientific progress* consists of discovering more and more general laws that govern the necessary behavior or properties of phenomena in nature and history.

(2) *Technical progress* is the widening of the scope in which human beings rationally control and consciously master their natural environment and socioeconomic circumstances.

(3) *Moral progress* constitutes succeeding sets of moral beliefs which are appropriate for and encouraging to technical progress.

Kautsky's Darwinistic Marxism

For Kautsky, Darwinism was the leading scientific theory of the day. Based on observations of natural phenomena, this theory provided an account of the evolutionary development of various species—from fossils to homo sapiens. Kautsky believed that Darwin put forward two basic claims. First, that human beings are members of the animal kingdom, wrought with a myriad of similarities and samenesses to other animals. Second, that the organic world is distinguished from the inorganic world by being adapted to an end or telos.

> When we study the organic world, it shows to us, in contrast to the inorganic, one very striking peculiarity: We find in it adaption to an end.[13]

And what is this end? The preservation of life. And according to Kautsky this preservation of life is to be understood as the preservation of the human species against the terrors of nature. Therefore this preservation requires the mastery and control of nature.

> But what is the work which the organs of the organism have to accomplish? This work is the struggle for life, that is, not the struggle with other organisms of the same kind, as the word is occasionally used, but the fight with the entire nature.[14]

Kautsky's appropriation of Darwin highlights the battle between human beings and nature, not the battles between the fittest people and ill-fated people. He does not deny that struggle between human beings plays an important role in the evolutionary development of history, but he claims that this struggle deserves a special category, that it is not the fundamental category of the struggle for existence. He is quite clear about this point:

War and competition are often regarded as the forms of the struggle for existence which fill the entire nature. In fact both arise from the technical progress of mankind and belong to its special peculiarity. Both are distinguished from the struggle for existence of the animal world therein, that the latter is a struggle of individuals or entire societies against the surrounding nature, a fight against living and non-living forces of nature in which those best fitted for the particular circumstances could best maintain themselves and reproduce their kind. But it is no fight for life or death against other individuals of the same kind, with the exception of a few beasts of prey, even with whom, however, the last kind of struggle plays only a secondary part in the struggle for life, and with the exception of the struggle for sexual selection. With man alone, thanks to the perfection of his tools, the struggle against individuals of the same kind to maintain themselves in the struggle for life comes to the fore. But even then there is a great distinction between wars and the struggle for existence.[15]

Kautsky views these two human activities—war and competition—as occasional interruptions of the perennial struggle for existence (or fight against nature). These interruptions or short-term battles within the human species occur primarily because of human conflict linked to the production of goods and services for human sustenance. Kautsky assumes, that is, that war and competition usually have economic causes.

Yet both human activities contribute in a positive way to the struggle for existence, the battle with nature. They both facilitate, in their own particular ways, human control over nature. War breeds "the strongest social cohesion" useful for uniting people against the forces of nature; competition serves as an effective incentive for developing the productive forces (or technological instruments for production) of society. Still, he believes, neither activity is permanent. They are only temporary activities that will someday be overcome. Therefore both have ultimately negative roles to play in human history. War ultimately leads to the self-destruction of the human race; competition, to unmanageable amounts of goods and services for the narrow social arrangements within which they are produced.

So Kautsky considers the struggle for existence the key to human history, the human fight against nature the central feature of human history, and human mastery and control over nature as the desirable goal of human history. This struggle for existence takes the form of divisions of labor efficacious for the optimal production of goods and services for human sustenance. The end or telos of human beings—the survival of the species—is inseparable from the division of labor in human societies.

> All organic beings are constructed and endowed more or less with a view to an end. The end which they serve is nevertheless not one which lies outside of them. The world as a whole has no aim. The aim lies in the individuals themselves, its parts are so arranged and fitted out, that they serve the individual, the whole. Purpose and division of labor arise together. The essence of the organism is the division of labor just as much as adaption to an end. One is the condition of the other end.[16]

This inextricable interweaving of the end of human beings—preservation of the species—and the divisions of labor leads toward the unique capacity of human beings: the capacity to produce the means of production for their sustenance. Just as adaptation to an end can serve to separate the organic world from the inorganic world, so the production of tools useful for producing goods and services can serve to separate human beings from other natural organisms.

> With the production of the means of production the animal man begins to become the human man; with that he breaks away from the animal world to found his own empire, an empire with its own kind of development, which is wholly unknown in the rest of nature, and which nothing similar is to be found there.[17]

This unique capacity permits human beings to lend support to their natural organs and, more importantly, to create technological tools or instruments for the production of goods and services for human sustenance. This *sui generis* human activity makes possible technical progress; it permits human control over nature.

> The technical progress forms from now on the foundation of the entire development of man. On that and not on any special divine spark rules by which man is distinguished from the animals.[18]

At this point, Kautsky introduces Marxist theory as the extension of Darwinism into the study of human societies and ethical matters. Marxist theory does for these spheres what Darwinian theory does for natural phenomena. Just as Darwin discovered in the natural world a necessary evolutionary development proceeding in accordance with general laws, so Marx discovered in human history a necessary evolutionary development proceeding in accordance with general laws.

By focusing on the distinctively human empire—the world of production, and the production of tools for production—Marxist theory becomes an essential mode of analysis for Kautsky. The division of labor, the precondition for this human empire, requires some set of social relations and hence a high dependence of people on one another for their survival.

> The discovery of the tool . . . made it possible that in a society certain individuals should exclusively use certain tools or any way so much oftener that they understand its use far better than any one else. Thus we come to a form of division of labor in human society . . . So much the greater the power of society over nature, so much the more helpless the individual outside society . . .
>
> Man is in his whole nature dependent on society, it rules him, only through the peculiar nature of this is he to be understood.
>
> The peculiar nature of society is, however, in a continual change, because in distinction to the animal society human society is always subject to development in consequence of the advance of their technology . . . Every society is modelled by the technological apparatus at its command, and the people who set it going, for which purpose they enter into the complicated social relations.[19]

For Kautsky, the major virtue of Marxist theory is that it provides a convincing account of this social change, discerns the general laws in history and those in capitalist society. Marxist theory shows that clear antagonisms result from social arrangements in which a small group of people appropriate the social surplus produced by a large group of laborers. This class conflict takes the form of a temporary interruption of the struggle for existence; it impedes the battle of human beings against nature. This interruption ends and the struggle for existence escalates when the basic condition for class conflict is removed: private property. Abolishing private property, overcoming class conflict, and overthrowing capitalist society would promote technical progress in that it would allow for the march of human control over nature to continue.

For Kautsky, the culprit is private property, not the division of labor (as it is with some Marxists).

> Not the abolition of division of labor, but certainly the abolition of all social distinctions and antagonisms which arise from the private property in the means of production and from the exclusive chaining down of the

mass of the people in the function of material production. The means of production have become so enormous, that they burst today the frame of private property . . . [upon] these grow the foundations for the abolition not of the division of labor, not of the professions, but for the antagonism of rich and poor, exploiters and exploited, ignorant and wise.[20]

Kautsky must preserve the division of labor because it is inextricably tied to his central notion of technical progress, as well as to the end or telos of human beings. And as divisions of labor become more and more sophisticated, highly skilled professionals will be needed for technical progress. Therefore Kautsky must defend the division of labor and professional distinctions and reject only class distinctions.

In fact, Kautsky can be seen as viewing the history of humankind as the history of the successions of divisions of labor, with each successive one more sophisticated than the previous one. This development ensures technical progress. Divisions of labor are the conditions under which the production of the means of production occur. They provide the occasion for the appearance and refinement of this unique human capacity. Yet the division of labor is not itself a unique human capacity: nonhuman animals have it. The unique human capacity usually presupposes the division of labor, but the two are not identical.

Kautsky's Ethical Naturalism

We have now reached the point at which we can examine Kautsky's naturalist argument for the objective status of socialist norms. It first should be pointed out that Kautsky is a moderate historicist and a hostile foe of extreme moral nihilism. He is vehemently opposed to banning the notions of objectivity and validity from moral discourse. For example, he states:

Other moralists have carried the idea of the moral regulations as simple customs still farther and described them as simple conventional fashions, basing this on the phenomenon that every nation, nay, each class, has its own particular moral conceptions which often stand in absolute contradiction to each other, that consequently an absolute moral has no validity. It has been concluded from this that morality is only a changing fashion, which only the thoughtless philistine crowd respect.[21]

As a naturalist, Kautsky has two ethical options: ethical naturalism or ethical nihilism. An ethical naturalist would claim that all facts are facts of nature and that any analysis of moral facts as facts of nature can be done in relation to human interests, needs, instincts, etc.; while an ethical nihilist would claim that all facts are facts of nature and then deny that there are any moral facts. This is the view Kautsky opposes.

For the ethical naturalist, moral judgments are assertions of fact and, just like any ordinary scientific factual assertion, can be justified by empirical inquiry. Kautsky's ethical naturalist view claims that moral norms ought to be understood as social instincts or impulses. These social instincts are grounded in human nature and take various forms owing to how people adapt to different and diverse circumstances. Since, he holds, all human societies possess these social instincts, the naturalistic basis for norms is ultimately universal.

> But not only are the social instincts something absolutely not conventional, but something deeply grounded in human nature, the nature of man as a social animal. . .[22]

Kautsky tries to justify the existence of social instincts on empirical grounds. He holds that social instincts rest upon the basic biological instinct of self-preservation. This basic biological instinct induces people to create social bonds which then cultivate social instincts. The social instincts consist of agreed-upon norms formed out of the social interaction of people. This social interaction is propelled by the biological instinct of self-preservation. And although the basic biological instinct is the motivating force for this social interaction and hence the creation of social instincts, the social instincts come to override the basic biological instinct.

> Among species of animals in whom the social bond becomes a weapon in the struggle for life, this encourages consequently social impulses which in many species and many individuals grow to an extraordinary strength, so that they can overcome the impulse of self-preservation. . .[23]

And what are the social instincts or moral norms common to people who have created social bonds? Kautsky provides a brief list of them, viewing them as necessary conditions for any community of animals. They are self-sacrifice for the community (what he calls altruism), courageous defense of the common interests of the community (bravery), submission and fidelity to the common will of the community (obedience and discipline), truthfulness in dealing with others, and susceptibility to the praise and blame of others. He concludes,

> These all are social impulses which we find expressed already among animal societies, many of them in a high degree.
>
> These social impulses are nevertheless nothing but the highest virtues, they sum up the entire moral code. At the most they lack the love for justice, that is the impulse for equality. For its development there certainly is no place in the animal societies, because they only know natural and individual inequality, and not those called forth by social relations, the social inequalities.[24]

Kautsky insists that these social instincts (or impulses) incorporate the grand moral principles that idealists attribute to either divine law or supersensuous worlds. Furthermore, he holds that the refusal to acknowledge the naturalistic, rather than metaphysical, foundations of such principles leads to either hard objectivism or extreme moral nihilism.

> The lofty moral law, that the comrade ought never to be merely a means to an end, which the Kantians look on as the most wonderful achievement of Kant's genius, and as the moral programme of the modern era, and for the entire future history of the world, that is in the animal world a commonplace. . .
>
> Because the moral law is the universal instinct, of equal force to the instinct of self-preservation and reproduction, thence its force, thence its power which we obey without thought, thence our rapid decisions, in particular cases, whether an action is good or bad, virtuous or vicious; thence the energy and decision of our moral judgment, then thence the difficulty to prove it when reason begins to analyze its grounds. . .
>
> Not from our organs of knowing, but from our impulses comes the moral law and the moral judgment as well as the feeling of duty and conscience.[25]

It is significant to note that the particular impulse which separates animal societies from human (animal) societies is the "impulse for equality." This instinct is tied to the unique human capacity to produce the means of production; it is manifest in different conceptions of equality appropriate for and encouraging to evolving divisions of labor in which such production takes place. In this way, the impulse for equality is dynamically related to technical progress.

Moral progress is dependent on technical progress because evolving divisions of labor require new conceptions of equality. Acceptable conceptions of equality contribute to the struggle for existence in that they regulate social institutions so that human conflict is minimized and more human energy is channeled toward the end or telos of human beings (namely, the preservation of the species).

The "impulse for equality" is the basis for socialist norms in the modern world, or in capitalist society. The impulse for equality would take the form of abolishing private property. And this abolition would, more than likely, require a political revolution. The abolition of private property is morally desirable because it would allow technical progress to flourish more than it presently does. This is so because, Kautsky holds, the capitalist system of production, with its commodities exchange, competition, and class divisions,

> has consequently a great economic importance, till it creates such gigantic productive forces that the framework of commodity-production becomes too narrow, as one time the framework of the primitive social or co-operative production became too narrow for the growing division of labor. The overproduction not less than the artificial limitation of production by employers' associations, shows that the time is past when competition as a spur to production helps on social evolution.[26]

For Kautsky, Marxist theory demonstrates that the general laws of capitalist society and the necessary developments in history require that the proletariat, with its aim of abolishing private property, overthrow the existing order and establish a society free of private property, namely, a socialist society. This process is demanded by the technical progress of humankind, with the "impulse for equality" as the moral justification of this progress:

> Thus there formed itself a foundation for the final realization of that moral conception already expressed by Christianity, though very prematurely, so that it could not be fulfilled, and which thus remained for the majority of Christians a simple phrase, the conception of the equality of men, a view that the social instincts, the moral virtues are to be exercised towards all men in equal fashion. This foundation of a general human morality is being formed not by a moral improvement of humanity . . . but by the development of the productive forces of man, by the extension of the social division of human labor, the perfection of the means of intercourse. This new morality is however, even today far from being a

morality of all men even in the economically progressive countries. It is in essence even today the morality of the class conscious proletariat . . .[27]

Kautsky's conception of science and his view of Marxist theory as having scientific status leads him to insist upon the necessity and inevitability of the triumph of the proletariat. Marxist theory discerns fundamental change in history and society. This change is understood

independent of the will of the individuals, and is necessarily determined by the given material conditions. Among these the technical factor is again the most important, and that phase whose development affects the method of production.[28]

So Kautsky's naturalist argument for the objective status of socialist norms can be put in the following way. Human beings are natural creatures, equipped with the basic biological instinct of self-preservation and adapted to the end of the preservation of the species. This basic biological instinct propels them into social interaction in which social instincts are cultivated; and the adaptation to the preservation of the species leads toward the struggle for existence or the mastery of and control over nature. These social instincts are moral norms which serve as requisite conditions for any community of animals. The unique human capacity is the production of tools or instruments for producing goods and services for human sustenance. This production is usually found within a particular division of labor. The unique human capacity makes possible technical progress, the human weapon in the human struggle for existence or control over nature. The more technical progress, the better the chance humankind can adapt to its end. The unique human "impulse for equality" promotes technical progress; it takes the form of various conceptions of equality which encourage the conscious mastery over nature. This encouragement constitutes the moral criteria, with its naturalistic basis, for deciding whether a state of affairs is desirable or not. In the last stages of capitalist society, private property, along with competition and class conflict, impedes technical progress. Therefore abolishing private property and overcoming class conflict— or establishing a socialist society—is morally desirable because it would encourage technical progress.

Kautsky believes this reasoning can be attacked in two ways. First, his Darwinist-Marxist framework can be attacked as unacceptable. This is an empirical matter, a rivalry between different theories about society, history, and the world. Second, his tacit assumption—that it is desirable that humankind should survive—can be refused. This is a normative matter, a question of ethics. This option is a real one only if one refuses to infuse normative content into the scientific fact of the basic biological instinct of self-preservation. Kautsky holds that the validity of this assumption is not a matter of purely philosophical debate. Instead this norm-laden fact is instinctual.

> The instinct of self preservation is the most primitive of the animal instincts and the most indispensable. Without it no animal species endowed in any degree with the power of self movement and a faculty of intelligence could maintain itself even a short time. . . Although many a suicide be philosophically grounded, we always, in every practical act of the denial of life, finally meet with disease or desperate social circumstances as the cause, but not a philosophical theory. Mere philosophizing cannot overcome the instinct of self preservation.[29]

Kautsky's ethical naturalism entails subordinating morality to technical progress and his instrumentalist conception of morality requires empirical inquiry to take on central significance. For example, he must be able to show, on empirical grounds, that the late stages of advanced capitalist society impede technical progress and that the abolition of private property and the overcoming of class conflict will promote technical progress. If these claims are not empirically confirmable, then we must reject their moral desirability. In this way, science undergirds his ethics.

Ethics and Science

If we give Kautsky the benefit of the doubt and assume for the moment that his claims can be empirically confirmed, does this make them morally desirable? This crucial question raises a more general query, namely, how does he perceive the relation of ethics to science?

Kautsky attempts to directly address this more general question. His response is highly ambiguous. On the one hand, he denies the autonomy of ethics. He views moral discourse as a domain of scientific inquiry, with ought-statements somehow arising from a scientific investigation which discerns necessity in historical and social phenomena. On the other hand, he draws a hard distinction between ethics and science, severing scientific claims from ethical ones. This ambiguity is illustrated in the following passage:

> Ethics must always be only an object of science; this has to study the moral instincts as well as the moral ideals and explain them; it cannot take advice from them as to the results at which it is to arrive. Science stands above Ethics, its results are just as little moral or immoral as necessity is moral or immoral.[30]

On first view, Kautsky weds moral judgments to empirical inquiry. Science, in some way (and he does not specify how) provides norms. A science of history and society somehow tells us where history is headed and what the good society ought to look like. This view is expressed here:

> Science has only to do with the recognition of the necessary. It can certainly arrive at prescribing a shall, but this dare only come up as a consequence of the insight into the necessary. It must decline to discover a "shall" which is not to be recognized as a necessity founded in the world of phenomena.[31]

But on second view, Kautsky separates moral discourse from scientific inquiry. Science is a value-free procedure that discerns necessity and has nothing to do with ought-statements. He states this view in this way:

> Even the Social Democracy as an organization of the Proletariat in its class struggle cannot do without the moral ideal, the moral indignation against exploitation and class rule. But this ideal has nothing to find in scientific socialism, which is the scientific examination of the laws of the development and movement of the social organism, for the purpose of knowing the necessary tendencies and aims of the proletariat class struggle.[32]

This ambiguity regarding the relation of ethics to science reflects Kautsky's own indecision as to what the role of philosophy is and ought to be. In short, I suggest Kautsky's ambiguity arises from his confused (and inconsistent) metaphilosophical vision.

It is the same as Kautsky's ambiguity regarding Kant. Kautsky lauds Kant because "through him did philosophy first become the science of science, whose duty it is not to teach a distinct philosophy, but how to philosophize."[33] This philosophizing, he suggests, consists of examining the process of knowing and explicating what it is to engage in methodical thinking. This extolment of Kant's metaphilosophical vision partially explains Kautsky's enthusiasm over Kant's epistemological project. Yet Kautsky is upset with Kant's moral philosophy primarily because it goes "beyond the facts," hence steps outside the boundaries of science.

> But Kant went farther than this, and his great philosophical achievement, the investigation of the faculties of knowledge, became itself his philosophical stumbling block.[34]

Kautsky's perception of Kant can best be seen from the vantage point of his positivist view of science and his naturalist view of ethics. First, he is enamored with "facts." And especially "facts" that yield necessary developments in history. He also is obsessed with foundations for these "facts." For him, Kant's epistemological project provides foundations for such "facts" while allowing for these "facts" to be subject to revision. For Kautsky, Kant's great philosophical achievement is to have undergirded a positivist view of science, preserved the sanctity of "facts," and permitted a dynamic or process view in science.

Second, Kautsky's extolment of "facts" and his search for their foundations leads him to take seriously the existence of moral facts. But he rejects Kant's attempt to undergird moral facts with a foundation different from that for scientific facts. He wants Kant's epistemological project without Kant's non-naturalist ethics. So, like a good ethical naturalist, Kautsky tries to reduce moral facts to scientific facts, norms to instincts. This would permit him to use the same foundation for moral facts as for scientific facts. And it is at this point that confusion sets in.

By siding with the Kantian epistemological project, Kautsky gets trapped in the philosophic quest for objectivity and search for foundations. And what he overlooks is that Kant's quest and search result in transcendental foundations for both science and ethics. Kautsky's ambiguity toward Kant is based on a misreading of Kant's consistent metaphilosophical vision. By utilizing Darwin and Marx as the major exemplars of scientists, Kautsky opts for radical historicists—or antifoundationalists—who shun the need for philosophic foundations (or a science of science) and are content with theoretic concerns. This leaves

Kautsky in a dilemma. If he goes completely with the Kantian project, he must choose a foundationalist conception of philosophy; if he follows Darwin and Marx, he must overcome this conception and choose radical historicism. Since he does not fully grasp what the Kantian project is, he ends up giving lip service to a conception of philosophy which his Darwinistic Marxism must reject, and he supports an anti-foundationalist viewpoint which Kant surely would abhor.

In fact, I believe that Kautsky's heart is with the Darwinistic Marxist view, but that his positivist view of science and his search for philosophic foundations prevent him from fully appreciating the radical historicist potential in the Darwinistic Marxist view. The best example of where his heart is can be found in his naturalist argument for the objective status of socialist norms. The crux of his argument is his understanding of scientific, technical, and moral progress. His instincts-talk provides out-of-place naturalist ornaments which are added because he thinks he must provide philosophic foundations for his ethical views. His central argument is a quite plausible one which employs value-laden terms such as technical progress and moral progress. Like any plausible argument, it appeals to factors which people consider important, e.g., survival, historical regression or progression, and provokes stimulating and intelligent responses. Admittedly, it is not a terribly convincing argument, but it does merit consideration without appealing to its philosophic foundations.

Like a good ethical naturalist, Kautsky is frightened by extreme moral nihilism and overly impressed by "scientific facts" or "scientific status." Both this fright and genuflection result from his acceptance of the philosophic quest for objectivity and search for foundations, the metaphilosophical vision that his heroes have abandoned.

◇ 6 ◇

The Hegelian Marxist Position: Lukács' Ontological Quest

Georg Lukács' *History and Class Consciousness: Studies in Marxist Dialectics* (1923) is one of the most influential Marxist texts published in this century. Written just prior to the publication of Marx's early *Economic and Philosophic Manuscripts* (delayed for over eighty years), Lukács' text played an important role in sparking the Hegelian renaissance which has swept through the Marxist intelligentsia in the past five decades. For our purposes, we shall view Lukács' book—and especially the longest essay in the work, entitled "Reification and the Consciousness of the Proletariat"—as the last major attempt to provide an objective basis for socialist norms in the Marxist tradition.

Hegel and the Dialectical Method

Lukács' viewpoint can be best understood by first examining briefly its Hegelian underpinnings. This Hegelian foundation is important because it plays a central role in how Lukács deals with ethical matters. The central feature of this Hegelian viewpoint is the dialectical method.

The dialectical method is a particular way of viewing the world. Specifically, it is a particular procedure of inquiry into the fundamental nature of reality, history, and society. The dialectical method claims that activity (human or divine) and hence process is at the center of reality, history, and society, and it holds that discernible contradictions and antagonisms are the chief determinants of change and transformation. For Hegel, the father of the modern dialectical method, this activity is

138

the activity of the *Weltgeist* (world spirit), and the change, the transformation, is primarily an affair of the consciousness of the *Weltgeist*.

I shall sketch crudely how Hegel employs the dialectical method in order to yield a dynamic, idealistic epistemology and a progressive philosophy of history. The aim of Hegel's *Weltgeist* is to achieve full self-consciousness by confronting alien objects and realizing that these objects are but alienated forms of its own consciousness. This process is propelled by the *Weltgeist*'s feelings of estrangement from the strangeness (or otherness) of the objects it confronts.

Knowing-mental labor is the basic activity that relates the *Weltgeist* to objects (or the objective world). This activity of knowing constitutes an antagonism between the *Weltgeist* and the objective world, between subject and object. This antagonism consists of the *Weltgeist* existing over against objects; it results in alienation, estrangement, homelessness on behalf of the *Weltgeist*—a situation that is overcome by the process of the *Weltgeist* conquering the strangeness or otherness of the object and thereby increasing its self-consciousness.

This process of overcoming the otherness of the object is the process of *Aufhebung,* a process of negation, preservation, and transformation. For Hegel, the *Weltgeist* negates, destroys, or annuls the otherness of the object; preserves, acknowledges, or realizes the object as but a form of consciousness; and hence transforms the alien object into an aspect of its own selfconsciousness.

Hegel's viewpoint is dynamic because it accents the process of becoming and transforms subject-object relations into an affair of the consciousness of the subject. The method therefore ultimately overcomes the subject-object distinction. Hegel's view, on this crude interpretation, is idealistic because it posits objects as but alienated forms of self-consciousness (on behalf of the *Weltgeist*).

The process of *Aufhebung*—of overcoming the otherness of the object and thereby increasing the self-consciousness of the *Weltgeist*—yields the augmentation of the self-activity of the *Weltgeist* in history. This augmentation takes the form of increased self-differentiation and self-disclosure of the *Weltgeist* in the world, through individuals, institutions, societies, and nations. The *Weltgeist* achieves its aim—full self-consciousness—through the desires and passions of individuals, the rise and fall of institutions, the appearance and disappearance of societies, and the ascent and descent of nations. This aim is synonymous with freedom in the world. The renowned Hegelian march of freedom in history is essentially the process of ever heightening self-consciousness of the *Weltgeist*. In this way, Hegel's dynamic, idealist epistemology is linked to his progressive philosophy of history.

The Hegelian idea of determinate negation is an integral part of the process of *Aufhebung*. It consists of a recognition (on behalf of a conscious subject) of the internal contradictions and antagonisms within a particular situation. This recognition is requisite for the first step in the process of *Aufhebung*, that of negation, destruction, annihilation. The process ends up yielding a determined outcome (or new stage or moment) which resolves the basic contradiction and antagonism in the revelant situation.

Marxist Dialectics and the Category of Concrete Totality

Lukács' understanding of the dialectical method differs from Hegel's at three points. First, he limits the scope of the dialectical method to history and society. He does not extend it into nature. Second, he replaces Hegel's historical agent, the *Weltgeist*, with the proletariat, the working class in capitalist society. Third and most importantly, he understands the notion of activity as praxis, as the reflective human transformation of the world.

In regard to the first point, it should be noted that this constitutes a break not only with Hegel, but also with the classical Marxist tradition. In later writing of Engels (including *Anti-Dühring*), it is claimed that the dialectical process of becoming occurs in nature as well as in history and society. For Lukács, Marxist dialectics is uniquely characterized by its application to only history and society. This application accents its distinctiveness, namely, its revolutionary aim, its practical import, its transformative function.

> It is of the first importance to realise that the method is limited here to the realms of history and society. The misunderstandings that arise from Engels' account of dialectics can in the main be put down to the fact that Engels—following Hegel's mistaken lead—extended the method to apply also to nature. However, the crucial determinants of dialectics—the interaction of subject and object, the unity of theory and practice, the historical

changes in the reality underlying the categories as the root cause of changes in thought etc.—are absent from our knowledge of nature.[1]

The second point is obvious. Marxist dialectics cannot take seriously some transcendental godlike entity like Hegel's *Weltgeist* or some trans-class community (if Hegel's *Weltgeist* is viewed in terms of intersubjectivity) as its chief historical agent. Marxist dialectics accepts a march of freedom in history, but it holds that in the capitalist era, it is embodied in the revolutionary praxis of the proletariat.

The third point is the most important one because it marks an attempt to move beyond Hegel's idealistic understanding of the *Weltgeist*'s activity to Marx's materialist view of the proletariat's praxis. We saw earlier that Hegel is an idealist in the sense that he holds objects to be mere forms of alienated consciousness. Therefore he becomes preoccupied with the ever-increasing consciousness of the *Weltgeist*, along with its overcoming of the "otherness" of objects. Lukács tries to sidestep this idealism by viewing the objective situations of the proletariat as real, as external to the proletariat, as more than a mere alienated form of consciousness (and this is a highly controversial point in Lukácsian scholarship). He becomes preoccupied with the self-consciousness (or class consciousness) of the proletariat, and he views their activity as possessing the potential for revolutionary political praxis and thus the possibility of reflectively changing the objective world, or their external socioeconomic circumstances. So just as subject-object relations in Hegel ultimately result in a higher form of self-consciousness for the *Weltgeist*, so the subject-object relation (proletariat-capitalist society) in Lukács results in a higher form of self-consciousness for the working class—revolutionary praxis is involved, and ultimately a new society, world, or stage in human history.

For Lukács, as for Hegel, the dialectical method makes ontological claims: that is, it makes claims about the fundamental nature of logical developments in reality. As we pointed out earlier, Lukács understands this reality solely in terms of history and society. For him Hegel's dialectical viewpoint

> throws an entirely new light on the problem of reality. If, in Hegel's terms, Becoming now appears as the truth of Being, and process as the truth about things, then this means that *the developing tendencies of history constitute a higher reality than the empirical "facts."*[2]

Marxist dialectics—or Marxist social theory which incorporates the dialectical method—discerns the basic contradictions and antagonisms of capitalist society. This is why it can reasonably project the developing tendencies of evolving capitalist society, why it can adopt a revolutionary attitude toward capitalist society.

> Marxism is the doctrine of the revolution precisely because it understands the essence of the process (as opposed to its manifestations, its symptoms); and because it can demonstrate the decisive line of future development (as opposed to the events of the moment).[3]

For Lukács, there are two basic reasons why Marxist dialectics can grasp the future development of history and society. First, Marxist dialectics holds fundamental contradictions and antagonisms to be the chief determinants of social change. Second, and more importantly, Marxist dialectics contains the category of concrete totality. This category highlights the present as a historical problem that must be viewed as an "aspect of a total social situation caught up in the process of historical change."[4]

The category of concrete totality is the central notion for Lukács' understanding of Marxist dialectics. In fact, it yields a methodological approach to viewing history and society which, for Lukács, distinguishes Marxism from bourgeois social science.

> It is not the primary economic motives in historical explanation that constitutes the decisive difference between Marxism and bourgeois thought, but the point of view of totality. The category of totality, all-pervasive supremacy of the whole over the parts is the essence of the method which Marx took over from Hegel and brilliantly transformed into the foundations of a wholly new science . . . proletarian science is revolutionary not just by virtue of its revolutionary ideas which it opposes to bourgeois society, but above all because of its method. *The primacy of the category of totality is the bearer of the principle of revolution in science.*[5]

Lukács believes that the category of concrete totality in Marxist dialectics distinguishes Marxism from bourgeois social science for two reasons. First, Marxism understands society as a whole of interrelated parts, while bourgeois social science separates these parts into isolated, atomic components. Therefore bourgeois social science cannot, as can Marxism, show the way in which productive forces, social relations, and individuals (as well as knowledge of the process of these relations) are inseparable elements within an evolving historical process. Marxism recognizes that capitalist society produces this self-serving way of perceiving itself, a perception which keeps the whole obscure and the process static.

> The fetishistic character of economic forms, the reification of all human relations, the constant expansion and extension of the division of labor which subjects the process of production to an abstract, rational analysis, without regard to the human potentialities and abilities of the immediate producers, all these things transform the phenomena of society and with them the way in which they are perceived. In this way arise the "isolated" facts, "isolated" complexes of facts, separate, specialist disciplines (economics, law, etc.) whose very appearance seems to have done much to pave the way for such scientific methods. It thus appears extraordinarily "scientific" to think out the tendencies implicit in the facts themselves and to promote this activity to the status of science.
>
> By contrast, in the teeth of all these isolated and isolating facts and partial systems, dialectics insists on the concrete unity of the whole. Yet although it exposes these appearances for the illusions they are—albeit illusions necessarily engendered by capitalism—in this "scientific" atmosphere it still gives the impression of being an arbitrary construction.[6]

Lukács holds that by ignoring the category of concrete totality, bourgeois social science ignores the historical, and ultimately ideological, character of its own perception of bourgeois society and of itself. It fails to see itself as but a historical product within a particular stage of history. This is precisely because it does not see capitalist society as such a product. In another long but rich passage Lukács reiterates this failure of bourgeois social science.

> The unscientific nature of this seemingly so scientific method consists, then in its failure to see and take account of the *historical character* of the facts on which it is based. . .
>
> The historical character of the "facts" which science seems to have grasped with such "purity" makes itself felt in an even more devastating manner. As the products of historical evolution they are involved in continuous change. But in addition they are also *precisely in their objective structure the products of a definite historical epoch, namely capitalism.* Thus when "science" maintains that the manner in which data immediately present themselves is an adequate foundation of scientific conceptualisation and that the actual form of these data is the appropriate starting point for the formation of scientific concepts, it thereby takes its stand simply

and dogmatically on the basis of capitalist society. It uncritically accepts the nature of the object as it is given and the laws of that society as the unalterable foundation of "science."[7]

The second reason the category of concrete totality in Marxist dialectics separates Marxism from bourgeois social science is that this category enables Marxism to adopt the standpoint of the proletariat.

> The category of totality, however, determines not only the object of knowledge but also the subject. Bourgeois thought judges social phenomena consciously, or unconsciously, naively or subtly, consistently from the standpoint of the individual. No path leads from the individual to the totality; there is at best a road leading to aspects of particular areas, mere fragments for the most part, "facts" bare of any context, or to abstract, special laws. The totality of an object can only be posited if the positing subject is itself a totality; and if the subject wishes to understand itself, it must conceive of the object as a totality. In modern society only the *classes* can represent this total point of view.[8]

And just as bourgeois social science is a historical product which reflects the biases and interests of the ruling class, so Marxist dialectics is a historical product which reflects the biases and interests of the working class.

> Thus the essence of the method of historical materialism is inseparable from the "practical and critical" activity of the proletariat: both are aspects of the same process of social evolution. So, too, the knowledge of reality provided by the dialectical method is likewise inseparable from the class standpoint of the proletariat.[9]

Lukács is not claiming that the simultaneous rise of the proletariat and the development of Marxist dialectics requires that only the proletariat use the dialectical method to grasp social reality. Nor is he implying that workers can *mysteriously* get in touch with social reality, while other classes cannot (in fact, he has a fairly sophisticated argument in favor of the latter claim, as we shall see in a future section). Rather, he is suggesting that anyone who adopts Marxist dialectics adopts the standpoint of the proletariat. This is so because Marxist dialectics puts forward a particular class analysis of capitalist society and requires participation in the revolutionary praxis of the working class.

> Historical materialism grows out of the "immediate, natural" life-principle of the proletariat; it means the acquisition of total knowledge of reality from this one point of view. But it does not follow from this that

this knowledge or this methodological attitude is the inherent or natural possession of the proletariat as a class (let alone of proletarian individuals). On the contrary. It is true that the proletariat is the conscious subject of total social reality. But the conscious subject is not defined here as in Kant, where "subject" is defined as that which can never be an object. The "subject" here is not a detached spectator of the process. The proletariat is more than just the active and passive part of this process: the rise and evolution of its knowledge and its actual rise and evolution in the course of history are just the two different sides of the same real process.[10]

Lukács' claim about the capacity of Marxist dialectics to grasp social reality is epistemic, and it therefore prompts the questions how he knows and how he would go about confirming this knowledge claim. Lukács seems to have two lines of answers to these questions. The first simplistic line holds that reality itself, the process of becoming itself, is dialectical. Therefore only Marxist dialectics can discern this process. Marxist dialectics grasps social reality because it correctly corresponds to the world, and it correctly corresponds to the world because both the world and the theory share a basic characteristic, namely, both are dialectical.

Two problems are immediately apparent in this reply, which appears to be mere verbal play. First, even if reality and theory were dialectical, it is not clear that both would have to be dialectical in the same way. Therefore, the question about whether the dialectical theory correctly corresponds to dialectical reality still remains. Second, and the more profound problem, the reply is circular. It claims that reality is inherently dialectical and then presents evidence for this claim guided by a theory that views reality only dialectically.

The second line of reply picks up where the first line leaves off. It holds that there is no noncircular way of talking about the relation of theory to reality. Any relevant statement about this relation will be non-neutral, it will already presuppose a particular theory about reality. It is impossible, Lukács suggests, to isolate reality from particular theories of reality, then to compare and adjudicate between these theories using a theory-free reality as the last court of appeal. So he believes that a certain kind of circularity is inescapable. Yet since a theory-free philosophic court of appeal is never available, he suggests that theories be tested in practice—that is, in the solutions they provide for common problems, the impetus they provide for promoting the march of freedom in history, the contribution they make to the higher development of humankind.

> . . . the historical process is something unique and its dialectical advances and reverses are an incessant struggle to reach higher stages of the truth, and of the (societal) *self-knowledge of man*. The "relativisation" of truth in Hegel means that the higher factor is always the truth of the factor beneath it in the system. This does not imply the destruction of "objective" truth at the lower stages but only that it means something different as a result of being integrated in a more concrete and comprehensive totality. Proletarian thought is practical thought and as such is strongly pragmatic. "The proof of the pudding is in the eating."[11]

This second line of reply is highly significant. It hints at a radical historicist conception of science and epistemology. We shall examine this significance, as well as its limitations, in the section entitled "Ethics and Dialectics."

Lukács' Critique of Bourgeois Social Science and Mechanical Marxism

We have already seen that Lukács criticizes bourgeois social science because it fails to see fundamental contradictions and antagonisms as the chief determinants of social change and, by ignoring the category of concrete totality, it does not acknowledge the interrelatedness and interconnectedness of social phenomena. The common denominator of both of these criticisms is that bourgeois social science views existing social forms of life as natural and permanent forms rather than as the temporary result of an underlying process in history.

We saw that this static bourgeois view of social reality worships isolated, atomic facts and focuses on specific, disparate parts of social reality. By this worship and focus, bourgeois social science tends to ossify social facts into frozen entities. In opposition to this view Marxist dialectics considers facts to be aspects of a certain discernible historical process.

> In this theory of reality which allows a higher place to the prevailing trends of the total development than to the facts of the empirical world, the antithesis we stressed when considering the particular questions raised

by Marxism (the antithesis between movement and final goal, evolution and revolution, etc.) acquires its authentic, concrete and scientific shape. For only this analysis permits us to investigate the concept of the "fact" in a truly concrete manner, i.e., in the social context in which it has its origin and its existence.[12]

Lukács believes that these historical trends are discernible by Marxist dialectics, with its employment of the dialectical method and its incorporation of the category of concrete totality. By grasping capitalist society as a whole, as a stage in the historical process, as a transient system of production with its own set of social relations, legal arrangements, and cultural beliefs, Marxist dialectics opposes the bourgeois worship of isolated facts and shows this worship to be narrow, myopic, and distorting.

> Thus only when the theoretical primacy of the "facts" has been broken, only when *every phenomenon is recognized to be a process,* will it be understood that what we are wont to call "facts" consists of processes. Only then will it be understood that the facts are nothing but the parts, the *aspects* of the total process that have been broken off, artificially isolated and ossified.[13]

This bourgeois worship of facts, this holding that "facts" lay bare social reality, is supportive of capitalist society because it presupposes a conception of social reality which views the present as static within the limits of undeniable, intransigent "facts." In this way, bourgeois social science has ideological import and serves as a legitimation of the existing order.

> Of course, it also becomes clear why in the reified thought of the bourgeoisie the "facts" have to play the part of its highest fetish in both theory and practice. This petrified factuality in which everything is frozen into a "fixed magnitude," in which the reality that just happens to exist persists in a totally senseless, unchanging way precludes any theory that could throw light on even this immediate reality.[14]

Bourgeois social science distorts the social reality it purports to reveal by ignoring the meaning of the "facts." It ignores this meaning by discarding the underlying process that allows one to understand these "facts." By remaining preoccupied with the "facts," bourgeois social science remains on the surface of social reality, it refuses to go beyond the world of immediate appearances.

If the facts are to be understood, this distinction between their real existence and their inner core must be grasped clearly and precisely. This distinction is the first premise of a truly scientific study which in Marx's words, "would be superfluous if the outward appearance of things coincided with their essence." Thus we must detach the phenomena from the form in which they are immediately given and discover the intervening links which connect them to their core, their essence. In so doing, we shall arrive at an understanding of their apparent form and see it as the form in which the inner core necessarily appears. It is necessary because of the historical character of the facts, because they have grown in the soil of capitalist society. This twofold character, the simultaneous recognition and transcendence of immediate appearances is precisely the dialectical nexus.[15]

Lukács' critique of bourgeois social science has a considerable bearing on his ethical standpoint. By dissolving the conception of "facts" that bourgeois social science depends upon he is, by implication, rejecting the bourgeois foundationalist view of science. And this bourgeois extolment of "facts," this foundationalist view of science, results in lower status for values. If normative statements are not objectively confirmable (as are factual statements) but are, rather, mere subjective responses to facts, then even though criticisms of existing social reality are not altogether eliminated, such criticisms are disarmed. If norms and values appear as less substantial than facts, as mere ideals that come from personal feelings or attitudes, then they have much less effect on people who do not already agree or prefer these ideals. In this way, the rigid is/ought and fact/value distinctions of bourgeois social science serve to lessen the impact of criticism of the status quo and to conceal the ideological bias of the "value-free" bourgeois social science obsessed with "facts."

But in the "facts" we find the crystalisation of the essence of capitalist development into an ossified, impenetrable thing alienated from man. And the form assumed by this ossification and this alienation converts it into a foundation of reality and of philosophy that is perfectly self-evident and immune from every doubt. When confronted by the rigidity of these "facts" every movement seems like a movement *impinging on them,* while every tendency to change them appears to be a merely subjective principle (a wish, a value judgment, a ought).[16]

Lukács' critique of bourgeois social science also provides a new conception of historical necessity within the Marxist tradition, and explicit rejection of mechanical Marxism. In the last chapter, we saw that Kautsky's view of historical necessity is based on the mechanical cause-effect determinism supported by Newtonian natural scientists of his day. It is a machine-like necessity that governs phenomena, independent of human will, consciousness, or choice.

Lukács' reformulation of the notion of historical necessity does not claim that a socialist regime is an inevitable outcome of capitalist society; it also does not imply that history is causally determined in such a way that the new emerging social arrangement will necessarily be morally desirable. Rather he holds that at a given point in history, the proletariat in capitalist society will be faced with a crucial choice: either to work for and establish proletarian control of the means of production or to remain under capitalist exploitation and oppression. He believes it is possible to make some reasonable predictions or projections as to how people will decide to act. Ripe objective socioeconomic circumstances can provide the occasion for the working class to act on the first choice. And this choice will be made if, under such circumstances, the proletariat achieves class consciousness—that is, if the working class attains a certain perception of itself, if it comes to see itself as a class involved in a historical process in which it can play a central role. In this way, historical necessity consists of ripe socioeconomic circumstances plus a particular collective choice on behalf of the proletariat.

> Only when the consciousness of the proletariat is able to point out the road along which the dialectics of history is objectively impelled but which it cannot travel unaided, will the consciousness of the proletariat awaken to a consciousness of the process, and only then will the proletariat become the identical subject-object of history whose praxis will change reality. If the proletariat fails to take this step the contradiction will remain unresolved and will be reproduced by the dialectical mechanics of history at a higher level, in an altered form and with increased intensity. It is in *this* that the objective necessity of history consists.[17]

This conception of the "objective necessity of history" differs from Kautsky's in that it accents the relative free choice of the proletariat. It is possible to predict or project what the proletariat will decide based on whether the necessary conditions (ripe socioeconomic circumstances) and sufficient conditions (class consciousness on behalf of the proletariat) are satisfied. Unlike Kautsky, Lukács allows for contingency and precludes rigid inevitability. He permits free will for historical agents.

> . . . a dialectical necessity is far from being the same thing as a mechanical, causal necessity . . .
>
> In addition to the mere contradiction—the automatic product of capitalism—a *new* element is required: the consciousness of the proletariat must become deed.[18]

Yet Lukács' view does not degenerate into an irrational voluntarism. Although it permits free choices of historical agents, it restricts these choices to particular alternatives. The choices are free in the sense that they are not determined by a mechanical, causal necessity, but they are contextual in that they are constrained by specific realizable options.

> History is at its least automatic when it is the consciousness of the proletariat that is at issue. The truth that the old intuitive mechanical materialism could not grasp turns out to be doubly true for the proletariat, namely that it can be transformed and liberated only by its own actions, and that "the educator must himself be educated." The objective economic evolution could do no more than create the position of the proletariat in the production process. It was this position that determined its point of view. But the objective evolution could only give the proletariat the opportunity and the necessity to change society. Any transformation can only come about as the product of the—free—action of the proletariat itself.[19]

Reification as the Starting Point

Lukács' notion of reification is the starting point for his treatment of ethical matters. He understands reification to be a social phenomenon which consists of socioeconomic circumstances under which producers' activity and the products produced by this activity result in a system of production and a set of social relations that control and dominate the producers. Reification is, for Lukács, both an objective state of affairs in capitalist society and a morally undesirable state of affairs.

On the one hand, reification incapacitates people. It renders people powerless. People may even discover the laws governing this reified world of objects and persons, but these laws confront them as natural, immutable, unalterable. These laws appear as invisible forces that generate their own power. They seem to stand outside human capacities to modify or transform them.

On the other hand, reification makes the productive activity of people a commodity that participates in the market exchange like any other consumer article. This commodity form of human labor is perceived as such by the buyer (capitalist) and the seller (worker). So the product produced by human labor and the labor itself are subject to market regulations. A reified society is one that satisfies all its needs in terms of commodity exchange or on the basis of market values. This is the kind of society Lukács finds morally undesirable, owing to its dehumanizing, "thingifying" effects on human beings.

Lukács begins with the notion of reification in his discussion of ethical matters because he believes any such discussion must begin with an objective state of affairs and a moral disposition toward it as seen through the lens of a social theory which correctly understands existing social reality and can reasonably predict or project the particular historical tendencies of this social reality. In short, any acceptable treatment of norms must start with an accurate social theory—and for him this means Marxist social theory.

For Lukács, Marxist dialectics somehow embodies normative and descriptive, evaluative and explanatory elements.

> . . . Marx's "humanism" diverges most sharply from all the movements that seem so similar to it at first glance. Others have often recognized and described how capitalism violates and destroys everything human. . .
>
> But this does no more than present the problem in a confused form and certainly does not point the way to a solution. The solution can only be discovered by seeing these two aspects [normative and descriptive] as they appear in the concrete and real process of capitalist development, namely inextricably bound up with one another: i.e. the categories of dialectics must be applied to man as the measure of all things in a manner that also includes simultaneously a complete description of the economic structure of bourgeois society and a correct knowledge of the present.[20]

According to Lukács, these "categories of dialectics" in some way unite is and ought, real and ideal, true and good. They serve as a conceptual net wide enough to capture a notion of human praxis guided by both an accurate social theory and objective norms. We shall explore in a later section how he believes a correct social theory illuminates what ought to be.

Norms as Negative Ideals or Historical Possibilities

On my interpretation, Lukács understands norms to be either negative ideals or historical possibilities. Both can be discerned by Marxist social theory about existing social reality. Both also constitute present or highly possible societal alternatives or moments of the historical process, stages in the march for freedom in history.

Norms as negative ideals consist of circumstances which it is good to overcome, realities it is desirable to transform. For instance, implicit in Lukács' view is the following negative ideal: overcome reification whenever and to whatever extent possible. This negative ideal refers to prevailing dehumanizing realities in capitalist society. It promotes the revolutionary praxis of the proletariat, the fundamental transformation of capitalist society.

Norms as historical possibilities provide alternative societal arrangements which are realizable in the near future. Marxist social theory discovers such possible historical alternatives to the present. As we noted earlier, for Lukács, the proletariat must choose between the present reified capitalist society or the new socialist regime. The latter choice, the revolutionary alternative, requires class consciousness; it demands that the working class perceive its needs and interests in such a way that only an alternative socialist society can satisfy them. The first choice, the reactionary alternative, consists of the proletariat refusing to perceive its needs and interests as requiring new norms, new historical possibilities, new societal alternatives. In short, Lukacs holds that the only option to capitalist society aside from conformity is to put forward a realizable alternative which will satisfy the needs and interests of people exploited and oppressed in this society.

So the collective choice of the proletariat is an ethical one in the sense that it consists of choosing one set of norms over another, one historical possibility over another, one societal arrangement over another. This choice also reflects a particular stage in the process of the proletariat's increasing self-consciousness, a process discernible by Marxist dialectics.

Hence dialectics is not imported into history from outside, nor is it interpreted in the light of history (as often occurs in Hegel), but is *derived* from history made conscious as its logical manifestation at this particular point in its development . . . it is the proletariat that embodies this process of consciousness. Since its consciousness appears as the immanent product of the historical dialectic, it likewise appears to be dialectical. That is to say, this consciousness is nothing but the expression of historical necessity. The proletariat "has no ideals to realise." When its consciousness is put into practice it can only breathe life into the things which the dialectics of history have forced to a crisis; it can never "in practice" ignore the course of history, forcing on it what are no more than its own desires or knowledge. For it is itself nothing but the contradictions of history that have become conscious.[21]

The proletariat "has no ideals to realize" in the sense that it does not propagate norms which are not closely connected and demonstratively continuous with the present, the ongoing historical process. The revolutionary proletariat is motivated by class consciousness, or by a particular perception of its needs and interests and how they can be satisfied. This perception propels the proletariat to overcome reification and transform existing capitalist society, hence opting for a new historical possibility or societal alternative, namely, a socialist regime.

Normative Discourse as the Parxis of Aufhebung

It should be apparent that Lukács is reluctant to put forward any independent philosophic criteria by which to deem socialist norms desirable. He seems to be, at this point, a radical historicist. He refuses to talk about norms in an abstract way, or as isolated from the historical process, the present system of production, social relations, legal arrangements, and the cultural way of life. He insists that one should always view people in concrete historical circumstances and then see how they go about making ethical choices.

Lukács adopts this viewpoint because he wants norms which are not only morally acceptable but also potent and effective—realizable in the near future. This is why it is crucial for him to begin with a negative ideal, a normative stance toward an objective state of affairs. His aim is to change the world, to transform existing social reality. Therefore, he starts with a particular description and explanation of this social reality which is also evaluative.

Any acceptable "ought-statement" for him must be tied to a particular theory of the phenomenon being evaluated, and it must come with a procedure or program which allows for its realization." If it is severed from the particular theory of social reality and from the way of transforming this social reality, it is rendered impotent, ineffective, innocuous.

> For precisely in the pure, classical expression it received in the philosophy of Kant it remains true that the "ought" presupposes an existing reality to which the category of "ought" remains *inapplicable* in principle. Whenever the refusal of the subject simply to accept his empirically given existence takes the form of an "ought," this means that the immediately given empirical reality receives affirmation and consecration at the hands of philosophy; it is philosophically immortalised.[22]

The disjoining of the ought-statement from a particular theory about the phenomenon being judged, the disjoining of the normative claim from a description and explanation of the state of affairs being evaluated, disarms the judgment and renders it harmless. The crucial role of theory—that of providing knowledge of the underlying process in historical and social reality—is overlooked or ignored. Just as bourgeois social science extols the "facts," the immediate appearance of social reality, and hence neglects the meaning of such "facts," so bourgeois moral philosophers generate justifications of norms (which either endorse or condemn capitalist society) without making explicit their particular social theory of capitalist society or pointing a way toward transforming this society. This is the major shortcoming of any bourgeois moral viewpoint.

> Thus every theory of the "ought" is left with a dilemma: either it must allow—the meaningless—existence of empirical reality to survive unchanged with its meaningfulness forming the basis of the "ought"—for in a meaningful existence the problem of an "ought" could not arise. This gives the "ought" a purely subjective character. Or else, theory must presuppose a principle that trancends the concept of both what "is" and what "ought to be" as to be able to explain the real impact of the "ought" upon what "is." For the popular solution of an infinite progression (toward virtue, holiness,) which Kant himself already proposed, merely

conceals the fact that the problem is insoluble. Philosophically it is not important to determine the time needed by the "ought" in order to reorganise what "is." The task is to discover the principles by means of which it becomes *possible in the first place* for an "ought" to modify existence. And it is just this that the theory rules out from the start by establishing the mechanics of nature as an unchangeable fact of existence, by setting up a strict dualism of "ought" and "is," and by creating the rigidity with which "is" and "ought" confront each other—a rigidity which this point of view can never eliminate.[23]

Lukács understands normative discourse to be the praxis of *Aufhebung*. As we recall, the process of *Aufhebung* is the process of a particular historical agent (*Weltgeist* or proletariat) acquiring increased self-consciousness, of overcoming alienation (or reification) and furthering the march of freedom in history. We saw that Hegel's idealistic viewpoint holds this three-step process to consist of negating, preserving, and transforming alien objects into aspects of the self-consciousness of the *Weltgeist*. We also saw that Lukács tries to adopt this viewpoint from a Marxist perspective, with the proletariat acquiring increased self-consciousness (or class consciousness) and thereby negating, preserving, and transforming reified socioeconomic circumstances into a situation of social freedom (or socialist society).

Lukács believes one should talk about norms in the following way. At any given time in history, there will be a certain system of production, a specific set of social relations and legal arrangements, and a specific cultural way of life accompanied by a normative discourse which contains various kinds of arguments that endorse or condemn the status quo, as well as principles about what kind of arguments are acceptable and valid. Since no one is a Cartesian disembodied ego or a pure consciousness in Kant's sense, since everyone grows up and lives in a particular society, one must start with the norms and values of one's society.

For a Marxist concerned first and foremost with understanding and changing the world, the aim of a normative discourse is to show that there is a discrepancy between the existing normative discourse, the norms and values generated from it, and the realities of the society. A Marxist analysis of existing capitalist society permits one to recognize this discrepancy. This recognition is the first step toward developing something, e.g., values, norms, political movement, to overcome the discrepancy. This recognition initiates the praxis of *Aufhebung*. The emphasis is not on realizing abstract principles justified by philosophical argument, but rather on overcoming concrete realities, e.g., reification, described and explained by Marxist social theory.

The notion of discrepancy is linked closely to the idea of contradiction. A discrepancy between the norms and realities in a given society points to the shortcomings of the society. These shortcomings result from the fundamental contradiction and antagonism of the society. So the recognition of the discrepancy between norms and realities in a society encourages people to search for the basic contradiction and antagonism in the society; it also begins the often long ordeal of transforming the society by overcoming the discrepancy, contradiction, and antagonism. And in capitalist society, this long ordeal is inseparable from the process of the proletariat acquiring increased self-consciousness, recognizing the discrepancy and the basic contradiction, and overcoming them.

By highlighting the ideas of discrepancy and contradiction, Lukács leaves himself open to the charge that his kind of criticism of a society—whether the society lives up to its own professed norms—amounts to a form of liberal revisionism. Liberal revisionism claims that society ought to live up to its own norms; it also presupposes that it can. Lukács holds that there is a discrepancy between the norms and realities of a society, that this discrepancy results from the fundamental contradiction and antagonism in the society; that the society cannot possibly overcome the discrepancy without resolving this contradiction and antagonism; and that the resolution of this contradiction and antagonism requires revolutionary change, fundamental social transformation.

For example, in capitalist society, there is a discrepancy between an egalitarian ethos and actual class inequality, between a libertarian ethos and actual social relations, which in the productive process amount to servitude. This discrepancy results from the basic contradiction and antagonism in capitalist society: the proletarian, working class, production vs. the private, capitalist, appropriation of profits.

An important difference between Lukács' viewpoint and the liberal revisionist viewpoint is that Lukács stresses the discrepancy between the general egalitarian ethos and the general realities of capitalist society, whereas the liberal revisionist focuses on the discrepancy between particular egalitarian principles and particular realities of capitalist society. For example, Lukács focuses on the notion of class equality—which capitalist society does not purport to uphold—that he derives from the society's ideological preoccupation with equality. He also highlights the idea of social freedom (workers' control and ownership of the means of production)—which capitalist society again does not claim to uphold—that he derives from the society's ideological obsession of freedom. The liberal revisionist, on the other hand, emphasizes legal equality and individual freedom—which capitalist society does attempt to uphold. Revolution is required to fulfill class equality and social freedom in capitalist society; reform is required to fulfill legal equality and individual freedom in capitalist society. This is the basic difference between Lukács' viewpoint and that of liberal revisionism.

Like Hegel, Lukács seems to think that there are only two alternatives to a present stage or moment in the process of *Aufhebung*. There is either the failure to recognize the basic contradiction and antagonism, with the result that the proletariat remains in a state of ignorance and submission, and the society in a state of reification; or there is the recognition of the contradiction and antagonism and the initiation of the process of overcoming and resolving them. The first choice constitutes human self-estrangement, human servitude; the latter choice, human self-consciousness, human freedom.

Again like Hegel, Lukács appears to think that the only result which proceeds from a recognition of the basic contradiction and antagonism in capitalist society is the further augmentation of human self-consciousness and human freedom. So if the proletariat recognizes the discrepancy between the egalitarian and libertarian ethos and the realities in capitalist society and ultimately resolves the contradiction and antagonism which produces this discrepancy, the new alternative established by the proletariat will amount to a giant step in the march of freedom in history.

Lukács' Hegelian reasoning as to why socialist norms are desirable goes as follows. Begin with the best available theory about existing social reality, namely, Marxist dialectics. This theory will tell one what the fundamental contradiction and antagonism is in this social reality, in this society. See how this contradiction and antagonism produces a serious discrepancy between the general ideas lauded, e.g., equality and freedom, and the realities of this society. The recognition of this discrepancy encourages one to develop something, e.g., norms, political movement, societal alternatives, to overcome it. And it can be overcome only by resolving the basic contradiction and antagonism. In capitalist society, the negative ideal (or undesirable concrete reality) to overcome is reification; the basic contradiction and antagonism is the private appropriation and proletarian production of profits. The praxis of *Aufhebung*—the political activity responsible for overcoming the negative ideal, resolving the basic contradiction and antagonism, and bringing about a new historical possibility or societal alternative—can be enacted only by the proletariat, the strategically located and systematically exploited class in the capitalist system of production. The proletariat can successfully engage in the praxis of *Aufhebung* only if there are ripe socioeconomic circumstances and if they acquire self-consciousness (or class consciousness). If the proletariat successfully engages in the praxis of *Aufhebung,* it will result in a political revolution which will establish a socialist regime, a higher stage of history.

Lukács' viewpoint contains an implicit critique of bourgeois normative discourse, a discourse that extols the idea of independent philosophic justification of norms or of autonomous philosophic criteria for evaluating norms. Bourgeois normative discourse is preoccupied with such justification and such criteria. This preoccupation makes exaggerated demands for the demonstration of discrepancies, contradictions, and antagonisms, and hence suppresses their significance. Bourgeois moral philosophers start with a social theory—derived from bourgeois social science—which overlooks or ignores the discrepancy between the egalitarian, libertarian ethos and the realities in capitalist society, and which overlooks the basic contradiction and antagonism in the society. When bourgeois moral philosophers do focus on discrepancies, they pinpoint trivial ones, namely, those discrepancies which can be overcome while keeping capitalist society intact. In this way, bourgeois moral philosophers become liberal revisionists.

At this point, we can proceed to Lukács' most controversial claim concerning normative discourse: that the philosophic justification of norms collapses into description and explanation of the historical process which demands and requires new norms, new historical possibilities, new societal alternatives. This claim forms the basis for his conception of norms as negative ideals (overcoming present undesirable objective realities) and historical possibilities (promoting new, desirable societal alternatives), as well as for his reluctance to engage in talk about philosophic criteria.

For Lukács, objectively grounding norms means two things. First, it means that an accurate social theory will describe and explain the dehumanizing concrete realities which should be overcome in capitalist society, e.g., reification. The theory further shows how this reification is inextricably linked to the basic contradiction and antagonism in capitalist society. Second, objectively grounding norms means that an accurate social theory can discern the historical tendencies of existing social reality. This discernment will reveal the particular historical possibilities realizable by human praxis in the near future. Objective social norms in this case are those which result from the revolutionary praxis of the proletariat which overcomes reification and class antagonisms in capitalist society. These norms regulate the alternative societal arrangements established by the class conscious proletariat. In this way, objectively grounding norms is not a matter of providing autonomous philosophic criteria or justifications lifted above and placed outside the historical and social context. Rather, it is a matter of explaining the process of the development of history which requires new norms.

Lukács does not provide a philosophic argument for socialist norms. Instead, he gives an historical explanation and assertion. He tries to explain how the historical process can possibly and will most likely proceed. In light of this explanation, he asserts that certain norms will be discarded and new ones required. These new ones—socialist norms—are desirable.

For Lukács, this historical explanation and assertion provides convincing reasons why a philosophic argument for socialist norms would presuppose an ahistorical viewpoint. It would assume an absolutist position, an Archimedian point, a hard objectivist perspective. He adds,

> And precisely this is the great danger in every "humanism" or anthropological point of view. For if man is made the measure of all things, and if with the aid of that assumption all transcendence is to be eliminated without man himself being measured against this criterion, without applying the same "standard" to himself or—more exactly—without making man himself dialectical, then man himself is made into an absolute and he simply puts himself in the place of those transcendental forces he was supposed to explain, dissolve and systematically replace.[24]

Marxist dialectics forces one to acknowledge that such an "absolute is nothing but the fixation of thought, it is the projection into myth of the intellectual failure to understand reality concretely as a historical process."[25] Such an absolutist, hard objectivist view is, ironically, tied to a relativist position; that is, any viewpoint which does not take historical change, development, and process seriously will yield either a hard objectivist or relativist perspective.

> At best, then, a dogmatic metaphysics is superceded by an equally dogmatic relativism.
>
> This dogmatism arises because the failure to make man dialectical is complemented by an equal failure to make reality dialectical. Hence relativism moves within an essentially static world . . . For it is one thing to relativise the truth about an individual or a species in an ultimately static world. And it is quite another matter when *the concrete, historical function and meaning* of the various "truths" is revealed within a unique, concretised historical process. Only in the former case can we accurately speak of relativism. But in that case it inevitably becomes dogmatic. For it is only meaningful to speak of relativism where an "absolute" is in some sense assumed.[26]

Ethics and Dialectics

A major difference between Lukács and the other two Marxist thinkers we have examined is that he refuses to look to the natural sciences as a model for how we acquire knowledge. Instead, Lukács looks to Hegel and the dialectical method. Lukács provides a refreshing break from the foundationalist view of science obsessed with finding eternal truths, hard "facts," or mechanical cause-effect necessity.

Yet despite Lukács' critical disposition toward traditional foundationalist views of science, he still does not hold a radical historicist view of science. Instead, he replaces the traditional foundationalist views with a new nontraditional foundationalist view of science. That is, he still remains preoccupied with being philosophically assured that necessity can be discerned and objectivity philosophically procured. He is just concerned with a different kind of necessity (dialectical necessity) and a different way of establishing objectivity (on ontological grounds).

Lukács embarks on an ontological quest for objectivity by trying to discover the "dialectics" inherent in the nature of historical and social reality. This quest produces, as we have seen, a powerful critique of traditional foundationalist views of science and ethics; but it also posits a new foundation: dialectics in history. And as we saw, Lukács' "categories of dialectics" unite is and ought, real and ideal, true and good. These "categories" are embodied—to be a bit rhetorical here—in the historical Logos, the privileged historical agent responsible for furthering the march of freedom in history: the class-conscious proletariat.

Lukács' nontraditional foundationalist view of science is best exemplified in his gallant struggle to show why the class-conscious proletariat can perceive the truth in capitalist society and why the bourgeoisie cannot, why this proletariat can grasp "those immanent meanings that necessarily inhere in the objects of bourgeois society,"[27] and the bourgeoisie cannot. In short, his view of science is best illustrated by his understanding of the notion of truth.

For Lukács, the basic reason why the class conscious proletariat can perceive the truth in capitalist society and the bourgeoisie cannot is because of the "differences between the social existence of the two classes."[28] But the complexity of his argument is found in his assessment of what these differences are and what supports them. Let us begin with the following passage.

> Of course, the knowledge yielded by the standpoint of the proletariat stands on a higher scientific plane objectively; it does after all apply a method that makes possible the solution of problems which the greatest thinkers of the bourgeois era have vainly struggled to find and in its substance, it provides the adequate historical analysis of capitalism which must remain beyond the grasp of bourgeois thinkers . . .
>
> But also, it appears that every method is necessarily implicated in the existence of the relevant class. For the bourgeoisie, method arises directly from its social existence and this means that mere immediacy adheres to its thought, constituting its outermost barrier, one that can not be crossed. In contrast to this the proletariat is confronted by the need to break through this barrier, to overcome it inwardly *from the very start* by adopting its own point of view.[29]

In this passage, Lukács makes it clear that the proletariat has access to a knowledge of capitalist society which the bourgeoisie cannot attain. We saw earlier how Marxist dialectics supports the proletarian viewpoint and yields this knowledge. But what is Lukács' philosophic justification for his claim that the proletariat can achieve objectivity and validity and grasp truth through its point of view while the bourgeoisie cannot? I shall try to show that Lukács' justification takes the form of a highly complex, slightly convoluted sociology of knowledge undergrided by Marxist dialectics. It is an ontological justification in that it rests upon certain claims about the fundamental nature and logical development of historical and social reality.

For Lukács, the proletariat has access to a knowledge of capitalist society which the bourgeoisie does not have because this society "employs the motor of class interests to keep the bourgeoisie imprisoned within this immediacy while forcing the proletariat to go beyond it."[30] The "immediacy" referred to in the passage is illusion; it is the surface or phenomenal appearance which conceals a noumenal reality.

The bourgeois viewpoint "is held fast in the mire of immediacy from which the proletariat is able to extricate itself"[31] because it is unable to perceive "the dialectical structure of the historical process in daily life."[32] That is, the bourgeois viewpoint refuses to see objects in capitalist society as the results of productive activity of subjects, and things as the products of mediated activity in social relations between people. The individualistic, atomic, specialized viewpoint of the bourgeoisie forces it to perceive

> the subject and object of the historical process and of social reality in a double form: in terms of his consciousness the single individual is a perceiving subject confronting the overwhelming objective necessities imposed by society of which only minute fragments can be comprehended. But in reality it is precisely the conscious activity of the individual that is to be found on the object-side of the process, while the subject (the class) cannot be awakened into consciousness and this activity must always remain beyond the consciousness of the—apparent—subject, the individual.[33]

The bourgeois viewpoint is forced to see "the subject and object of the social process. . . in a rigidly twofold form, each external to the other."[34] It does not see any interaction between them. Therefore it ignores the activity which mediates between them. In this way, the bourgeois viewpoint precludes the possibility of stressing process and the development of the subject and object; it stultifies and ossifies the relation between subject and object, hence distorting the reality of capitalist society.

The opposite, Lukács claims, holds for the proletariat's viewpoint.

For the proletariat social reality does not exist in this double form. It appears in the first instance as the pure *object* of societal events. In every aspect of daily life in which the individual worker imagines himself to be the subject of his own life he finds this to be an illusion that is destroyed by the immediacy of his existence.[35]

The existence of the worker is so objectified and reified that he or she cannot help but see him/herself as a saleable object, a commodity. There is no double vision here, only the realization that the worker is "no more than a cipher reduced to an abstract quantity, a mechanical and rationalised tool."[36] The worker exemplifies the most extreme reified character of capitalist society, a mere element of the movement of commodities and an impotent observer of it. The capitalist also experiences this split, but perceives it differently.

> But for his consciousness it necessarily appears as an activity (albeit this activity is objectively an illusion), in which effects emanate from himself. This illusion blinds him to the true state of affairs, whereas the worker, who is denied the scope of such illusory activity, perceives the split in his being preserved in the brutal form of what is in its whole tendency a slavery without limits. He is therefore forced into becoming the object of the process by which he is turned into a commodity and reduced to a mere quantity.
>
> But this very fact forces him to surpass the immediacy of his condition. For as Marx says, "Time is the place of human development." The quantitative differences in exploitation which appear to the capitalist in the form of quantitative determinants of the objects of his calculation, must appear to the worker as the decisive, qualitative categories of his whole physical, mental and moral existence.[37]

This long passage is crucial in that it contains the central formulation Lukács employs in order to distinguish the proletariat's viewpoint from the bourgeois viewpoint: the ability and capacity to move from quantity to quality, from objectification or reification to self-consciousness. As with Hegel's *Weltgeist,* this move is not only an augmentation of the self-consciousness of a particular historical agent; it also is a perception of what the object really is, a penetration into the essence of the object. Lukács notes,

> The transformation of quantity into quality is not only a particular aspect of the dialectical process of development, as Hegel represents it in his philosophy of nature and, following him, Engels in the *Anti-Dühring.* But going beyond that, as we have just shown with the aid of Hegel's *Logic,* it

means the emergence of the truly objective form of existence and the destruction of those confusing categories of reflection which had deformed true objectivity. . .[38]

So the proletariat's viewpoint is objective and true, while the bourgeois viewpoint is not because the social existence of the latter precludes a move from quantity to quality, from being objectified to achieving self-consciousness, from false perceptions to true perceptions.

> For the social existence of the proletariat is far more powerfully affected by the dialectical character of the historical process in which the mediated character of every factor receives the imprint of truth and authentic objectivity. . .[39]

At this point Lukács seems to uphold two contradictory claims: that all knowledge about historical and social reality has an ideological character, and that a certain knowledge, i.e., Marxist theory of capitalist society, is objective and true. Of course, much depends on what he understands "objectivity" and "truth" to mean. And he is a bit ambiguous about their meanings. He wavers between a crude radical historicist understanding of them and a moderate historicist (or soft objectivist) understanding of them. The former is illustrated by the following passage:

> In the period of the "pre-history of human soceity" and of the struggles between classes the only possible function of truth is to establish the various possible attitudes to an essentially uncomprehended world in accordance with man's needs in the struggle to master his environment. Truth could only achieve an "objectivity" relative to the standpoint of the individual classes and the objective realities corresponding to it.[40]

The moderate historicist understanding of "objectivity" and "truth" he adopts takes seriously social location in the productive process as a starting point for the epistemological perceptions of classes, but then it goes on to appeal to a notion of "relevance to reality" which allows one to adjudicate between rival class perceptions. The criterion of truth here is relevance to a dialectical, dynamic reality. In a revealing passage he states,

> The solution proposed by Marx in his *Theses on Feuerbach* is to transform philosophy into praxis. But, as we have seen, this praxis has its objective and structural preconditions and complement in the view that

reality is a "complex of processes." That is to say, in the view that the movements of history represent the true reality; not indeed a transcendental one, but at all events a higher one than that of the rigid, reified facts of the empirical world, from which they arise. For the reflection theory this means that thought and consciousness are oriented towards reality but, at the same time, the criterion of truth is provided by relevance to reality. This reality is by no means identical with empirical existence. This reality is not, it becomes.[41]

The chief problem with Lukács' view here is that, despite his acute observations about the circular character of the relation of theory to reality, he still clings to the realist, objectivist dream—that of appealing to a reality (in his case, a dialectical reality) which allows us to adjudicate between competing theories about reality. He makes this mistake when he writes:

> It is true that reality is the criterion for the correctness of thought. But reality is not, it becomes—and to become the participation of thought is needed.[42]

And it becomes quite apparent what problematic he believes he has overcome—and the metaphilosophical vision to which he adheres—when he adds,

> We see here the fulfilment of the programme of classical philosophy: the principle of genesis means in fact that dogmatism is overcome (above all in its most important historical incarnation: the Platonic theory of reflection).[43]

Lukács cannot adopt a radical historicist view or an anti-foundationalist view in epistemology and science because he remains tied to a conception of philosophy which promotes the quest for objectivity and search for foundations. His Hegelian perspective, which often sounds like a radical historicist view, calls into question traditional foundationalist views, but it ultimately yields a nontraditional foundationalist view: a view which adopts an anti-Platonic ontology, an ontology of becoming. This ontology consists of the inherent dialectical nature of social reality and the logical development of history discernible by Marxist dialectics.

What Lukács does not realize, as does the radical historicist, is that the philosophic quest for objectivity and search for foundations—be it based on an ontology of being or becoming—is ultimately Platonic.

That is, the very notion of an "ontology" itself is a Platonic remnant whose justification requires philosophic (i.e., objectivism/relativism, necessity/contingency, etc.) moves similar to those of Plato. In other words, any philosophic inquiry into the fundamental nature or logical development of an x is an heir to Plato, an homage to the quest for objectivity. Such inquiries are precisely what is called into question by the radical historicist. Any form of philosophic essentialism is an anathema to radical historicism.

There is nothing wrong with Lukács arguing for the acceptance of Marxist dialectics with its ontology, i.e., claims about what is under-a-Marxist-description; but it is unacceptable, to the radical historicist, to argue for Marxist dialectics (and the proletariat's viewpoint) because of its ontology, i.e., claims about what *really* is. "Reality" (be it conceived as dynamic or static) cannot serve as a last court of appeal for the choice between theories about reality; rather, it is always part of such theories people must choose in order to solve problems, insure survival, overcome unpleasant circumstances, etc. Of the three Marxist thinkers we have examined, Lukács seems to see this most clearly, but his preoccupation with "fulfilling the programme of classical philosophy" lands him right back into the trap of foundationalism, despite the radical historicist moves he often seems to make.

◇ 7 ◇

Conclusion:
Marx vs. the Marxist Philosophers

The major difference between Marx and the Marxist philosophers regarding approaches to ethics is that Marx is not bothered by charges of moral relativism, whereas the philosophers are bothered by such charges. Marx views charges of moral relativism as defensive reflexes of those captive to the vision of philosophy as the quest for certainty, the search for foundations. And, of course, Marx's radical historicist viewpoint calls this vision of philosophy into question. Engels, Kautsky, and Lukács—each in his own way—take the charges of moral relativism seriously and therefore attempt to put forward philosophic foundations for the objectivity of socialist norms. How does one account for this major philosophic difference between Marx and the Marxist philosophers regarding approaches to ethics?

Despite their radical historicist Marxist heritage, as I have pointed out, Engels, Kautsky, and Lukács adopt a moderate historicist viewpoint. They fail to put forward a radical historicist perspective primarily because they remain captive to the vision of philosophy as the quest for certainty, the search for foundations, because they retain foundationalist conceptions of epistemology and science that rest upon linking the foundations of knowledge to varying notions of philosophic necessity. For Engels, philosophic necessity is based on the dialectical laws of thought, nature, and history; for Kautsky, philosophic necessity is based on undeniable facts; and for Lukács, philosophic necessity is based on the dialectical nature of historical and social reality. Lukács fundamentally differs from Engels and Kautsky in that he refuses to employ the methods of the natural sciences as the model for how we acquire knowledge. Yet his use of the dialectical method for acquiring

167

knowledge of history and society presupposes the German idealist distinction between the *Naturwissenschaften* and *Geisteswissenschaften* which itself presupposes a foundationalist conception of epistemology and science.

In contrast to the Marxist philosophers, Marx discards any notion of philosophic necessity after he adopts the radical historicist viewpoint. Of course, he continues to talk about necessity (or, better yet, inevitability) in his later works, but his necessity is no longer philosophic necessity (which serves as the basis for valid knowledge claims or true representations of reality), but rather historical necessity, always subsumed under his theoretic formulations or within his value-laden description of historical reality and its projected tendencies. As I have tried to show, Marx's discarding of any notion of philosophic necessity is a highly conscious and intentional act owing to a metaphilosophical move he believes he is forced to make if he takes seriously historical consciousness and the conventional status of dynamic social practices and human activities. This metaphilosophical move consists of rejecting the vision of philosophy as the quest for certainty and the search for foundations and hence dispelling the gravity of charges of relativism. The basic difference between Marx and Engels, Kautsky, and Lukács is that the latter three never make this metaphilosophical move.

The central question now arises why Engels, Kautsky, and Lukács never see this move made by Marx, or if they see the move, why they fail to put forward criticisms of it? I think it is clear that Engels, Kautsky, and Lukács understood themselves to be emulating Marx; therefore they believe they are making moves *similar* to Marx's. But if this is so, why then do they not make Marx's crucial metaphilosophical move?

In the cases of Engels and Kautsky, I believe the answer to this question is a simple one. Engels and Kautsky were amateur philosophers in the sense that neither had the time to think deeply about the Western philosophical tradition nor the talent to seriously grapple with the assumptions and presuppositions of the dominant vision of philosophy in the West. Therefore their humble attempts to relate Marx's thought to this tradition result in their viewing Marx's thought as critical of this tradition yet ultimately assimilated into it. They see Marx as critical of past attempts to arrive at philosophic foundations or grounds for knowledge claims (or ethical norms) and as putting forward a new historicist viewpoint which arrives at new philosophic foundations or grounds; they do not realize that Marx is calling into question the idea of any search for philosophic foundations or grounds.

The case of Lukács is a bit more complex. Lukács is a sophisticated thinker and serious philosopher who understands quite well the philosophical tradition in the West. In fact, his critique of mechanical Marxism and its understanding of philosophic necessity is precisely his rejection of amateur Marxist philosophers (like Engels and Kautsky) who uncritically look to the natural sciences as a model for how we acquire knowledge about history and society. In short, his critique is a general rejection of the capitulation of mainstream nineteenth-century European philosophy to a positivist conception of epistemology and science. His attempt to link Marx's thought to Hegelianism is an attempt to unwed Marx's thought from any positivist conception of epistemology and science. In fact, by linking Marx's thought to Hegelianism, Lukács wants to make Marx part and parcel of the grand Hegelian revolution in philosophy which called question any positivist search for philosophic foundations. Lukács believes Marx made a crucial metaphilosophical move and Lukács understands this move to be a Hegelian one. Therefore, like Engels and Kautsky, though in a more interesting and sophisticated way, Lukács sees Marx as critical of a particular, i.e., positivist, search for philosophic foundations and as putting forward a new historicist viewpoint—namely, a Hegelian one—which arrives at philosophic foundations.

The crucial role in Marx's philosophic development, as our explication has shown, was played by Hegel, not by positivism. Therefore, it is not surprising that Lukács' Hegelian reading of Marx's thought more closely resembles Marx's viewpoint than the interpretations of Engels and Kautsky. Yet it is important to note that the evolution of Marx's philosophical development is never highlighted or accented by either Engels, Kautsky, or Lukács. Indeed many of the texts, e.g., *Philosophic and Economic Manuscripts,* necessary for any reconstruction of Marx's philosophical development were not available (or had not been discovered). The inability—as well as the refusal—to take seriously Marx's philosophical development and hence his ultimate disposition toward the vision of philosophy as the search for foundations results, for Engels, Kautsky, and Lukács, in the *misreading* of Marx's metaphilosophical move of calling into question any philosophic search for foundations.

They ultimately view the move as a rejection of one particular kind of philosophic search and an embarkation on another search—more historicist yet still philosophic. It is this misreading of Marx's metaphilosophical move which separates Marx from the Marxist philosophers, his radical historicist viewpoint from their moderate historicist perspectives, and ultimately his rejection of philosophic aims from their attempts to fulfill philosophic aims. The failure of the Marxist philosophers is that they ultimately remain philosophers, whereas Marx's radical historicist metaphilosophical vision enables him to stop doing philosophy and to begin to describe, explain, and ultimately change the world.

Notes

Chapter 1: Radical Historicism

1. Cf. Gilbert Harman, "What Is Moral Relativism?" in *Values and Morals,* ed. A. I. Goldman and J. Kim (Holland, 1978), pp. 146–48; and William K. Frankena, *Ethics,* 2d ed. (Englewood Cliffs, N.J., 1973), pp. 109–110.

Chapter 2: Marx's Road to Radical Historicism

1. Cf. William W. Johnston, "Karl Marx's Verse of 1836–1837 as a Fore-shadowing of His Early Philosophy," *Journal of the History of Ideas* 28 (1967): 259–68; and Leonard P. Nessell, Jr., "Marx's Romantic Poetry and the Crisis of Romantic Lyricism," *Studies in Romanticism* 16, no. 4 (Fall 1977): 509–34.
2. Karl Marx and Frederick Engels, *Collected Works,* Volume 1 (New York, 1975), p. 11.
3. Ibid., pp. 11–12.
4. Ibid., p. 12. Cf. Donald R. Kelley, "The Metaphysics of Law: An Essay on the Very Young Marx," *American Historical Review* 83, no. 2 (April 1978): 350–67.
5. Ibid., p. 12.
6. Ibid.
7. Ibid., p. 15.
8. Ibid.
9. Ibid.
10. Ibid., p. 17.
11. Ibid., p. 18; emphasis added.

12. Ibid.
13. Ibid., p. 19.
14. Ibid., p. 61.
15. Ibid., p. 62.
16. Ibid.
17. Ibid., p. 70.
18. Ibid., p. 71.
19. Ibid., p. 85.
20. Ibid.
21. Ibid., p. 86.
22. Ibid., p. 204.
23. Ibid.
24. Ibid., p. 206.
25. Ibid., p. 207.
26. Ibid., p. 205.
27. Ibid., p. 209.
28. Ibid., p. 195.
29. Ibid., pp. 195–96.
30. Ibid., pp. 196–97.
31. Ibid., p. 197.
32. Ibid., p. 231.
33. Ibid., pp. 233–34.
34. Ibid., p. 234.
35. Ibid., p. 245.
36. Ibid., p. 247.
37. Ibid., p. 242.
38. Ibid., p. 253.
39. Ibid., p. 254.
40. Ibid., p. 255.
41. Ibid., p. 337.
42. Ibid., pp. 344–45.
43. Ibid., p. 348.
44. Ibid.
45. Ibid., pp. 348–49.
46. *Writings of the Young Marx on Philosophy and Society,* ed. and trans. Lloyd D. Easton and Kurt H. Guddat (Garden City, N.Y., 1967), p. 212.
47. Ibid., p. 213.
48. Ibid., p. 214.
49. Ibid., pp. 214–15.
50. Ibid., p. 241.

51. Ibid., p. 251.
52. Ibid., p. 252.
53. Ibid., p. 256.
54. Ibid., p. 257.
55. Ibid., pp. 257–58.
56. Ibid., pp. 262–63.
57. Ibid., p. 264.
58. Ibid., p. 266.
59. Ibid., p. 268.
60. Ibid., p. 270.
61. Ibid., pp. 270–71.
62. Ibid., pp. 271–72.
63. Ibid., p. 272.
64. Ibid., p. 276.
65. Ibid., p. 279.
66. Ibid., p. 281.
67. Ibid., p. 284.
68. Ibid., p. 316.
69. Ibid.
70. Ibid., p. 321.
71. Ibid., pp. 322–23.
72. Ibid., p. 289.
73. Ibid., p. 291.
74. Ibid., p. 297.
75. Ibid.
76. Karl Marx, *Early Writings,* trans. and ed. T. B. Bottomore (New York, 1964), p. 168.
77. Ibid., p. 171.
78. Ibid.
79. Ibid., p. 173.
80. Ibid., p. 191.
81. Ibid., p. 193.
82. Ibid., p. 127.
83. Ibid., p. 128.
84. Ibid., p. 158.
85. Ibid., p. 132.
86. Ibid., pp. 164–65.
87. Ibid., pp. 193–94.
88. Ibid., p. 167.
89. Ibid., p. 155.

90. Ibid., pp. 173–74.
91. Ibid.

Chapter 3: Marx's Adoption of Radical Historicism

1. Karl Marx and Frederick Engels, *Collected Works*, Volume 5 (New York, 1976), p. 6.
2. Ibid., p. 6.
3. Ibid., p. 7.
4. Ibid.
5. Ibid., pp. 7–8.
6. Ibid., p. 8.
7. Max Stirner, *The Ego and His Own*, ed. and introd. John Carroll (New York, 1971), p. 39.
8. Ibid., p. 54.
9. Ibid., pp. 58–59.
10. Ibid., p. 61.
11. Ibid., pp. 72–73.
12. Ibid., pp. 104–105.
13. Ibid., p. 105.
14. Ibid., p. 114.
15. Ibid., p. 121.
16. Ibid., pp. 138–39.
17. Ibid., p. 205.
18. Marx and Engels, *Collected Works*, Volume 5, p. 23.
19. Ibid., pp. 23–24.
20. Ibid., p. 30.
21. Ibid.
22. Ibid., p. 37.
23. Ibid., p. 39.
24. Ibid., p. 41.
25. Ibid., p. 98.
26. Ibid., p. 128.
27. Ibid., p. 129.
28. Ibid., p. 247.
29. Ibid., p. 455.
30. Ibid.
31. Ibid., p. 456.
32. Ibid., p. 464.

33. Ibid., p. 460.
34. Ibid., p. 469.
35. Ibid., p. 479.
36. Ibid., pp. 479–80.
37. Ibid., p. 492.
38. Ibid., p. 514.
39. It is highly significant that Marx's next book, *The Poverty of Philosophy* (written January–June 1847) was regarded by him as the first scientific presentation of his new social theory and also recommended by him as an introduction to *Capital*. The title indeed is a pun on the work the book criticizes—Proudhon's *The System of Economic Contradictions: The Philosophy of Poverty*. But the title also expresses his newly arrived at attitude toward philosophy (and ethics).
40. Marx and Engels, *Collected Works,* Volume 5, p. 50.
41. Ibid., pp. 53–54.
42. Ibid., p. 54.
43. Ibid., p. 39.
44. Ibid., p. 45.
45. Ibid., p. 59.
46. Ibid., p. 60.
47. Ibid., p. 61.
48. Ibid., p. 432.
49. Ibid., p. 247.
50. Ibid., p. 439.
51. Ibid.
52. Ibid., p. 49.
53. Ibid., p. 81.
54. Karl Marx, *Capital,* ed. Frederick Engels, Volume 3 (New York, 1967), p. 817.
55. Karl Marx, *Capital,* ed. Frederick Engels, Volume 1 (New York, 1967), p. 10.
56. Ibid., p. 20.
57. Ibid., pp. 17, 72.
58. Ibid., p. 8.
59. Karl Marx, *Grundrisse,* trans. Martin Nicolaus (New York, 1973), p. 106; emphasis added.
60. *The Marx-Engels Reader,* ed. Robert C. Tucker (New York, 1972), pp. 385, 386, 388.
61. Ibid., pp. 388–89.

Chapter 4: The Classical Marxist Position

1. Frederick Engels, *Anti-Dühring* (New York, 1972), pp. 104–105.
2. Ibid., p. 105.
3. Ibid., pp. 103–104.
4. Ibid., p. 117.
5. For a similar line of argument, see Roberto Mangabeira Unger, *Knowledge and Politics* (New York, 1975), pp. 238–48.
6. Engels, *Anti-Dühring,* pp. 97, 98, 99.
7. Ibid., p. 98.
8. Ibid., p. 100.
9. Ibid., p. 31.
10. Ibid., pp. 15–16.
11. Ibid., p. 126.
12. Ibid., p. 125.

Chapter 5: The Positivist Marxist Position

1. My selection of Kautsky over Eduard Bernstein, the famous defender of democratic socialism and reformist economism, may surprise some. But those familiar with the works of these two theorists will agree that Kautsky far outshines Bernstein in regard to theoretical (as opposed to strategic) matters. Bernstein's well-known dictum "Back to Kant" remained, for the most part, merely a slogan. There is little serious treatment of ethical problems in Bernstein's writings and his major attempt to synthesize Kantian ethics and socialist ideals ended in disaster, viz., his essay "Is Scientific Socialism Possible?" It indeed is true that Bernstein's emphasis on ethical ideals for socialist movements is more pronounced than that of Kautsky. It also is true that Bernstein more fully recognized the need for a well-worked-out normative viewpoint to complement the scientific analysis of capitalist society than did Kautsky. Yet Bernstein would yield little fruit in this study because he neither formulated a philosophic justification for socialist ethical ideals nor gave these ideals any substantive content. For further elaboration of this view of Bernstein, see George Lichtheim, *Marxism* (New York, 1964), pp. 259–300, and Peter Gay's classic work, *The Dilemma of Democratic Socialism* (New York, 1952).
2. Karl Kautsky, *Ethics and the Materialist Conception of History,* trans. John B. Asken (Chicago, 1907), p. 202.
3. Ibid., pp. 15–16.

4. Ibid., p. 17.
5. Ibid., p. 39.
6. Ibid., pp. 40–41.
7. Ibid., pp. 46–47.
8. Ibid., pp. 65–66.
9. Ibid., p. 58.
10. Ibid., pp. 55–56.
11. Ibid., p. 64.
12. Ibid., pp. 60–61.
13. Ibid., p. 71.
14. Ibid., p. 73.
15. Ibid., pp. 152–53.
16. Ibid., pp. 71–72.
17. Ibid., pp. 120–21.
18. Ibid., pp. 122–23.
19. Ibid., pp. 130–31, 132–33.
20. Ibid., pp. 204–205.
21. Ibid., p. 178.
22. Ibid.
23. Ibid., pp. 94–95.
24. Ibid., pp. 95–96.
25. Ibid., pp. 96, 97, 98.
26. Ibid., p. 154.
27. Ibid., pp. 159–60.
28. Ibid., p. 164.
29. Ibid., pp. 85, 86.
30. Ibid., p. 203.
31. Ibid., pp. 202–203.
32. Ibid., p. 202.
33. Ibid., p. 40.
34. Ibid.

Chapter 6: The Hegelian Marxist Position

1. Georg Lukács, *History and Class Consciousness: Studies in Marxist Dialectics,* trans. Rodney Livingstone (Cambridge, 1968), p. 24n.
2. Ibid., p. 181.
3. Ibid., p. 258.
4. Ibid., p. 162.

5. Ibid., p. 27.
6. Ibid., p. 6.
7. Ibid., pp. 6, 7.
8. Ibid., p. 28.
9. Ibid., pp. 20–21.
10. Ibid., p. 21.
11. Ibid., pp. 188, 198.
12. Ibid., p. 183.
13. Ibid., p. 184.
14. Ibid.
15. Ibid., p. 8.
16. Ibid., p. 184.
17. Ibid., p. 198.
18. Ibid., p. 178.
19. Ibid., pp. 208–209.
20. Ibid., pp. 190–91.
21. Ibid., pp. 177–78.
22. Ibid., p. 160.
23. Ibid., p. 161.
24. Ibid., pp. 186–87.
25. Ibid., p. 187.
26. Ibid.
27. Ibid., p. 163.
28. Ibid.
29. Ibid., pp. 163–64.
30. Ibid., p. 164.
31. Ibid., p. 163.
32. Ibid., p. 165.
33. Ibid.
34. Ibid.
35. Ibid.
36. Ibid., p. 166.
37. Ibid.
38. Ibid.
39. Ibid., p. 164.
40. Ibid., p. 189.
41. Ibid., pp. 202–203.
42. Ibid., p. 204.
43. Ibid.

◇ *Index* ◇